P9-CFX-355

 Taylor's Guides to Gardening

David Michener
and Nan Sinton

FRANCES TENENBAUM, Series Editor

꽃 Taylor's Guide to

Ground Covers

**MORE THAN 400 FLOWERING
AND FOLIAGE GROUND COVERS
FOR EVERY GARDEN SITUATION**

HOUGHTON MIFFLIN COMPANY

BOSTON   NEW YORK   2001

Library of Congress Cataloging-in-Publication Data

Michener, David.
    Taylor's guide to ground covers: More than 400 flowering and
foliage ground covers for every garden situation / [David Michener,
Nan Sinton].
      p. cm.
    ISBN 0-618-03010-7
    1. Ground cover plants.   I. Sinton, Nan.   II. Title.
    SB432.M53 2002
    635.9'64—dc21   2001039566

Cover photograph by Steven Still
Book design by Anne Chalmers
Typefaces: Minion, News Gothic

Printed in Singapore

TWP 10 9 8 7 6 5 4 3 2 1

❧ Contents

✖Introduction

❦A FRESH LOOK AT GROUND COVERS

Ground Covers at Work

Carpets, rugs, mats, or floors—no matter how you think of ground covers, gardeners agree that without them, no garden picture is complete. Ground covers are planted to make thick mats and broad, dramatic sweeps. They cover the ground under trees, around shrub masses, along paths and driveways, and under or around accent features such as benches, birdbaths, and statuary. Whether they are perennials, ground-hugging vines, or low shrubs, ground covers naturally form thick stands of foliage that, once established, require little maintenance. Their ability to spread by runners, offshoots, and even low-spreading branches that root at the tips means that they will grow together to cover an area even when the initial planting is comparatively sparse. Not only are these plants beautiful, but they also can transform many problem spots into featured areas. Their tight growth makes them ideal for erosion-prone slopes and soils. The densely interwoven roots, stems, and foliage bind the soil, slow down water, and halt soil creep. On level surfaces, all these features help make the ground cover weed-free. Although you can look at ground covers from many vantage points, it is helpful to sort them into either foliage ground covers or flowering ground covers that have attractive foliage both in and out of bloom.

Leaves of foliage ground covers are predominantly green, but some are blue-green, purple-bronze, yellow, or strongly marked with white. In all cases, foliage color and texture establish the "look" of the ground cover. Having masses of green foliage is important. It is restful to the eye and helps set off nearby flowering plants and views. Many foliage ground covers also have attractive flowers, fruits, or autumn colors. Think of periwinkle *(Vinca)* with blue or white flowers, bearberry *(Arctostaphylos uva-ursi)* with pink flowers and red berries, ground-covering junipers *(Juniperus)* with gray-blue berries, lily turf *(Liriope)* with black berries, and Virginia creeper *(Parthenocissus quinquefolia)* with bright red, orange, or even purple fall foliage.

Flowering ground covers are usually chosen for a period of dramatic bloom. Anyone who has seen great masses of daylilies *(Hemerocallis)* blooming on a bank, cascading billows of moss pinks *(Phlox subulata)*

Epimedium × versicolor 'Sulphureum' massed as a ground cover does multiple tasks. The height of the foliage marks the stairs without hiding the stones, the bright foliage color highlights the Berberis thunbergii at the top, and the tidy, heart-shaped foliage hides the peony bases. All this from one ground cover massed abundantly.

transforming a rocky slope into a bower, or a woodland under-planted with sweeps of astilbes *(Astilbe)*, barrenworts *(Epimedium)*, or foamflowers *(Tiarella)* understands that ground covers with an intense peak of bloom can be breathtaking. But flowering ground covers, to be satisfactory, must have clean and healthy foliage for the rest of the garden's season and not die down like spring-flowering bulbs or native spring flowers and leave vast bare spots. Fortunately, many ground covers and bulbs are compatible, leading to two seasons of color for the garden area.

Preparing to Plant

So you've decided that you need ground covers in your garden. Most likely, something else is already growing where your new plants will go, even if it's turf. Your first task is to mark all the edges of the new bed—a hose or stakes and twine are useful for this. When you've created a pleasing shape, stand back and look at it from all perspectives, including, if possible, an upstairs window. If the bed is where you will see it from the street or along the driveway, get in your car and check to make sure it looks right from inside the vehicle. Once you are satisfied with the shape, it's time to clear the entire area that is going to be planted. You will need to be thoroughly rid of the plants you are removing, including their roots. This is especially important with turf, as fragments left behind will make your ground cover look weedy. Dig the bed at least 12 inches deep, more for shrubs. At this point, you'll begin to realize what kind of soil you have and how to improve it so that your plants will thrive.

GOOD SOIL, THRIVING PLANTS

Amending the soil is an important step in helping your ground cover get established and spread. In almost all cases, adding organic matter to the soil helps. Well-rotted manure, compost, rotted wood chips, bark mulch, and shredded leaves break down to microscopic particles that help retain both moisture and the dissolved minerals and nutrients that are in the soil. These same particles also help aerate the soil. An unseen but vital benefit of decaying organic matter is the increase of bacteria, fungi, tiny insects, and earthworms in the soil. The relationships between them and the plants result in a healthy, holistic system that cannot be developed in any other way.

If you have clayey soil, incorporating sand or fine gravel such as poultry grit (available in bulk from feed stores) or builder's sharp sand (not beach sand), as well as gypsum (look for the last two in hardware and garden stores), is as important as adding organic matter to the soil.

Clay has an amazing ability to stick to itself, to prevent air from entering, and to shrink when it dries. All these activities are traumatic to tender, growing roots. Mixing in sand or fine gravel, gypsum, and organic matter reduces this self-sticking tendency. The resulting soil is much better aerated, holds much more water, and is less likely to shrink when it dries.

For soils that are too gravelly and sandy, try adding well-rotted animal manure, compost, rotted wood chips, bark mulch, or shredded leaves, as the rough organic matter improves the soil's ability to hold water. Fresh wood chips are often easily obtained from tree-pruning crews, but these chips need to decompose for at least several months before being used. If you do not have the space for a pile of fresh wood chips to age on your property, rotted wood chips are often available from civic recycling centers or garden contractors. Well-rotted manure is available in bags from garden centers, and in several regions of the country, stables and farms gladly give it away for free.

Good soil is the Holy Grail of gardening. What is meant by "good soil" varies regionally depending on climate, but gardeners agree that most plants thrive in soil that holds moisture, drains freely, and has many tiny air spaces.

Buying the Plants

For any gardener, the first step in planting a ground cover is to figure out which plants you want to buy. If possible, go to a public garden or nursery and decide what you like best. The next step is to measure the area you want to plant and figure out how many plants you need to fill it. This can get tricky. Are you buying many small plants or fewer larger ones? Deciding which plants to use depends not only on price but also on what is in stock at the nurseries. Let's look at each step in detail.

WHICH PLANTS?

As you visit nurseries or order plants by mail or on the Internet, you will encounter many names not listed in the main entries in the Encyclopedia of Plants. Check the index to see if a plant you are considering is listed here under another name. Many plants are sold under more than one name, and we have attempted to include as many names as possible. For example, if you look at the main Encyclopedia entry for *Sedum spurium* 'Schorbuser Blut', you will see that it is also listed as 'Dragon's Blood'.

What if a plant species or cultivar you are considering is not included in the Encyclopedia of Plants? The best way to judge whether it will thrive in your garden is to look at the entries here for the entire genus. As long as the genus grows in your climate zone, then some of the species are likely to do well there. But be aware that this is how exotic invasive pests have infiltrated the country — some do too well here because they have left their disease and insect problems "at home." (Invasive species are considered on page 16.)

If the flower color of a ground cover is important, make your choices from the photographs and descriptions in the Gallery of Plants. If a specific shade is critical to you, it's often best to make the final selection at a nursery, where you can see the ground cover in late bud to full bloom. Such plants are almost always in the larger (more expensive) sizes.

HOW MANY PLANTS?

Once you have made your selections, you will need to figure out how many plants to buy. First, measure the area you want to plant. Area is figured in square feet in the United States and in square meters in Canada. For a rectangular area, multiply length by width. For an irregularly shaped area, measure it as several adjacent rectangles. Figure the area of each rectangle, then add these figures together to come up with the total square feet or meters. For a circular area, multiply the radius (the distance from the center to the edge) squared times 3.14.

Once you know the area to be planted, you can move on to plant size. Here your budget and what is available come into play. It may be confusing to find that a particular ground cover is available in many different sizes. In general, the less soil on the plants you purchase and the smaller the size, the more frequently you will need to water and weed until the plants are established. Smaller plants are usually much cheaper, but once these plants start growing, they will colonize with amazing speed and effectiveness. At the opposite extreme, larger plants may withstand more neglect in the beginning, but it will take time for them to fuse into a mass.

The number of plants needed to cover 100 square feet at specific planting distances is calculated in the table on page 6. Gardeners are often surprised by how many small plants set close together it takes to cover an area. This table gives you a ballpark estimate of the numbers needed. Don't worry if you end up buying "extra" plants in the smaller sizes. You will be able to use them to thicken the planting. In all cases, your initial planting will look better if you purchase slightly more plants than estimated. Remember that these numbers assume that you are planting in square grids — as if you were placing a plant in the center of every square floor tile. If you like a geometric look, plant by the grid. If you like a more flowing, naturalistic look from the very beginning, you must have uniform coverage but not perfectly straight lines. Think of ripples on a pond or fan-shaped cobblestone patterns. Keep your spacing fairly even as you plant by using some sort of measuring stick—your hand, a trowel, a stick, or even a yardstick with the planting distance marked. Use this "stick" each time you position a new plant. Start planting at the back of the bed and work your ripples or fan shapes forward. Use extra plants to fill in holes that emerge from slight misalignments, to fill in spaces around smaller plants, or to thicken the planting at the very front.

Approximate Numbers of Plants for Ground Covers

Distance Between Plants	Plants per 100 Square Feet
4 inches	900
6 inches	400
8 inches	225
10 inches	145
12 inches	100
15 inches	65
18 inches	45
24 inches	25
36 inches	9 to 11

Getting Plants Growing

It is critical to add a light layer of mulch, about 1 inch deep, as soon as the plants are in the ground. Mulches reduce the soil water that is lost to evaporation, thus retaining moisture for the tender roots that the new plants are sending out. Except in dry climates, organic mulches are much more helpful than inorganic ones (such as ornamental stone or gravel) because an organic mulch will break down over time and further build the soil. Mulches also keep the soil cool and promote root growth by shading the soil from direct sunlight. In addition, mulches help suppress the germination of weed seeds. Another benefit of mulches on slopes— and few gardens are truly flat—is that they trap rain and irrigation water as it is applied and thus help the soil absorb the water. Without a mulch, the water will make small erosion channels, which will grow quickly, leading to both the water running off and the soil washing out of the bed.

Once the ground cover is planted, it should need little attention during the first year, other than periodic weeding and adequate watering. If the ground cover is new to you, or the garden site is new, pay particular attention to any early signs of plant stress, such as yellowing or curling of leaves. This stress is usually caused by either too little or too much water. Check to see whether the soil is moist by pulling back the mulch in a small area and feeling the soil. Remember to take a trowel and sample the soil several inches deep. The soil should be moist but not wet.

If the soil is dry, there is too little water. Remedy the situation immediately with regular deep watering with a sprinkler. Watering by hand is inadequate, as the water is applied too quickly and for too short a time to penetrate deeply. If the soil under the mulch is soggy, you have poor drainage. The plants show the same symptoms as when water stressed because the roots are drowning—water has filled the soil's air spaces and the roots cannot survive. In this case, stop watering immediately. If the soil does not dry out within 2 or 3 days, lift the plants and hold them in pots or trays, or even move them temporarily to a drier part of the garden. Replant them once you have fixed the drainage problem. To do this, you might try making raised beds, incorporating sand or fine gravel into the soil, or installing drainage tile. If the soggy conditions cannot be fixed, you will need to find a ground cover that tolerates wet conditions. Some moisture-loving plants are cinnamon fern *(Osmunda cinnamomea)*, ostrich fern *(Matteuccia struthiopteris)*, mazus *(Mazus reptans)*, Japanese sweet flag *(Acorus gramineus)*, and yellow root *(Xanthorhiza)*.

If your new ground cover is planted at the beginning of the growing season, you can speed up its establishment by fertilizing it on a regular basis. Use an organic fertilizer that has been diluted to one-quarter to one-half of the recommended strength (these are tender young plants). Fish emulsion works well. Lightly spray the foliage every 4 weeks, trying to do this when the weather is cloudy or early or late in the day. Stop all fertilizing at least 8 weeks before the expected first frost date for your area so that your plants will stop active growth before winter.

After a growing season has passed, your new ground cover should be well established and need only occasional weeding and supplemental watering. It is good to add a light dressing of new organic mulch (up to an inch if there are bare spots between plants, otherwise less) during the ground cover's dormant season at least every several years. Not only will this renew the mulch, but the organic material will also slowly break down to continue enriching and improving the soil. This routine top-dressing will provide the needed nutrients and require you to fertilize less frequently or not at all.

Some ground covers need additional care to perform best. Bedstraw *(Galium)*, lily turf *(Liriope)*, and yarrow *(Achillea)* will perform better in the long run if they are severely pruned back once a year. This can be done quite effectively by setting a power lawn mover on its highest setting and mowing the ground cover just before it breaks dormancy at the beginning of the growing season. This is also the time to apply a top dressing of mulch. Other ground covers, such as astilbes *(Astilbe),* coralbells *(Heuchera),* and lady's mantle *(Alchemilla),* will perform best if the old clumps are dug up and divided every several years. In these cases, the vigorous outer parts are divided or cut off of the mass and replanted, while the old decaying centers are thrown away or composted. This renewal process can go on indefinitely and will provide additional plants for you to place in new or renovated garden areas, as well as to share with neighbors and friends.

Making More Plants

Gardeners propagate ground covers for many reasons—personal satisfaction is one and "bragging rights" another. This is also done to increase existing plants, as some may be difficult to find, others have sentimental value, and many gardeners enjoy sharing their favorite plants with friends. Finally, it saves money but not always time. Whatever your motives, long-term success depends on using your healthy new plants in appropriate, well-prepared sites. Before you begin propagating your ground covers, estimate how many new plants you will need (see the table on page 6) and decide if you really want to produce and care for the necessary number of plantlets. It is one thing to enjoy producing a few dozen plants for a plant sale, but it is quite another to create hundreds for a new project.

How do you produce healthy new plants? Each propagation method has its advantages depending on ease of production, number of "mother plants" in your garden, season of the year, and your time commitments and interests.

Plants are propagated vegetatively or by seeds. Common methods of vegetative propagation are cuttings, divisions (including offsets), layers, and suckers. These methods have several advantages over seeds—uniformity of the new plants, the speed with which these plants develop, and the fact that plants can be propagated throughout much of the growing season when seed germination might be difficult. In addition, these vegetative propagation methods need not hurt the mother plants. The original mass of ground cover is usually in fine form after the propagation material has been taken.

Seed propagation is used in special cases where seedlings come up in an existing ground cover mass with no effort by the gardener. Seedlings are transplanted to their new site before the mother plants overcome them. Hellebores *(Helleborus)*, violets *(Viola)*, and wild gingers *(Asarum)* are all well known for their seedling production in sites where they are happy.

CUTTINGS

Of all the types of cuttings, stem cuttings are the top choice of most gardeners. Stem cuttings are just that—sections of young, pliable stems with several leaves attached. The trick is to fool the stem section into sending out new roots—rather than new leaves—at selected nodes (there is always a node where a leaf attaches to the stem). To do this, fill pots or flats with well-drained garden soil or a commercial soil mix and moisten the soil. Then take the cuttings with two to several nodes—use a sharp knife or clippers to make clean cuts—and plunge the cuttings into a bucket of water so that they do not dry out while you are working. Poke a hole in the planting medium (your finger or a pencil will do), and take the leaf (or leaves) off the bottom node(s) of the cutting. Dip this leafless node into a rooting compound (available at garden centers), put it in the soil hole, and press the soil firmly around the buried node. The rest of the leafy stem remains above ground. When the pot or tray is full, water well and place it out of full sun or strong wind. You may wish to make a temporary enclosure for the new cuttings with clear or fogged plastic and short stakes to keep the humidity high and drying winds away, but be careful not to overheat the cuttings with the high temperatures that can build up in such enclosures. Ground covers that are easy to root in this way include ivy *(Hedera)*, pachysandra *(Pachysandra terminalis)*, and periwinkle *(Vinca)*.

DIVISIONS

Divisions and offsets are much easier to produce than cuttings and are typically used for ground covers that spread from well-defined crowns. These need to be dug just as the new leaves are beginning to show in the spring, and the vigorous new growth is cut ("divided") from the old, dying centers. These small but vigorous sections, which include roots, stems, and growing points, are replanted. There are usually many more sections to plant than there were plants in the beginning. Try this with barrenworts *(Epimedium)*, coralbells *(Heuchera)*, hostas *(Hosta)*, lady's mantle *(Alchemilla)*, and navelworts *(Omphalodes)*.

   Ground covers that spread by running stems and roots to make thick masses are easy to propagate by division in a much more casual manner.

Dig square, shovel-width plugs several inches deep to include numerous roots and stems. Plant these square plugs in the newly prepared area—the plugs have enough substance to reestablish themselves as if little has happened. Fill the holes in the original ground-cover area with compost or other garden soil, then cover them with mulch. The existing ground cover will recover very quickly. This type of division works well with ivy *(Hedera)*, pachysandra *(Pachysandra terminalis)*, lily-of-the-valley *(Convallaria)*, lily turf *(Liriope)*, periwinkle *(Vinca)*, and ribbon grass *(Phalaris)*.

Offsets are the easiest divisions to use. Some ground covers produce new plantlets with great regularity at the end of runners or root segments. Late in the season or early the following year, the newly developed plants can be severed from the mother plant and taken with a small amount of attached soil to a new site. Examples include barren straw-

A generous, weedproof planting of Liriope spicata *holds a difficult bank beneath a grove of redleaved Japanese maples adjacent to a turf path. The composition works by playing with foliage textures and colors. The* Liriope *bridges the dramatic leaves of the maple to the soft green of the turf path. The size of the* Liriope *mass is critical to the success of the scene.*

berries *(Waldsteinia)*, ajugas *(Ajuga)*, mazus *(Mazus)*, ostrich fern *(Matteuccia struthiopteris)*, wild strawberry *(Fragaria virginiana)*, and woodland phloxes *(Phlox divaricata, P. stolonifera)*.

Layers and suckers are sometimes used to propagate woody ground covers. Layers are formed when a stem that is still attached to the mother plant is shallowly buried and develops its own roots. Later, it can be cut from the mother plant. This is a slow process, but nicking the stem and using rooting compounds (as with cuttings) can speed it up. As you begin the process, it helps to bring in a shovelful of good soil and use it around the buried stem so that the roots can grow without immediate competition. After several months, check carefully to see if roots have formed. Once roots are well established, cut the layer from the mother plant and move it to a new site. Be certain to cut back some of the stem and leaves if there are too many for the new roots to support. Layers need very careful attention during establishment, as it is easy to disturb them before they are settled into their new home, and they dry out quickly. Examples of woody ground covers that may be layered include bearberry *(Arctostaphylos uva-ursi)*, lowbush blueberry *(Vaccinium angustifolium)*, stephanandras *(Stephanandra)*, and some prostrate junipers *(Juniperus)*.

Suckers are vigorous shoots of woody plants that can be split from the mother plant while retaining part of the root system. To take suckers, insert a sharp shovel close to the mother plant so that there is as large a root section as possible remaining with the sucker. Cut around the sucker with the shovel and tease up the soil block and sucker. If the sucker was vigorous and the roots are few, cut the top back to balance the roots. Plant immediately in the new site. Often the sucker will grow as if nothing happened. Examples of plants that can be propagated this way include blackberries *(Rubus)*, coralberry *(Symphoricarpos orbiculatus)*, sumacs *(Rhus)*, and wild roses *(Rosa)*.

Using Ground Covers to Solve Problems

Cars, utilities, dense shade, and foot traffic create difficult sites around homes. All of these areas are exactly where most homeowners feel the greatest need for carpets of ground covers. It helps to understand why these sites are difficult when you are selecting ground covers.

Of all the problem categories, "near cars" is the worst. No matter how carefully marked, cars somehow cross over the edge of a driveway into the planted area. This is especially damaging when the ground is damp, as the air is driven out of the soil, which becomes so tightly compacted that it cannot support plant life. Only redigging the soil will break up its crushed structure and allow proper aeration and drainage for subsequent root growth. A less obvious influence of cars is their toxic compounds. Motor oil and various mechanical fluids drip onto the surface over time and are washed over to the bed. In low but chronic doses, they stunt the plants' growth. In wintry zones, even if you do not salt your driveway, cars carry salt in the frozen masses that cling to the wheel wells and underbody. To add insult to injury, snowplows often run into ground covers and damage them by breaking branches and even gouging up the frozen earth and plants. Take special care to select very rugged ground covers in these sites and to prepare the soil particularly well.

Ground covers native to seaside and brackish environments are often naturally tolerant of a certain amount of road salt. Most of these plants require full to near-full sun and good drainage. Plants tolerant of salty sites in sun include the old-fashioned orange daylily *(Hemerocallis fulva*—single and double forms), periwinkle *(Vinca),* some campanulas *(Campanula takesimana),* as well as bearberry *(Arctostaphylos uva-ursi)* and junipers *(Juniperus),* provided splashed salts are washed off promptly. In severe sites, wild and ornamental forms of *Rosa rugosa* can be massed. As a ground cover, *R. rugosa* must be shorn within several inches of the ground late each winter before the buds develop. The resulting roses are spectacular.

Gloomy shade is found in gardens under dense trees and under decks. These two types of deeply shaded sites are slightly different. Under surface roots and dense shade of specimen trees, ground covers face three chronic challenges: gloomy shade, dry soil (the trees absorb the moisture first), and poor soil (again because the trees obtain the nutrients first). The trees most likely to create these situations include evergreen conifers such as hemlocks, some pines, redwoods, and spruces, as well as broad-leaved evergreen trees such as eucalyptuses, live oaks, and magnolias. The deciduous trees that typically create these sites are beeches and many maples, especially red, silver, and Norway maples. For these trees, especially if the branching is low and the trees are large, the optimal solution may be a weed-free treatment such as leaf mulch, wood chips, a decorative specialty mulch such as cocoa bark, or gravel. It may be possible to plant some early-spring bulbs at the edges of such sites.

The area under a deck, especially when seen from a window under the deck, is especially difficult, as plants always grow toward the light. Place them too far back, and the result will be weak, spindly stems that lean toward the light. Locate them too far forward, and they will not creep back into the deeper shade. One solution is to have a nonliving

Golden-foliaged Lamium macula-tum *'Aureum' appears chartreuse in light shade, an effect intensified by the dark, heart-shaped leaves of* Brunnera. *In shade, bright foliage creates the effect of shafts of sunlight.*

cover, perhaps stones or wood chips, in the deepest shade behind the ground cover so that the entire effect is one of intention rather than partial success. Plants growing under decks will bloom poorly, if at all, so the ground cover needs to be selected for its attractive foliage.

Modern living presents an array of challenging utility sites for ground covers. Frequently encountered problem sites are next to air conditioners, below dryer vents, and in shallow soil over buried utility boxes. Ground covers look best when the mass grows uniformly well, not when only one section performs well. Air conditioners cool the house but blast the plants nearby with artificial arid wind. For an air conditioner to operate well, it is important that tall plants be kept at least 1 to several feet away from the unit so that air flows freely. Air conditioners are best screened with fences and shrubs at the proper distance, and ground covers should be planted to suppress any weeds around these barriers and to create a tidy appearance. Likewise, dryer vents near foliage can overheat leaves with blasts of hot air. Some low members of the mint family, including catmints *(Nepeta)* and thymes *(Thymus),* perform well in these sites if the areas are sunny and well drained. If your air conditioner or dryer vent is in a moist and shady site, it is important to remember that the air currents will dry and heat the immediate area. Woodland natives will perform poorly, and tough, low perennials such as ajugas *(Ajuga),* creeping Jenny *(Lysimachia nummularia),* ivies *(Hedera),* and lily turfs *(Liriope)* are better choices. Be aware that some air conditioners create such harsh conditions that no plants will survive close to them. In these cases, use a stone mulch.

Utility covers near ground level are features of many modern homes. Access is typically needed only on rare occasions, and so these covers can be masked by low ground covers. When the utility cover is hidden or buried, mark the site within the bed by an object such as a stone or a bird-bath, and plant the entire area with an assertively spreading ground cover. Low ground-covering shrubs that regenerate well, such as roses *(Rosa)*, stephanandras *(Stephanandra)*, and yews *(Taxus)*, are good choices. When access is needed, the branches can be moved or pruned, and the plants will regrow quickly. With herbaceous ground covers, of course, the plants can be divided and the area replanted.

Walkway edges present special problems. People may not stay on the path, or plants may encroach on the walkway. In both cases, the plants lose. If the pathway is too narrow, widen it. Ground covers planted along a walkway should not create tripping hazards or have low branches that will snag skin, clothes, or the sides of grocery bags. When leaves and stems grow near the edges of a walkway, they should be pliable, or ener-getic children and pets may snap them off. Cotoneasters *(Cotoneaster)*, junipers *(Juniperus)*, roses *(Rosa)*, and stephanandras *(Stephanandra)* are often used as ground covers next to walkways, especially on steep slopes and staircases. Though beautiful soon after establishment, the stems of these plants will quickly grow forward and encroach on the walkway. It is best to set these shrubs back and edge the walkway with a softer, pliable

The low, crisp green foliage and white flowers of Galium odora-tum *contrasts well with the height of the woody plants and the muted blue-gray gravel path. The sweep of* Gal-ium *unifies the entire area and draws one along the path.*

ground cover that is hardy in your area. The tapestry produced by a mix of ground covers creates a distinctive and welcoming effect.

Hardiness Matters

Listen to a group of gardeners discussing plants, and you are likely to hear the term "hardiness zone." What they are talking about is the severity and length of cold a plant will tolerate in an average winter. The right ground covers for your garden are those that thrive in your hardiness zone, as well as in the microclimates in your garden. You can locate your hardiness zone on the USDA Hardiness Zone Map on page 357. In temperate regions of North America, plants considered hardy in your zone and colder will usually survive in your garden. Plants from warmer zones will usually not survive in your garden without special siting and care, if at all. (The temperate regions include most of the continent except desert areas and regions where the native vegetation is dominated by cacti and succulents or by broad-leaved evergreen trees and shrubs, such as evergreen oaks and magnolias.) In subtropical and strongly Mediterranean-type climates (those in the Deep South, on the Gulf Coast, and in parts of California), plants from colder hardiness zones may not tolerate the warm season because of those plants' physiological need for a specific winter dormancy period or their inability to thrive in hot weather. In these warm climates, special siting and care can help you enlarge your plant palette.

Gardeners revel in surprising their friends by growing plants that are not expected to survive in their particular hardiness zones. These gardeners succeed in this "zonal denial" by finding the perfect microsite in their gardens that is as much as one hardiness zone warmer or cooler. The soil next to a south- or west-facing masonry wall is slightly warmer in the winter due to the retained heat, especially if the wall is heated from the back, such as a house foundation where there is a full basement. Large expanses of pavement also change the microsite conditions. Pavement absorbs significant heat during sunny days and in turn heats up and dries out adjacent beds more quickly than areas just a few feet away. This desiccation can be particularly stressful to plants in winter, when lack of humidity and the relatively warm soil work together to dry out leaves and roots even more.

By contrast, soil in the north shadow of a wall or building is slightly cooler, and plants that are happy in cooler climates may thrive there. Likewise, sites adjacent to large bodies of water tend to have microsites that are slightly milder and with delayed seasons. The larger the body of water, the farther inland the effect extends. In the fall, this warming is due to the heat given off by the water as it slowly cools and then freezes— prolonging the growing season and holding off the first killing frosts. In the spring, the reverse is true, as the cold water takes longer to warm to summer temperatures, thus keeping the site cooler. In all of these cases, you can experiment with a wider variety of plants. Use the Encyclopedia of Plants to guide your selection.

Conditions Can Change

Sometimes an established ground cover will go into decline through no fault of its own. Over the years, sites change for many reasons—the growth or loss of trees, additions to buildings, and the like. Ground covers that thrived several years before, perhaps when you bought your home, may now perform poorly even though you have made no changes in the garden area. As you plan your ground-cover plantings, think of how the amount and intensity of shade and root competition will change as a result of the growth of existing trees and large shrubs. Are some of the trees and shrubs likely to be removed and thus change the light level so that another selection would perform better? Likewise, if there are new trees, are they growing so quickly that the sun-loving ground covers you are considering will need to be replaced in a few years, whereas a selection that is more tolerant of both sun and shade would perform better over the long run?

Did you know that some evergreen ground covers will survive in colder climates by shedding their leaves in winter? If you are an adventuresome gardener and want to experiment with these plants, your knowledge of microsites in your garden can help you guess where you might pull off this feat. Evergreen species of barren strawberries (*Waldsteinia*), cranesbills (*Geranium*), evening primroses (*Oenothera*), lily turfs (*Liriope*), true strawberries (*Fragaria*), roses (*Rosa*), and wild gingers (*Asarum*) are candidates to try. However, these are the exceptions, so don't expect most evergreen ground covers to live if they lose their foliage. Most will die, either outright or by going into permanent decline.

INVASIVE EXOTICS

The term "invasive exotic" refers to a plant from a distant land that has been introduced as an ornamental and, once established in the garden, has "leapt the wall" into the natural landscape and escaped. This is not a problem if establishment is rare, if plants quickly die out, or if they grow only under exceptional circumstances and spread no farther. Alas, just as starlings and English sparrows, introduced to North America so that youths could see the birds mentioned in Shakespeare, have become invasive pests, so too have some ornamental plants. An important ecological and horticultural issue in selecting ground covers is determining whether the plant is an invasive pest in your area.

All invasive species are native plants somewhere on Earth. What makes invasive species so ecologically damaging is that they have few, if any, natural controls on their growth in specific environments. As a result, they can dominate an area to the extent that native plants are challenged to survive. A major consequence is that the forest or grassland development in that area is arrested, and the invasive exotic maintains a chokehold on the site, with unknown ecological consequences. Some invasive exotics, such as kudzu *(Pueraria lobata)* and Japanese honeysuckle *(Lonicera japonica),* are well known as rampant ground covers.

Should you plant a certain ground cover even if it can be invasive in other parts of the country? The answer is a qualified yes. Remember that vigorous and spreading ground covers are not invasive under all circumstances. Plants that are invasive in one climate or region are often not invasive in another, nor are they likely to become so, since they have unique soil, hardiness, and water requirements.

Learn which species are invasive pests in your area and avoid them as ground covers. The best reference on this topic is the Brooklyn Botanic Garden's *Invasive Plants: Weeds of the Global Garden.* As more plant species are introduced, and as more of our countryside is disturbed by development and ecological stresses, it is likely that additional species will be found to be invasive in particular areas. Listed below are the ground covers known to be invasive in specific regions of North America.

Berberis thunbergii (Japanese barberry) is invasive in some parts of the Mid-Atlantic region and Midwest.

Carpobrotus edulis (ice plant) has escaped extensively in coastal California—a cautionary note for other members of Aizoaceae.

Coronilla varia (crown vetch) is a serious pest in the Northeast and Midwest.

Cotoneaster (several species) is invasive in parts of coastal California and occasionally escapes in other parts of the country.

Cytisus scoparius (Scotch broom) is not included in this book because it is an extremely invasive species in the Pacific Northwest and may have the potential to be so in other parts of North America.

Euonymus alatus (burning bush) has escaped cultivation throughout much of the East and Midwest.

Euonymus fortunei (wintercreeper) has become an invasive pest in the Chicago area and may become one in regions with similar climates.

Gypsophila paniculata (baby's breath) has escaped around Lake Michigan, where it is now well entrenched.

Hedera helix (English ivy) is a serious pest in humid parts of the Pacific Northwest, California, and the South.

Lonicera japonica (Japanese honeysuckle) has become established and invasive throughout much of temperate North America east of the Rockies.

Nandina domestica (heavenly bamboo), but not the dwarf forms listed here, has escaped to the pine woodlands of the southeastern United States.

Phalaris arundinacea (ribbon grass) invades and persists in a wide variety of moist habitats, from prairies in the Midwest to mountain and alpine habitats in the West.

Vinca minor (myrtle) and *V. major* (bigleaf periwinkle) are distinctive "exotic squatters" in several regions of North America. They are very persistent, sometimes being the only indicators in woodlands of long-abandoned farmsteads. In favorable sites, the massive vegetative colonies continue to spread and show no signs of dying out, but they do not appear to spread by seed into new locations, as is true of exotic invasives.

✿ DESIGN ISSUES

Stylish Solutions

Every garden, including your garden, fits at least one broad garden style, and some gardens have areas with separate styles. Think of garden styles as breezes moving a weathervane — the weathervane can't point north and south at the same time, but it can swing to a point between north and west. Some of the major "compass points" of garden styles work for opposite aesthetic purposes. A garden can't be formal and naturalistic at the same time, but it can be formal and contemporary, naturalistic and con-

Any ground cover can work in very different situations and styles provided its
cultural requirements are met. Santolina chamaecyparissus is important in
these very distinct gardens. Next to the
ocean (above), the repeating mounds of
silvery gray foliage with bright yellow
flowers is the constant in the cottage
perennials. Next to the formal terrace
(right), two foliage colors of Santolina
are massed and treated as a serpentine
ribbon separating the terrace from the
turf.

temporary, formal and romantic, romantic and naturalistic, and on and on.

Fortunately for the gardener, there are many design styles. In addition, there are subtle influences that give a garden a sense of a specific culture, such as Chinese, English, French, or Japanese. No one style, or combination of styles, is more "right" than another, but some are more appealing to individual gardeners. Learn how to read this vocabulary of styles and use it in your own garden to your advantage.

One of your main design decisions—one that ground covers will reinforce—is how formal or naturalistic you want your garden to look. Formal styles are based on geometric patterns, often reflecting the architecture of your home. In these styles, plantings may be symmetrical or abstract, but plant placement and rigorous maintenance always show that you are in control. Naturalistic styles, by contrast, try to mimic the plant combinations as they are found in the landscape—think of a woodland or meadow scene. In these styles, plantings reflect site conditions and flow organically over the ground. Your hand is less obvious, although design and maintenance are still essential. Many garden styles combine formal and naturalistic elements, but it is always helpful to determine whether your garden breeze is blowing, so to speak, predominantly from the north or the south.

Broad, sweeping masses of low plants are thought of as the "estate look," combining well with contemporary architecture but also enhancing older homes. Drive through an established neighborhood in any part of the country, especially in the East, Midwest, and Deep South, and you may well see massed ground covers such as cast-iron plant *(Aspidistra elatior)*, pachysandra *(Pachysandra terminalis)*, or periwinkle *(Vinca)* complementing spring-blooming shrubs. The estate style emphasizes generous plantings, a restricted plant palette, and simplicity of maintenance.

The opposite extreme, the "cottage look," has become popular in the past several decades, especially among enthusiastic plant collectors. Think of the cottage look as quilting with plants, where you assemble many different but compatible elements into a pleasing whole. You may have seen gardens where ground-covering masses of daylilies *(Hemerocallis)*, hostas *(Hosta)*, or pinks *(Dianthus)* on closer inspection turn out to be composed of blocks of individual selections.

Naturalistic styles are patterned after plants as they are found in nature. These styles combine plants based on similar ecological needs, such as sun or shade, wet or dry. Plants are arranged as they are in nature, even though the species may come from different continents. A naturalistic style does not require that you use only native plants. One of the advantages of naturalistic styles is that you can use spring ephemerals in your ground covers. Spring ephemerals are plants that perform magnificently early in the year, such as dogtooth violets *(Erythronium)* and May apples *(Podophyllum),* then retreat into dormancy once the hot weather arrives.

One of the most famous examples of a garden in which ground covers and spring ephemerals are used superbly and on a grand scale is Winterthur in Delaware. In the naturalistic woodlands at Winterthur, the season begins with early bulbs — snowdrops, crocuses, winter aconites — under tall tulip poplars and beeches. These are followed by a tapestry of spring-blooming Jacob's ladder *(Polemonium),* woodland phloxes *(Phlox divaricata, P. stolonifera),* and windflowers *(Anemone nemorosa, A. apennina).* As these fade, waves of ferns such as *Osmunda,* hostas *(Hosta),* and lilies *(Lilium)* take over, and the woods are underplanted with periwinkle *(Vinca).* This is "time-sharing" on a grand scale. The early bloomers are not cut back, but instead disappear behind the later foliage. Vigor is maintained by annual applications of a chopped-leaf mulch and careful hand weeding of unwanted seedlings. You can adapt these ideas even to a small space.

In the mid-twentieth century, the American firm of Oehme van Sweden & Associates interpreted a naturalistic ecological style from Germany for North American gardens. This became the movement to make "bold, romantic gardens" using ornamental grasses and thousands of plants of a

In the grand naturalistic garden at Winterthur, the tapestry of ground covers in-cluding Anemone apennina, Mertensia vir-ginica, *and* Phlox divaricata *shares the scene with the foliage of wild-flowers and com-plements the col-orful masses of azaleas.*

single species arranged to create grand sweeps. What makes this contemporary and romantic style effective as well as distinctive is its textural compositions, in which large expanses of foliage and seed heads are considered essential elements throughout the year. Behind the carefully chosen palette is rigorous attention to plant compatibility, both culturally and aesthetically. These gardens erase the distinction between "perennials" and "ground covers"—the look is simply a matter of scale and intent.

Just as you can copy Winterhur's naturalistic woodland style with spring ephemerals, you can borrow the bold, romantic style of Oehme van Sweden. First, assess your site for its light requirements, soil conditions, and hardiness zone. Then check the Encyclopedia of Plants for selections that meet those conditions. Once you have made your initial list, you must be ruthless. Massed perennials used as ground covers for a bold, romantic look will make an even stronger design statement if you plant sweeps of a limited range of plants.

If your site is sunny, consider massing lamb's ears (*Stachys byzantina* 'Silver Carpet') backed by sedum (*Sedum* 'Herbstfreude' ['Autumn Joy']) and yarrow (*Achillea* 'Moonshine'). Build up the textures from front to back and side to side, with the low, fuzzy *Stachys* acting as the unifying river of color that winds between the islands of *Sedum* and *Achillea*. The recurring waves of silvery foliage will light up a sunny, gravelly slope. Complete the picture with grand drifts of roses *(Rosa rugosa),* and you will have a year-round, long-lived design in which the similar habitat requirements of the plants can be easily met.

Perhaps you have a partly shaded site. If so, consider bergenias *(Bergenia)* or lady's mantle *(Alchemilla)* boldly braided through with astilbes *(Astilbe)* and hostas *(Hosta)* for a pleasing composition. It's important to have a range of foliage sizes in the composition but not in each genus. Consider hostas with smaller foliage, such as 'Blue Cadet' or *Hosta plantaginea,* rather than attention-grabbing hostas such as 'Sum and Substance', unless your site is very large. Lay them out in a zigzag pattern so that the ground will fill in more quickly, rather than in a straight line. Think of arranging your family for a group portrait so that everyone can be seen, and you'll get the idea of how to place the plants.

Foliage Sets the Mood

Once you have decided that you want to use ground covers in your garden, you have two choices, regardless of style. You can simply use what is hardy, available, and cheap, or you can select the right ground covers to make a design statement. Selecting the right ground covers, whether foliage or flowering, means thinking about the moods you want the garden to evoke. These moods—such as contemplative or exciting, lively or serene—are largely set by foliage features and the size of plant masses.

We are all familiar with glossy and matte finishes on photographs, and exactly the same effects occur with ground-cover leaves when seen *en masse*. Glossy foliage is lively and vibrant, whereas matte foliage is soothing. Plants look matte or glossy depending on their leaf surface, shape, and size. Ground covers are seen as very glossy when the leaves look polished, regardless of leaf size. Examples are bergenias *(Bergenia)*, Confederate jasmine *(Trachelospermum jasminoides)*, European wild ginger *(Asarum europaeum)*, and periwinkle *(Vinca)*. Ground covers are seen as relatively glossy when the leaves have some luster and are held close to each other and roughly parallel to the ground, as in some forms of ajugas *(Ajuga)* and ivies *(Hedera)*. Ground-cover leaves are seen as matte when they are hairy (lamb's ears *[Stachys]* and spurge *[Euphorbia myrsinites]*); when the leaves are held at various angles to the ground (astilbes *[Astilbe]*, foamflower *[Tiarella]*, and lily-of-the-valley *[Convallaria]*); when there are numerous small leaves or leaflets (barrenworts *[Epimedium]*, bedstraw *[Galium]*, stephanandras *[Stephanandra]*, and thyme *[Thymus]*); when the leaf edges are curled or crisped (numerous forms of hostas *[Hosta]* and ivies *[Hedera]*); or when there are arching stems (many junipers *[Juniperus]*). Leaves appear especially matte when they have at least two of these characteristics—think of the silver leaves of beach

The silver foliage of Stachys byzantina *'Silver Carpet' is deftly used in two ways along a path. The narrow, silver ribbon highlights the dark, clipped hedge while its hillside planting is in scale to the large, naturalistic conifers.*

wormwood *(Artemisia stelleriana)* or the fan-shaped, dull green leaves of lady's mantle *(Alchemilla)*. Long, curving leaves are always seen as matte because the eye can't focus on all the arching shapes. Daylilies *(Hemerocallis)*, lily turf *(Liriope)*, sedges *(Carex)*, and most grasses are typical examples here.

Although color choices are often among the first to come to mind, they should follow after you have determined the mood of the garden. Colors strongly influence a garden's mood. Green is among the most soothing and refreshing colors, and the human eye is more sensitive to subtle shades of green than to any other color. Dark green is the key to making a garden seem calm and contemplative. By contrast, foliage that is variegated with white, silver, or golden yellow (as in most of the 'Picta' and 'Variegata' cultivars, as well as in many others) brightens an area and causes more visual excitement. This brightness makes the garden stimulating and lively. Purple or bronze foliage appears to absorb light and creates the effect of dark shadows. The rich tones of purple or bronze leaves can be used either to intensify the dark greens or to highlight the yellows, whites, and silvers.

The scale of ground-cover plantings affects the garden's mood and reflects your design style. Numerous small groups of plants make the scene active (think of the cottage garden style), but the same plants arranged in large, flowing masses can be naturalistic, dramatic (think of the bold and romantic style), or serene (think of the estate style). In a large garden, masses of ground-cover shrubs are especially useful for creating sweeping drifts in proportion to the space and views. Imagine that you are making layers, and place these large shrub masses amid equally bold sweeps of low ground covers. Instead of using the shrubs as specimen plants, treat them as if they were perennials to be massed in a group — only much larger. Now create irregular masses — but make a trial run first by using stakes as markers rather than dragging the shrubs around. It's much kinder to your back, and to the plants' roots, to move the stakes. Use small stakes and mark the center point where you think each plant should go. Step back and look at the stakes from all angles, rearrange them until the layout looks right, and when you are satisfied, start planting. Because shrubs have a rigid woody structure, remember to "face" them so that their branches will blend together.

The pleasure of gardening with ground covers comes from several sources. One pleasure is learning the diverse array of plants that serve well as ground covers in your region — especially those that go beyond the "expected" ground covers in your neighborhood. Another pleasure comes from experimenting with your garden's style by selecting different plants. Your increased awareness of foliage colors and textures will lead you to new discoveries of plant combinations that work for you. And, of course, there is the great fun of sharing ground covers you have propagated with family and friends.

Whether you are a neatnik or a naturalistic gardener, ground covers will tidy up your garden, hide the mulches, define bed edges, direct foot traffic, and set the mood. Finding the right ground covers is like finding the right carpet, rug, or flooring for a room. Far from being an afterthought, they are critical elements that set off everything around them, from house, to paths, to trees, lawn, and flowers. Gardening with ground covers opens new horizons.

Gallery
of Plants

◄ *Acanthus mollis*
Bear's Breeches
Partially shaded sites; may go dormant in hot, humid weather

Well-drained soil

Handsome, large-scale ground cover with evergreen leaves

Zones 7 to 10

P. 154

▼ *Acanthus spinosus*
Bear's Breeches
Nearly full sun to bright shade

Well-drained soil

Handsome, dissected leaves that are somewhat spiny

Zones 7 to 9

P. 154

► *Achillea* 'Coronation Gold'

Yarrow

Full sun required

Well-drained soil

Plants form slowly; spreading, low to medium-height masses of gray, finely cut foliage. Bright yellow flowers in midsummer are carried well above the foliage.

Zones 3 to 8

P. 156

► *Achillea* 'Moonshine'

Yarrow

Full sun needed for best performance

Well-drained soil

Plants form slowly; spreading, low to medium-height masses of silvery foliage. Pale yellow flowers complement the foliage.

Zones 3 to 8

P. 156

▲ *Acorus gramineus*
'Variegatus'

Japanese Sweet Flag

Full sun to partial shade

Constantly moist to nearly aquatic soils, prefer-
ably with above-average organic content
and high fertility

Slowly spreading, low, rhizomatous masses develop to form a lush, grasslike sward

Zones 6 to 9

P. 158

▼ *Aegopodium podagraria*
'Variegatum'

Goutweed, Bishop's Weed

Sun to deep shade

Any soil

Forms aggressive, vigorous medium-height
masses that will choke out most other
plants. Useful in dry shade where little else
will grow.

Zones 2 to 9

P. 159

▲ *Ajania pacifica*

Full sun to light shade

Moist, fertile, well-drained soil

Variegated foliage on sprawling, medium-height plants makes for attractive mass plantings. Tiny yellow flowers are produced in late summer.

Zones 7 to 10

P. 160

▼ *Ajuga genevensis*

Ajuga

Partial shade

Tolerates more alkaline and drier soils than most other ajugas

Moderate low spreader with attractive blue flowers — ajugas are good companion ground covers to spring bulbs

Zones 4 to 9

P. 161

▲ *Ajuga reptans* 'Burgundy Glow'

Ajuga

Partial shade; in full sun needs constant moisture

Moist but well-drained soil

Fast, low-growing spreader; lustrous bronze to bronze-green foliage and blue flowers

Zones 4 to 9

P. 161

▼ *Ajuga reptans* 'Pink Beauty'

Ajuga

Partial shade; in full sun needs constant moisture

Moist but well-drained soil

Fast spreader; mats of green leaves make three-season carpet

Zones 4 to 9

P. 162

▲ *Ajuga reptans* 'Pink Beauty'
Ajuga

Partial shade; in full sun needs constant moisture

Moist but well-drained soil

Fast spreader; in early summer light pink flowers are carried above mats of green leaves

Zones 4 to 9

P. 162

▼ *Ajuga reptans* 'Variegata'
Ajuga

Partial shade; in full sun needs constantly moist soils

Moist but well-drained soil

Fast spreader grown for its carpet of creamy white and green leaves

Zones 4 to 9

P. 162

▲ *Alchemilla mollis*

Lady's Mantle

Nearly full sun to partial shade depending on climate

Well-drained, moisture-retentive soil

Clump-forming and assertively self-seeding where well sited; bold, lime green leaves and clouds of tiny chartreuse flowers in early summer

Zones 4 to 8

P. 163

▼ *Anemone tomentosa*

Grape-leaf Anemone

Partial shade

Moist and organic soil

Spreading, tall perennial forms large masses with clean, green leaves and pink flowers in late summer

Zones 4 to 8

P. 165

▶ *Antennaria dioica*

Pussytoes

Full sun; does best in regions with cool summers

Well-drained soil

Mat-forming perennial with gray-green leaves and small, fuzzy flower heads spreads slowly for an excellent small-scale ground cover

Zones 3 to 8

P. 166

▶ *Arabis ferdinandi-coburgi*

Rock Cress

Full sun to partial shade; does best where summers are not hot and muggy

Well-drained soils required; slightly alkaline soils preferred

Cascading, low perennial ground cover for rock walls, gravels, and moderate slopes

Zones 4 to 9

P. 167

▲ *Arctostaphylos densiflora* 'Howard McMinn'

Vine Hill Manzanita, Sonoma Manzanita

Full sun; does best in the western states

Acidic, well-drained soil

Evergreen shrub to 5 feet tall but forming broader mounds because of stems that may root as they touch the ground

Zones 7 to 10

P. 168

▼ *Arctostaphylos* 'Emerald Carpet'

'Emerald Carpet' Bearberry

Full sun; does best in western states

Acidic, well-drained soil

Low-growing evergreen shrub makes a bright green carpet punctuated by small white flowers early in the growing season

Zones 8 to 10

P. 169

▲ *Arctostaphylos uva-ursi* 'Massachusetts'

Bearberry, Kinnikinnick

Full sun; one of the best selections for cool maritime gardens on the Atlantic Coast

Acidic, well-drained soil

Low-growing evergreen shrubs spread slowly to form dense but not quite prostrate mats

Zones 4 to 7

P. 169

▶ *Arctostaphylos uva-ursi* 'Vancouver Jade'

Bearberry

Full sun; does best in western states

Acidic, well-drained soil

Fast-growing low shrub with glossy, evergreen leaves

Zones 4 to 7

P. 169

▲ *Ardisia japonica*
Marlberry
Partial shade; does best in western states

Moist, organic soils of at least average fertility

Slow-growing but effectively spreading low evergreen shrub with dark green leaves and red fruits in winter

Zones 7 to 10

P. 170

▼ *Arenaria montana*
European Sandwort, Mountain Sandwort
Full sun

Alkaline, gritty to sandy soil

Lax stems covered with short, grasslike leaves support clouds of white flowers in spring

Zones 4 to 8

P. 171

▲ *Artemisia* 'Silver Brocade'

Beach Wormwood

Full sun

Gravelly dry soils with perfect drainage

Compact, slowly spreading plants with silvery cut foliage create stunning drifts and masses

Zones 4 to 8

P. 173

▼ *Asarum caudatum*

Western Wild Ginger

Partial to full shade

Rich, moist soil high in organic content

Spreads slowly by rhizomes to form a low carpet of heart-shaped leaves

Zones 6 to 9

P. 174

▲ *Asarum europaeum*

European Wild Ginger

Partial to full shade

Rich, moist, well-drained soil

Spreads slowly by rhizomes but self-seeds where conditions are right to create a low evergreen carpet of heart-shaped leaves

Zones 5 to 8

P. 174

◄ *Aspidistra elatior*

Cast-iron Plant

Partial to deep shade

Moist, well-drained, humus-rich soil

Slowly spreads by underground stems to form a low-maintenance, medium-height mass of stout, evergreen leaves

Zones 8 to 10

P. 176

▶ *Aster divaricatus*

White Wood Aster

Partial shade to nearly full sun

Moist, well-drained soils — plants grown in wet soils are often taller and ranker

Runs rapidly by underground stems to form large, spreading colonies to over 3 feet tall covered with small, white flowers in early fall

Zones 3 to 8

P. 177

▼ *Astilbe chinensis* 'Pumila'

Partial shade

Rich loams that never fully dry

Moderate spreader; plants form low, weed-suppressing mats with pale lavender flowers in fall; most tolerant *Astilbe* for dry sites

Zones 4 to 8

P. 178

◄ *Astilbe* 'Sprite'

Partial shade

Moist, rich loams that never fully dry

Very slowly spreading with finely cut dark
green foliage and pale pink flowers

Zones 4 to 8

P. 179

▼ *Athyrium filix-femina*

Lady Fern

Partial to full shade

Moist, organic soil

Vigorous, fast-spreading colonizer with deciduous fronds to 3 feet tall

Zones 5 to 9

P. 180

▲ *Athyrium niponicum* var. *pictum*

Japanese Painted Fern

Partial to full shade

Moist, organic soil

Foliage close-up shows complex and attractive coloration

Zones 4 to 9 (with protection at its southern limits)

P. 180

▼ *Athyrium niponicum* var. *pictum*

Japanese Painted Fern

Partial to full shade

Moist, organic soil

Nonspreading but effectively massed so its short attractive fronds marked with green, silver, and purple create a complex, eye-catching composition

Zones 4 to 9 (with protection at its southern limits)

P. 180

▲ *Aubrieta* hybrid 'Red Carpet'

Rock Cress
Full sun; performs best in climates with cool
  summers
Well-drained soil
Slowly spreading herbaceous mat with purplish
  flowers in spring
Zones 4 to cool 7
P. 181

▼ *Aurinia saxatilis*

Basket-of-gold
Full sun
Well-drained, acidic soil
Cascading perennial mats with bright yellow
  flowers in spring
Zones 4 to 6
P. 182

▲ *Baccharis pilularis* 'Twin Peaks'

Coyote Bush

Full sun

Good drainage required

Fast-growing, low-spreading shrub with bright green, fire-resistant leaves; this is a male selection so there are no seed heads

Zones 7 to 10

P. 184

▼ *Berberis thunbergii* 'Kobold'

(Inset: Small, bright yellow flowers in spring are followed by attractive slender red fruits in fall.)

Full sun to light shade

Very tolerant of a wide range of soil conditions

Low to medium-high shrub with deciduous dark green leaves

Zones 4 to 8

P. 185

◀ *Bergenia ciliata*

Partial to full shade

Moist, rich, medium to heavy soil

Nonspreading plants that are massed for their large, elegant, rich green foliage

Zones 7 to 9

P. 186

▼ *Bergenia cordifolia*

Heart-leaved Bergenia

Partial to full shade

Moist, rich, medium to heavy soil

Nonspreading to slowly spreading perennial massed for its bold, glossy, dark evergreen leaves

Zones 3 to 5 (deciduous), 6 to 9 (evergreen)

P. 187

▲ *Bergenia* 'Silberlicht'

Partial shade

Moist, rich, medium to heavy soil

Use where the white flowers work with the overall color scheme of the garden or to highlight the dark leaves

Zones 3 to 5 (deciduous), 6 to 9 (evergreen with ample water)

P. 187

▼ *Brunnera macrophylla* 'Langtrees'

Siberian Bugloss, Dwarf Anchusa

Partial to full shade

Any fertile garden soil that never dries out

Medium-tall, slowly spreading perennial

Zones 3 to 9

P. 188

▲ *Calamintha nepeta*

Full sun to lightly filtered shade

Dry, well-drained soils of average fertility — in rich soils the plants may be leggy and short-lived

Lax-stemmed perennials to barely woody spreading shrubs grown for their aromatic foliage and tiny white, pink, or blue flowers

Zones 4 to 8

P. 188

▼ *Callirhoe involucrata*

Wine Cups

Full sun; does best where summers are dry

Well-drained soil

Sprawling but nonspreading low perennial with surprisingly large flowers — massed plants cascade over the ground and walls

Zones 6 to 9

P. 189

▲ *Calluna vulgaris*
Scotch Heather

Full sun; performs poorly in regions with high
  summer humidity and hot nights

Well-drained, acidic soil

Low evergreen shrubs with needlelike leaves
  and small, urn-shaped flowers in summer

Zones 5 (with protection) to 8

P. 190

▼ *Campanula carpatica*
'Blue Clips'
Carpathian Bellflower

Full sun to light shade

Good, well-drained soil

Low, creeping perennial forms mats highlighted
  with bright blue flowers in summer

Zones 4 to 8

P. 191

▲ *Campanula portenschlagiana*

Dalmatian Bellflower

Full sun to light shade

Good, well-drained soil

A vigorous, spreading perennial with deciduous to evergreen foliage (depending on winter severity) and deep blue flowers in summer

Zones 4 to 8

P. 192

◄ *Campanula takesimana*

Sun to partial shade

Good, well-drained soil

An invasive perennial; forms blankets of low to medium foliage that chokes out other plants; large, pendent speckled flowers in summer

Zones 4 to 8

P. 192

▸ *Carex glauca*

Blue Sedge

Partial shade to nearly full sun

Dry to moist soil

Nonspreading masses add dramatic foliage texture and color to the garden

Zones 5 to 9

P. 193

▾ *Carex muskingumensis*

Palm Sedge

Partial shade to sun

Moist but not soggy soil

Slowly spreading perennial with distinctive deciduous foliage gives the garden a tropical look

Zones 4 to 8

P. 193

▲ *Carex nigra*

Black Sedge

Partial to deep shade

Moist but not soggy soil

Nonspreading perennial massed for its glossy
green foliage

Zones 6 to 9

P. 194

◄ *Ceanothus griseus*
var. *horizontalis*

Carmel Creeper

Full sun to very light shade; best used in western states

Acidic, well-drained soil

Low, spreading, evergreen shrub well suited to
cover slopes and rough ground; pale blue
flowers in late winter

Zones 7 to 10

P. 195

▲ *Cerastium tomentosum*

Snow-in-summer

Full sun; performs best where summers are not hot and humid

Friable to sandy, well-drained soils

Fast-spreading low perennial with small gray leaves and clouds of tiny white flowers

Zones 3 to 8, but not reliably perennial in hot, humid regions

P. 196

▼ *Ceratostigma plumbaginoides*

Plumbago

Full sun to bright shade; performs best in warm climates

Well-drained and never wet soil

Low, tough, spreading perennial with green leaves that have a red to bronze cast in fall; stunning blue flowers in summer

Zones 6 (marginal as a ground cover) to 10

P. 197

◄ *Chamaemelum nobile*

Chamomile

Full sun to very light shade

Well-drained soils of average fertility

A small-scale lawn alternative—provided there is very little foot traffic—with bright green, aromatic leaves and daisylike flowers

Zones 5 to 9; unsuitable where summers are muggy

P. 198

▼ *Chrysogonum virginianum*

Green and Gold

Partial shade—can tolerate sun in the North

Moist and at least slightly acidic soil with above-average organic content

Low-growing, deciduous woodland native with showy yellow flowers in spring

Zones 6 to 8

P. 200

▲ *Cistus salviifolius*
Sage-leaf Rock Rose

Full sun; grows best in western states

Well-drained soil

Rugged, evergreen, fire-retardant low shrub masses well to cover slopes; showy white flowers with yellow markings

Zones 8 to 10

P. 201

▼ *Comptonia peregrina*
Sweet Fern

Full sun; grows best in cool climates

Poor, well-drained soil

Distinctively aromatic, fernlike foliage on low, colonizing shrubs; effective for naturalizing; intolerant of disturbance one established

Zones 3 to 7

P. 202

◄ *Convallaria majalis*

Lily-of-the-valley

Partial shade; rapidly spreading perennial does best in cool climates

Average garden soils—amazingly tough once established

Deciduous perennial spreads indefinitely, creating a low mass of broad green leaves and, in spring, sprays of fragrant, small pendent white flowers (the bright red berries are toxic and should be kept away from infants)

Zones 4 to 9

P. 203

◄ *Convolvulus cneorum*

Silverbush

Full sun

Sandy to clayey well-drained soil

Small shrubs with silvery foliage and silky white flowers mass well to make dramatic sweeps by themselves or with companion ground covers

Zones 8 to 10

P. 204

▲ *Convolvulus sabatius*
(Inset: flowers)

Ground Morning Glory

Full sun

Sandy to clayey well-drained soil

Trailing perennial with silvered leaves and
lavender-blue flowers; excellent for covering
banks, rocky slopes, and draping over walls

Zones 8 to 10

P. 204

▼ *Cornus canadensis*

Bunchberry

Partial shade

Rich, moist, organic, strongly acidic soil

Stunningly beautiful, low, creeping ground
cover for naturalizing in cool northern gardens; small, white flowers are followed by
red fruits and dramatic fall foliage

Zones 2 to 5

P. 205

◄ *Coronilla varia*

Crown Vetch

Full sun

Poor, dry, well-drained soil

An aggressively invasive pest in some parts of the country where it was introduced to stabilize road cuts. Useful for its soft green deciduous foliage and attractive flowers in summer but only if it can be prevented from escaping.

Zones 4 to 8

P. 206

▼ *Cotoneaster apiculatus*

Cranberry Cotoneaster

Full sun to light shade

Average, neutral to acidic, well-drained soil

Low, mat-forming shrub with attractive red fruits held well into winter

Zones 4 to 8

P. 208

▲ *Cotoneaster horizontalis*

Rockspray Cotoneaster

Full sun to light shade

Average, well-drained soil

Low-growing evergreen to semievergreen shrub
with attractive branching structure and
handsome small red fruits in fall

Zones 5 (4 with careful siting) to 8

P. 208

▼ *Cotoneaster procumbens*

Full sun to light shade

Average, well-drained soil

Ground-hugging evergreen shrub forms a
glossy carpet

Zones 7 to 8

P. 209

▲ *Cyrtomium falcatum*
Holly Fern

Partial to full shade

Moist soil; must never dry out

Handsome, rugged ferns form dark, medium-
height evergreen masses that complement
many other plants

Zones 8 to 10

P. 210

▼ *Daboecia cantabrica*
Irish Heath

Full sun; performs best in cool maritime climates on both coasts

Organic, acidic, and well-drained soil

Use in low, naturalistic drifts with heaths
(Erica) and heathers *(Calluna)*

Zones 6 to 8

P. 211

▸ *Dalea greggii*
Trailing Indigo Bush

Full sun; performs best where summers are hot and dry

Well-drained, alkaline soil

Excellent low, ground-covering shrub with pearly gray foliage and amethyst flowers in spring

Zones 8 to 10

P. 212

▸ *Daphne × burkwoodii*
'Carol Mackie'

(Inset: flowers)

Full sun to partial shade

Porous and well-drained soil—plants are intolerant of wet soils and easily drowned (as by automatic sprinklers)

Fragrant white flowers on small to medium-size deciduous shrubs that form eye-catching masses of variegated foliage—use where the fragrance will be enjoyed but the toxic to lethal attractive fruits are out of reach of children

Zones 5 to 8

P. 213

▲ *Daphne cneorum* 'Ruby Glow'

Garland Daphne

Full sun to partial shade

Neutral to alkaline, porous and well-drained soil—plants are intolerant of wet soils and easily drowned (as by automatic sprinklers)

Intensely fragrant rich pink flowers on small deciduous shrubs; use where the fragrance will be enjoyed but the toxic to lethal attractive fruits are out of reach of children

Zones 5 to 8

P. 213

▼ *Dennstaedtia punctilobula*

Hay-scented Fern

Partial shade; nearly full sun at the northern limit

Slightly dry, rocky, stony soil

Assertively spreading deciduous fern with fragrant (when crushed) fronds provides a "been here forever" feel; avoid areas with high foot traffic

Zones 3 to 8

P. 215

▶ *Dianthus* 'Bath's Pink'

Full sun

Fast-draining, calcareous to neutral soil

The most heat- and humidity-tolerant *Dianthus* for ground-covering purposes, with grayish foliage and clove-scented pink flowers

Zones 4 to 8

P. 216

▼ *Dianthus deltoides*

Maiden Pink

Full sun

Fast-draining, calcareous to neutral soil

Low, slowly spreading perennial with deciduous, blue-gray grasslike leaves forms bold masses with white, pink, or red flowers

Zones 4 to 8

P. 216

▲ *Dianthus gratianopolitanus* 'Tiny Rubies'

Pink, Cheddar Pink

Full sun, especially popular in northern New
  Mexico, Colorado, and adjacent areas

Fast-draining, calcareous to neutral soil

Spreading, grassy, dwarf, narrow-leaved
  mounds covered in spring with bright rose-
  pink flowers

Zones 4 to 8

P. 216

▼ *Dicentra eximia*

Bleeding Heart

Partial shade

Rich, loamy soil that never dries out

Slowly spreading perennial with dissected, fernlike foliage and flowers in spring

Zones 4 to 9

P. 217

▶ *Dicentra formosa*
Bleeding Heart

Partial shade

Rich, loamy soil that never dries out

The best spreader of the species, the pale to deep rose flowers are produced through much of the growing season

Zones 4 to 9

P. 217

▶ *Dicentra* 'Luxuriant'
Bleeding Heart

Partial shade

Rich, loamy soil that never dries out

Slowly spreading perennial with dissected, blue-gray foliage and dark pink to purplish red flowers

Zones 4 to 9

P. 217

▲ *Dichondra micrantha*
Pony-foot

Partial shade to sun

Moist but not wet, average soil

Warm-climate lawn substitute forms spreading, almost-prostrate mats of small, rounded to heart-shaped leaves

Zones 9 (8 with protection) to 10

P. 218

▼ *Dryopteris marginalis*
Marginal Wood Fern

Partial shade

Moist, organic, acidic, above-average fertility

Slowly spreading, long-lived perennial fern with deciduous fronds makes an impressive stand when massed; surprisingly tolerant of occasional drought once established

Zones 5 to 9

P. 220

▶ *Duchesnea indica*
Barren Strawberry, Mock Strawberry

Partial to deep shade — tends to burn in full sun

Well-drained but not dry soil; not particular regarding pH

Fast-spreading, deciduous, low ground cover with strawberry-like leaves and yellow flowers in spring

Zones 5 to 8 (tolerant of warmer zones with cool summers)

P. 221

▶ *Epigaea repens*
Mayflower, Trailing Arbutus

Light shade

Highly acidic, organic, well-drained, and moist but not wet soil

Small-scale, almost-prostrate, evergreen ground cover with fragrant flowers in spring for naturalistic gardens

Zones 3 to 5 or 6

P. 222

◄ *Epimedium alpinum*
Barrenwort, Bishop's Hat
Partial shade

Well-drained but not dry, acidic soil

Spreading perennial with deciduous foliage and creamy yellow flowers in spring; relatively tolerant of dry shade once established

Zones 4 to 8

P. 223

◄ *Epimedium × perralchicum*
'Frohnleiten'
Barrenwort, Bishop's Hat
Light shade

Well-drained but not dry, acidic soil

Slow-spreading evergreen perennial with acid yellow flowers in spring

Zones 5 to 8

P. 224

▸ *Epimedium × versicolor* 'Sulphureum'

Barrenwort, Bishop's Hat

Light shade

Well-drained but not dry soil

One of the best barrenworts for use as a ground
cover, as the foliage masses choke out weeds;
lemon yellow flowers in spring

Zones 5 to 8

P. 224

▸ *Erica carnea* 'Vivellii'

Winter Heath

Full sun; best in maritime regions with cool
summers

Acidic, well-drained but not dry soil

Mass plantings form attractive, low, evergreen,
naturalistic drifts with small, deep red flowers in early spring

Zones 5 to 8

P. 225

▲ *Euonymus fortunei*
'Silver Queen'

Wintercreeper

Full sun to partial shade

Ordinary, well-drained garden soil

Dense, vigorously spreading, almost-prostrate,
    evergreen shrub forms extensive weed-free
    mats

Zones 4 to 9

P. 227

◄ *Euphorbia amygdaloides*
var. *robbiae*

Wood Spurge

Partial shade

Well-drained soil

Slowly spreading, low, dark green, evergreen
    ground cover masses well in woodland set-
    tings and shady garden sites

Zones 6 to 9

P. 228

▲ *Euphorbia cyparissias*

Cypress Spurge

Sun to light shade

Well-drained, dry soil

Aggressively spreading low perennial with running underground stems; forms extensive
finely textured stands of blue-gray foliage

Zones 6 to 8

P. 228

▼ *Euphorbia griffithii*

Spurge

Sun to light shade

Well-drained soil

Tall perennial forms distinctive masses in large-
scale landscapes

Zones 6 to 8

P. 228

▲ *Euphorbia myrsinites*
(Inset: flowers)

Spurge

Full sun

Well-drained soil

Distinctive stems of fleshy, waxy, blue-green leaves carpet the ground and cascade over walls — few other ground covers have this dramatic presence

Zones 6 to 9

P. 228

▼ *Euphorbia polychroma*

Cushion Spurge

Full sun to light shade; can't take high heat and summer humidity

Well-drained soil

The hardiest ground-covering euphorbia spreads assertively to form light green masses with acid yellow bracts in late spring to early summer

Zones 4 to 7

P. 229

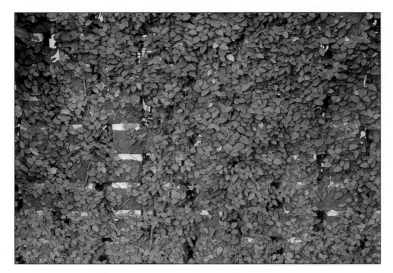

▲ *Ficus pumila*

Creeping Fig

Light shade; will not climb well on extremely hot walls

Moist, well-drained, loamy soil

Vigorous, tough, evergreen ground cover and climbing vine forms nearly flat mats that cover almost any surface

Zones 9 to 10

P. 230

▼ *Forsythia* 'Arnold Dwarf'

Full sun

Average garden soil

Tough, low deciduous shrub roots as it grows; useful in difficult sites in cold climates

Zones 3 to 8

P. 231

▲ *Forsythia viridissima* 'Bronxensis'

Full sun

Average garden soil

Tough, low deciduous shrub roots as it grows; useful in difficult sites in cold climates

Zones 3 to 8

P. 231

▼ *Fragaria chiloensis*

Chilean Strawberry

Full sun

Well-drained moist soil

Vigorously spreading, low evergreen ground cover with white flowers in spring and bland fruits in early summer

Zones 5 to 10

P. 232

▲ *Fragaria* 'Pink Panda'

Full sun to light shade

Well-drained moist soil

Small-scale ground cover with distinctive bright
     pink flowers

Zones 5 to 8

P. 232

▶ *Galax urceolata*

Partial to full shade

Moist, organic, acid soil

Elegant, low evergreen ground cover forms
     slowly spreading mats when well sited;
     striking spikes of white flowers in early
     summer

Zones 5 to 8

P. 234

◄ *Galium odoratum*

Sweet Woodruff, Ladies' Bedstraw

Partial shade

Well-drained but moist soil; will perform
    poorly in either compacted or loose soils

Persistently spreading, low, deciduous foliage
    makes for a light airy mass with clouds of
    tiny, white flowers in spring

Zones 4 to 8

P. 235

▼ *Gaultheria mucronata*

Chilean Pernettya

Nearly full sun to light shade; does best in west-
    ern states

Moist but well-drained acidic soil

Low, suckering evergreen shrub with shiny
    leaves and handsome (but toxic) berries

Zones 7 to 9

P. 236

▲ *Gaultheria shallon*

Salal

Sun to light shade; does best in western states

Moist but well-drained acidic soil

Spreading shrub with tough, evergreen leaves
and dark berries

Zones 7 to 9

P. 237

▼ *Gazania rigens*

Trailing Gazania

Full sun

Well-drained but not dry soil

Effective, low, spreading cover for slopes and
banks with attractive bright flowers

Zones 9 to 10

P. 238

◀ *Gelsemium sempervirens*
Carolina Jessamine
Full sun to light shade

Grows best in acidic, well-drained, moist, fertile soils

Moderately fast-growing vine that climbs and spreads indefinitely; glossy, evergreen leaves and stout, yellow flowers

Zones 8 to 10

P. 239

◀ *Genista pilosa*
Broom
Full sun

Well-drained soil

Low-growing, evergreen ground cover with bright yellow flowers; useful on banks and slopes

Zones 6 to 9

P. 240

▲ *Genista sagittalis*

Broom

Full sun

Well-drained soil

Distinctive, small-scale ground cover with almost-prostrate, flattened, photosynthetic
stems and small, bright yellow, pea-shaped
flowers

Zones 6 to 9

P. 240

▶ *Geranium × cantabrigiense*

Geranium, Cranesbill

Partial shade; more tolerant of warm, humid
climates than most geraniums

Moisture-retentive, well-drained soil

Vigorous to moderate rate of spread with fragrant foliage and pink flowers

Zones 5 to 8

P. 241

▲ *Geranium himalayense*
'Johnson's Blue'

Geranium, Cranesbill

Full sun to partial shade

Moisture-retentive, well-drained soil

Classic selection to make spreading masses
highlighted by relatively large, blue flowers

Zones 5 to 8

P. 241

▼ *Geranium macrorrhizum*
'Album'

Geranium, Cranesbill

Partial shade

Well-drained soil

One of the best geraniums for dry shade; plants
spread to form patches; leaves are fragrant
when brushed; flowers white with a pink
blush

Zones 4 to 8

P. 242

▲ *Geranium macrorrhizum* 'Bevan's Variety'

Geranium, Cranesbill

Partial shade

Moisture-retentive, well-drained soil

Similar to *macrorrhizum* 'Album', except the flowers are deep magenta

Zones 4 to 9

P. 242

▼ *Geranium macrorrhizum* 'Ingwersen's Variety'

Geranium, Cranesbill

Partial shade

Moisture-retentive, well-drained soil

Similar to *macrorrhizum* 'Album', except the foliage is light green and the flowers pale pink

Zones 4 to 9

P. 242

▲ *Geranium × oxonianum* 'Claridge Druce'

(Inset: close-up)

Geranium, Cranesbill

Partial shade

Moisture-retentive, well-drained soil

Slowly spreading, ground-covering geranium with magenta pink flowers highlighted with dark veins

Zones 5 to 8

P. 242

▼ *Geranium phaeum* 'Samobor'

Mourning Widow Geranium

Partial to full shade

Moisture-retentive, well-drained soil

Excellent geranium for shade, colonizes extensively even in dry areas; foliage has distinctive deep brown markings and bronze-red flowers

Zones 5 to 8

P. 242

▲ *Geranium sanguineum*
Bloody Cranesbill

Full sun to partial shade

Moisture-retentive, well-drained soil

Low, spreading geranium forms thick, weed-proof mats highlighted by bold magenta flowers

Zones 4 to 9

P. 242

▼ *Gypsophila repens* 'Rosea'
Creeping Baby's Breath

Full sun; not tolerant of hot, muggy summers

Well-drained, friable to gravelly, alkaline soil

Low-growing foliage supports clouds of pink flowers in early to midsummer; exceptionally attractive where the frothy floral display can spill down hills or along pathways

Zones 3 to 9

P. 243

▲ *Hebe pinguifolia*

Full sun; best in maritime climates

Moist but well-drained, organic soil

Mounding small shrub masses well to add gray-green foliage in the landscape, white flowers in early summer

Zones 8 to 10

P. 245

▼ *Hedera canariensis* 'Gloire de Marengo'

Algerian Ivy

Partial shade; may burn in full sun

Average garden soil

Very adaptable; somewhat coarse in texture; variegated ground cover best used where large masses are seen at a distance

Zones 8 to 10

P. 246

▲ *Hedera colchica*

Persian Ivy

Partial shade; may burn in full sun

Average garden soil

Attractive, evergreen ivy useful in warm climates; numerous named cultivars allow selection for leaf shape and color

Zones 7 to 10

P. 246

▼ *Helianthemum nummularium* 'Wisley Pink'

Full sun

Superbly well-drained soil; intolerant of winter dampness in the soil

Low mats of rooting stems host gray foliage and pink flowers

Zones 6 to 9

P. 248

▲ *Helianthemum nummularium* 'Wisley Primrose'

Full sun; best where summers are dry

Superbly well-drained soil; intolerant of winter dampness in the soil, as is the case with organic-rich soils

Low mats of rooting stems host gray-green foliage and pale yellow flowers

Zones 5 to 9

P. 248

◄ *Helleborus niger*

Christmas Rose

Partial shade

Alkaline to neutral soil

Clump-forming ground cover with attractive evergreen leaves; flowers in late winter to early spring

Zones 4 to 9

P. 249

▲ *Helleborus orientalis*
Lenten Rose

(Inset: Hellebore flowers appear before most
  spring bulbs; numerous named selections,
  including hybrids, are available and all are
  attractive as ground covers.)

Partial shade

Alkaline to neutral soil

Clump-forming and, when well sited, freely re-
  seeding, evergreen ground cover

Zones 4 to 9

P. 249

▼ *Hemerocallis fulva*
Daylily, Orange Daylily, Tawny Daylily

Full sun to very light shade

Ordinary soil; drought tolerant once established

Vigorously spreading to invasive perennial with
  long-persistent roots forms extensive masses
  over time; orange flowers in early summer

Zones 4 to 9

P. 251

▲ *Hemerocallis* 'Hyperion'

Full sun to very light shade

Not particular about soil

An elegant, old-fashioned, tall daylily that
spreads less vigorously than the naturalized
species; attractive fragrant yellow flowers in
early summer

Zones 4 to 9

P. 252

◀ *Hemerocallis* 'Stella de Oro'

Full sun to light shade

Not particular about soil

Modern, low selection makes low, tough
masses; golden yellow flowers rebloom
through the summer, though not as abundantly as during the initial flowering peak

Zones 5 to 9

P. 252

► *Heuchera*
'Cathedral Windows'

Alumroot

Partial shade

Average soil but not subjected to prolonged dry
   periods

Purplish green deciduous leaves mass to make
   bold sweeps in the landscape with clouds of
   tiny greenish white flowers in early summer

Zones 4 to 9

P. 253

▼ *Heuchera micrantha* var.
diversifolia 'Palace Purple'

Partial shade; full sun with adequate moisture

Average soil but should not be subjected to prolonged dry periods

Dramatic, eye-catching foliage commands attention, especially when used in bold,
   sweeping masses

Zones 4 to 9

P. 253

▲ *Heuchera micrantha* var. *diversifolia* 'Palace Purple'
Chocolate-colored leaves and tiny pale flowers are both most effective when massed

P. 253

◄ *Heuchera* 'Ruby Veil'

Alumroot

Partial shade

Average soil but should not be subjected to prolonged dry periods

Similar use as 'Cathedral Windows', only here the red veins highlight the paler foliage

Zones 4 to 9

P. 253

▲× *Heucherella* 'Bridget Bloom'

Partial shade

Average, moisture-retentive soil

Deciduous perennial ground cover with green foliage and pink flowers; use in masses in conditions similar to the parents *(Heuchera* and *Tiarella)*

Zones 4 to 9

P. 253

▼ *Hosta* 'Allan P. McConnell'

Hosta

Partial shade

Moist, rich soil

Excellent small-leaved hosta with a white edge and purple flowers in summer

Zones 4 to 9

P. 255

◄ *Hosta* 'Blue Cadet'

Hosta

Partial shade

Moist, rich soil

Spreading hosta with small, blue-green leaves
and lavender flowers in late summer

Zones 4 to 9

P. 255

▼ *Hosta* 'Ginko Craig'

Hosta

Partial shade

Moist, rich soil

Vigorous grower with narrow, white-edged
leaves and lavender-purple flowers in summer

Zones 4 to 9

P. 256

▲ *Hosta* 'Golden Tiara'

Hosta

Partial shade

Moist, rich soil

Vigorous, compact clumps bearing small green
leaves with a golden edge and deep lavender
flowers in summer

Zones 4 to 9

P. 256

▶ *Hosta lancifolia*

Hosta

Partial shade

Moist, rich soil

Quickly spreading hosta with narrow, dark
green leaves and lavender-violet flowers in
late summer

Zones 4 to 9

P. 255

▲ *Hosta plantaginea*

Hosta

Partial shade

Moist, rich soil

Substantial, spreading hosta with glossy, light green, heart-shaped, elegant leaves over-topped with fragrant white flowers in late summer

Zones 4 to 9

P. 255

▼ *Houttuynia cordata* 'Chameleon'

Sun to partial shade

Invasive in any moist soil high in organics or fertility

A spreading, invasive plant best massed where it can be completely restricted; multicolored deciduous foliage is eye-catching, but plants overwhelm any companion plantings

Zones 6 to 9

P. 257

▸ *Hydrangea anomala* ssp. *petiolaris*

Climbing Hydrangea

Partial shade

Average, moist soil

Mounding, deciduous ground cover with attractive white flowers best in large-scale plantings and over uneven ground; will climb walls and trees in preference to sprawling and rooting in the ground: for best ground cover, prune out any climbing stems

Zones 5 to 9

P. 258

▸ *Hypericum calycinum*

St. Johnswort

Full sun to partial shade

Any fertile, well-drained soil

Semievergreen small shrub spreading by rhizomes useful for stabilizing banks; bright yellow flowers in summer

Zones 6 to 9

P. 259

◄ *Iberis sempervirens*

Evergreen Candytuft

Full sun

Well-drained, sandy to gravelly soil

Low, evergreen ground cover with bright white
   flowers in spring

Zones 6 to 9

P. 260

▼ *Ilex crenata* 'Helleri'

Japanese Holly, Box-leaved Japanese
Holly

Full sun to light shade

Acid to slightly acid soils

Nonspreading, small-leaved, evergreen shrub
   masses to create dark foliage pools in the
   garden

Zones 6 to 9

P. 261

▲ *Ilex glabra* 'Compacta'

Inkberry

Full sun to light shade

Acid to slightly acid soil

Nonspreading, evergreen shrub masses to form
dark green foliage accents in the garden

Zones 4 to 9

P. 262

▼ *Ilex* 'Red Sprite'

Swamp Holly

Full sun to light shade

Moist to wet but not waterlogged soil

Deciduous shrub masses well to produce a
spectacular fruit display

Zones 3 to 9

P. 262

▲ *Indigofera kirilowii*

Full sun

Well-drained, fertile loam

Slowly spreading low shrub stabilizes banks beneath its mass of pealike foliage and pink, cotton-candy flower masses

Zones 6 to 10

P. 263

▼ *Iris cristata*

Dwarf Crested Iris

Partial shade

Moist, rich, organic soil

Dwarf creeping mats of iris foliage bear incongruously large blue and white flowers in spring; excellent for carpeting moist shady areas but will go dormant in summer

Zones 3 to 8

P. 264

▲ *Iris pseudacorus*
Yellow Flag
Full sun
Moist to submerged rich, organic soil
Masses to form dramatic foliage feature at
water's edge
Zones 5 to 9
P. 264

▼ *Iris pumila*
Dwarf Bearded Iris
Full sun to light shade
Any well-drained, moist garden soil
Creeping dwarf mats; numerous color selec-
tions available
Zones 4 to 8
P. 264

◄ *Iris tectorum*

Japanese Roof Iris

Full sun

Moist, rich, organic, acidic soil

Massed in sunny sites, clumps will spread moderately quickly; a wide range of color selections are available

Zones 6 to 9

P. 264

▼ *Juniperus horizontalis* 'Wiltonii'

Creeping Juniper

Full sun

Well-drained soil

Low-maintenance (once established), mat-forming blue juniper does well on slopes and many hot, dry, difficult sites

Zones 3 to 9

P. 266

▲ *Juniperus sabina*

Savin Juniper, Sabin Juniper

Full sun

Well-drained soil

Slowly growing blue-green foliage but will not
tolerate hot climates

Zones 4 to 7

P. 267

▼ *Juniperus squamata* 'Blue Star'

Single-seed Juniper

Full sun

Well-drained soil

Slowly growing, low, blue foliage makes a distinctive element on many hot, dry, difficult
sites

Zones 4 to 8

P. 267

▲ *Lamium galeobdolon*

Yellow Archangel

Light to deep shade

Any garden soil

Fast-spreading, low deciduous ground cover forms spreading colonies with attractive, silver-variegated foliage and bright yellow flowers in spring—an excellent ground cover for dry shade

Zones 4 to 8

P. 268

▼ *Lamium maculatum*

(Inset: 'Aureum' has golden yellow foliage with white marks)

European Spotted Dead Nettle

Partial shade

Rich, moist loam

Clump-forming, herbaceous ground cover with mottled foliage makes attractive masses

Zones 4 to 8

P. 268

► *Lantana* 'Spreading Sunset'

Lantana

Full sun and good air circulation on the foliage

Well-drained soil

Invasive in parts of the country; birds spread the plants by eating the fruits and passing the seeds; excellent tough bank stabilizers where bright flowers are desired

Zones 8 to 10

P. 270

► *Leiophyllum buxifolium* var. *prostratum*

Box Sand Myrtle

Full sun to light shade

Porous, loamy soil

A distinctive, small-leaved ground-covering evergreen shrub for naturalistic or small-scale applications; the clusters of tiny white flowers are best seen at close range

Zones 6 to 8

P. 271

◄ *Leucothoe axillaris*

Fetterbush, Dog Hobble

Partial to full shade

Moist, rich, organic, acidic soil

Arching-stemmed, suckering shrub colonizes areas to create a glossy, dark green understory beneath large trees; attractive clusters of ivory white flowers in late spring

Zones 6 to 9

P. 272

▼ *Liriope muscari*

Lily Turf

Light to full shade

Rich, moist soil

Spreading, grasslike foliage makes bold, solid green masses

Zones 7 to 10

P. 274

▶ *Liriope spicata*

Creeping Lily Turf

Light to full shade

Rich, moist soil

Slowly spreading but persistent, evergreen perennial ground cover stabilizes large areas and is well suited to underplanting large shrubs and trees

Zones 6 to 10

P. 274

▼ *Lonicera japonica*

Japanese Honeysuckle

Full sun to partial shade

Any soil

An aggressive, invasive vine with extremely fragrant flowers forms irregular and extensive colonies over rough ground and slopes but will overwhelm most other plants in the area; useful on difficult sites if the invasiveness is not a long-term issue

Zones 4 to 9

P. 275

▲ *Luzula nivea*
Snowy Wood Rush
Partial to full shade

Well-drained rich soil

Nonspreading clusters of distinctive, hairy leaves make a strong statement when massed in the shade garden and complement other foliages

Zones 4 to 8

P. 276

▼ *Lysimachia clethroides*
Gooseneck
Partial shade to full sun

Moist soil

Aggressive and invasive perennial ground cover forms extensive colonies with clean foliage and arching white flower masses in early summer

Zones 4 to 8

P. 277

▲ *Lysimachia nummularia*
Creeping Jenny

Sun to light shade; constant moisture needed in full sun and warm climates

Moist soil

Extremely fast-spreading deciduous mats of green leaves choke out most weeds (and companion plantings); yellow flowers in spring

Zones 4 to 8

P. 278

▼ *Mahonia repens*
Creeping Grape Holly

Light shade; protect from winter sun at northern limits or foliage will burn

Well-drained, moisture-retentive, acidic soil

Low, slow-spreading evergreen shrublet with handsome bluish green foliage that reddens in winter; stunning as a massed planting

Zones 6 to 9

P. 279

◀ *Maianthemum kamtschaticum*

Deerberry

Partial shade; best in cool maritime climates

Rich, moist, acidic soil

Low deciduous foliage carpets the ground in slowly spreading colonies; tiny white flowers in spring

Zones 4 to 8

P. 280

▼ *Matteuccia struthiopteris*

Ostrich Fern

Partial shade; plants will collapse in windy or occasionally dry sites

Cool, wet to damp, organic, acidic soil

Quickly spreading fern with dramatic crowns of deciduous foliage 3 to 5 feet tall

Zones 3 to 8

P. 281

▶ *Mazus reptans*
Mazus

Partial shade; full sun if constantly moist

Moist, organic soil

Fast-spreading, prostrate, deciduous ground cover with attractive flowers in spring to early summer; excellent among stepping-stones in moist sites

Zones 5 to 8

P. 282

▼ *Microbiota decussata*
Siberian Carpet Juniper

Partial shade to full sun

Well-drained soil

Low-growing evergreen for massing in shadier sites than junipers as well as in full sun; foliage is not prickly so can be used near walkways

Zones 4 to 7

P. 283

▲ *Mitchella repens*
Partridgeberry

Partial shade

Moist, well-drained, organic, acidic soil

Small-scale, prostrate, evergreen ground cover with pink to white flowers in spring and attractive red fruits later in the season

Zones 3 to 7

P. 284

▼ *Myoporum parvifolium*
Full sun

Average, well-drained soil

Heat-tolerant, prostrate, evergreen shrub reaching many feet covers slopes and rough sites; several selections differ in leaf size

Zones 9 to 10

P. 285

▲ *Nandina domestica*
'Harbor Dwarf'

Heavenly Bamboo

Light shade

Moist soils

Massed to show their graceful, glossy, colorful
foliage and bright fruit, these small shrubs
spread slowly and are surprisingly tough

Zones 7 to 10

P. 286

▼ *Nepeta × faassenii*

Persian Catmint

Full sun to very light shade; best where summers are not long, hot, and muggy

Well-drained soil

Attractive, low perennial (often woody at the
base) planted in masses creates a gray-
leaved, mounding ground cover with small
blue flowers

Zones 4 to 9

P. 287

◄ *Oenothera fruticosa*
Sundrops

Nearly full sun to partial shade; blooms best in
    areas with hot summers

Well-drained but barely moist soil

Assertive, rapidly spreading, deciduous herba-
    ceous ground cover to nearly 2 feet tall
    topped with bright yellow flowers in mid-
    summer

Zones 4 to 9

P. 289

▼ *Oenothera speciosa*
'Siskiyou'
Mexican Evening Primrose, Prairie Evening Primrose

Full sun

Well-drained soil

Spreading, deciduous herbaceous ground cover
    forms mats several feet across with fragrant
    large crepe-paper–like pink flowers

Zones 5 to 9

P. 289

▲ *Omphalodes cappadocica*
Navelwort, Blue-eyed Mary
Partial shade

Well-drained, gritty and gravelly soil

Slowly spreading deciduous ground cover with sturdy, heart-shaped leaves and numerous small blue flowers in early summer

Zones 6 to 9

P. 290

▶ *Omphalodes cappadocica* 'Starry Eyes'
Starry Eyes Navelwort
Partial shade

Well-drained, gritty and gravelly soil

Slowly spreading deciduous ground cover with sturdy, heart-shaped leaves and numerous stunningly deep blue flowers bordered in white in early summer

Zones 6 to 9

P. 290

▲ *Ophiopogon planiscapus* 'Nigrescens'

Black Mondo Grass

Partial shade

Moist, well-drained, slightly acidic soil

Very slowly spreading evergreen with the blackest foliage of any ground cover

Zones 1 to 10

P. 291

◄ *Osmunda cinnamomea*

Cinnamon Fern

Light to partial shade; requires cool summers in warmer hardiness zones

Moist to swampy organic soils

Large deciduous fern, spreads to form colonies if conditions are correct; masses add a primeval quality to the garden

Zones 3 to 8

P. 293

▶ *Osteospermum fruticosum*

Freeway Daisies

Full sun

Excellent drainage required

Low, dense mats of evergreen leaves; named selections have flowers in several bold colors

Zones 9 to 10

P. 294

▼ *Pachysandra procumbens*

Allegheny Mountain Spurge

Partial shade; must have cool summers in
warmer hardiness zones

Moist, organic-rich, acidic soil

Slowly spreading, small-scale, deciduous
ground cover with matte green leaves
marked with earth tones; flowers in spring

Zones 5 to 8

P. 295

◄ *Pachysandra terminalis*

Pachysandra

Light to full shade; most selections burn in full
    sun even with adequate moisture

Moist, well-drained soil

Spreading, dense, low evergreen carpet with
    glossy green leaves; extremely tough once
    established

Zones 5 to 8

P. 295

◄ *Parthenocissus quinquefolia*

Virginia Creeper

Full sun to partial shade; best as a ground cover
    in partial shade

Not particular about soil

Quickly spreading naturalistic deciduous
    ground cover with stunningly beautiful fall
    colors (especially on plants in nearly full
    sun); will vigorously climb trees or walls—
    to maintain as a ground cover, cut back all
    branches at they begin to climb

Zones 4 to 9

P. 297

▶ *Parthenocissus tricuspidata*

Boston Ivy

Full sun to partial shade; best as a ground cover in partial shade

Not particular about soil

Vigorous climber best suited to covering walls and tree trunks; large leaves have spectacular fall colors, especially in sunny locations

Zones 4 to 9

P. 297

▼ *Paxistima canbyi*

Partial shade

Moist, well-drained soil

Small evergreen shrub masses for a naturalistic, informal effect

Zones 5 to 7

P. 298

◄ *Phalaris arundinacea* var. *picta*

Ribbon Grass

Full sun to partial shade

Moist, rich soil

Rapidly spreading variegated grass is an invasive exotic in some regions; creates weed-free, deciduous masses of indefinite spread and to 2 feet tall

Zones 3 to 9

P. 299

▼ *Phlox divaricata* ssp. *laphamii* 'Chattahoochee'

Partial shade

Moist but well-drained, humus-rich soil

Low, vigorously spreading, deciduous, flowering ground cover with mauve-blue flowers in spring

Zones 4 to 8

P. 300

▲ *Phlox subulata*
Moss Pink
Full sun

Very well-drained soil

Low, spreading, prickly mats with evergreen,
needlelike leaves; brilliantly colored flower
masses in spring

Zones 4 to 8

P. 301

▶ *Pleioblastus auricomus*
Yellow-stripe Bamboo
Full sun to light shade

Well-drained soil

Vigorously spreading low bamboo with fluorescent yellow foliage forms bold color statements

Zones 7 to 10

P. 302

▲ *Plumbago auriculata*

Cape Plumbago

Full sun to light shade

Excellent drainage; otherwise not particular about soil

Sprawling ground cover for banks and slopes in warm climates

Zones 9 to 10

P. 303

◄ *Potentilla tridentata* 'Minima'

Wine-leaf Cinquefoil, Trident Cinquefoil

Full sun

Sandy, well-drained soil

Small selection of a quick-growing ground cover for banks and rocky situations

Zones 3 to 7

P. 304

▲ *Pratia angulata*

Light shade

Moist, organic soil that never dries out

Small-scale ground cover for moist sites with
blue, rose, or white flowers

Zones 8 to 10

P. 305

▼ *Prunella grandiflora*

Showy Self-heal

Full sun to partial shade

Any soil

Easy ground cover for woodland and naturalistic gardens

Zones 4 to 8

P. 306

◄ *Pulmonaria angustifolia*
Lungwort
Partial shade

Well-drained, moist, rich soil

Low, slowly spreading, deciduous masses with
    dark green leaves and deep blue flowers in
    spring

Zones 4 to 8

P. 307

▼ *Pulmonaria* 'Excalibur'
Lungwort
Partial shade

Well-drained, moist, rich soil

Slowly spreading, deciduous plants with dra-
    matically silvered foliage and red flowers
    that fade to pink create bright masses in
    shade gardens

Zones 4 to 8

P. 308

▲ *Pulmonaria saccharata*
'Mrs. Moon'

Lungwort

Partial shade

Well-drained, moist, rich soil

A classic lungwort for massing with strongly sil-
ver-spotted leaves, pink flower buds, blue
flowers

Zones 4 to 8

P. 308

▶ *Pyracantha koidzumii*
'Santa Cruz'

Firethorn

Full sun; best in western states

Well-drained soil

Low-growing shrub masses to cover dry banks;
bright fruits in fall provide color notes

Zones 8 to 10

P. 309

▲ *Rhaphiolepis indica*

Indian Hawthorn

Full sun to light shade

Not particular about soil

Masses to form a large-scale, evergreen bank up to 5 feet tall; several named cultivars are more compact than the species

Zones 8 to 10

P. 310

◄ *Rhododendron*
'Delaware Valley White'

Rhododendron

Partial shade; some direct sun needed for best bloom; popular selection in the Mid-Atlantic region

Moist, organic, acidic soil

White-flowering evergreen selection masses to cover a large area under high-branched trees

Zones 6 to 8

P. 311

▲ *Rhus aromatica* 'Gro-low'
Fragrant Sumac

Full sun to light shade

Not particular about soil

Spreading colonizer stabilizes banks; brilliantly
    colored fall foliage

Zones 6 to 9

P. 313

▶ *Rosa banksiae* 'Lutea'
Lady Banks Rose

Full sun

Rich, fertile soil with adequate moisture
    through the growing season

Cascading ground cover (evergreen in mild
    winters) to nearly 15 feet in spread

Zones 8 to 10

P. 314

◄ *Rosa* 'Bonica'

Full sun

Rich, fertile soil with adequate moisture
through the growing season

A Meidiland introduction; medium-size rose
with double, pink flowers masses extremely
well

Zones 5 to 10

P. 315

◄ *Rosa* 'Paulii'

Full sun

Rich, fertile soil with adequate moisture
through the growing season

Old-fashioned scrambling rose covers slopes
and banks with nearly impenetrable masses
to 4 feet tall; mildly fragrant white flowers

Zones 4 to 8

P. 315

▸ *Rosa rugosa*

Full sun

Rich, fertile soil with adequate moisture through the growing season; will tolerate leaner soils than most roses and considerable salt spray from the ocean or highway deicing mixtures

Suckering shrubs form nearly indestructible, floriferous masses; can be rejuvenated by annual pruning to near the ground before new growth emerges

Zones 3 to 8

P. 314

▸ *Rosa* 'White Meidiland'

Full sun

Rich, fertile soil with adequate moisture through the growing season

Low, ground-covering rose to only 2 feet tall with white flowers

Zones 5 to 10

P. 315

▲ *Rosmarinus officinalis*
'Prostratus'

Rosemary

Full sun

Well-drained soil

Low, evergreen, aromatic shrub cascades down
slopes and over walls; pale blue flowers

Zones 7 (with dry summer heat) to 10

P. 317

◄ *Rubus pentalobus*

(Inset: *R. pentalobus* 'Emerald Carpet')

Creeping Raspberry

Full sun; tolerates partial shade but less
vigorous

Well-drained, fertile acidic soil

Dense, low mat of crinkly leaves; can be evergreen in warm, maritime climates

Zones 7 to 9

P. 318

▲ *Sagina subulata* 'Aurea'
(Inset: flowers)

Irish Moss, Pearlwort
Partial shade

Damp, well-drained soil

Creeping plants form prostrate mats easily mistaken for an unusual golden moss until in bloom; flowers small, white

Zones 4 to 8

P. 319

▼ *Salix repens*

Creeping Willow
Full sun

Moist, organic, acidic soil

Low, deciduous, spreading shrub to over 2 feet tall; masses well along streams and in low, damp areas

Zones 4 to 8

P. 320

◄ *Salvia blepharophylla*

Eyelash Sage

Partial shade

Rich, well-drained soil

Spreading perennial forms masses to 18 inches
    tall; flowers scarlet

Zones 9 to 10

P. 322

◄ *Salvia chamaedryoides*

Germander Sage

Full sun

Well-drained, average soil

Low shrub to 2 feet tall masses well; flowers
    light blue

Zones 7 to 9 in dry climates

P. 322

▲ *Santolina chamaecyparissus*

Lavender Cotton

Full sun

Well-drained soil

Masses provide aromatic mounds with tight foliage and bright yellow, buttonlike flowers

Zones 7 to 9

P. 323

▼ *Sarcococca hookeriana* var. *humilis*

Dwarf Sweet Box, Himalayan Sweet Box

Partial to full shade

Moist, acidic organic soil

Small, slowly spreading evergreen shrub with inconspicuous, fragrant white flowers

Zones 7 to 9

P. 324

▲ *Sasa veitchii*

Partial shade

Moist soils; quite tolerant of heavy soil

Decisively but slowly spreading low bamboo
  with attractive leaves that have a striped appearance in winter

Zones 6 to 9

P. 325

▼ *Saxifraga stolonifera*

Strawberry Begonia

Partial to full shade

Moist, organic, rich soil

Low, stoloniferous, deciduous perennial with
  handsome foliage wherever the stolons root;
  flowers small, white

Zones 6 to 9

P. 326

▶ *Saxifraga umbrosa*
'Variegata'

London Pride

Light shade

Moist, rich soil

Forms architectural rosettes of green foliage
marked with yellow; clusters of small pink
flowers held on wiry stalks

Zones 6 to 9

P. 327

▼ *Scaevola aemula*
'Blue Wonder'

Fan Flower

Full sun to partial shade

Well-drained soil

Low-sprawling perennial (annual outside of
hardiness range) creates carpets of bright
green leaves, prolific blue flowers

Zones 9 to 10

P. 328

▲ *Sedum acre*

Mossy Stonecrop

Full sun

Not particular about soil

Rampantly growing, almost-prostrate, small-
leaved succulent can become weedy; flowers
bright yellow

Zones 3 to 8

P. 329

▼ *Sedum kamtschaticum*

Full sun

Well-drained soil

Slowly spreading, low succulent has dark,
semievergreen leaves and bright orange-yellow flowers

Zones 3 to 8

P. 329

▲ *Sedum spectabile* 'Herbstfreude'

Showy Stonecrop

Full sun

Well-drained soil

Bold mounds of succulent foliage and rose-pink flower heads up to 2 feet tall make this a favorite for massing

Zones 5 to 8

P. 330

▼ *Sedum spurium* 'Schorbuser Blut'

Dragon's Blood Stonecrop

Full sun

Well-drained soil

Low, spreading sedum with bronze-red foliage spreads moderately fast and makes a definite color statement; bright red flowers reinforce the drama

Zones 4 to 8

P. 330

▲ *Senecio aureus*
Golden Groundsel
Partial shade to full sun

Moist, well-drained soil

Effective naturalizer along open woodland streams, moist meadow openings, and garden areas that emulate these environments

Zones 5 to 8

P. 331

▼ *Stachys* 'Big Ears'
Lamb's Ears
Full sun in temperate climates

Coarse, well-drained loams

Robust, large-leaved selection is best suited for large-scale plantings

Zones 4 to 8

P. 332

▶ *Stachys byzantina*
'Silver Carpet'

Lamb's Ears

Full sun

Coarse, well-drained loams

A nonflowering selection of the spreading,
   woolly-white-leaved perennial; makes a
   bold contrast to many foliage masses

Zones 4 to 8

P. 332

▶ *Stachys macrantha*

Big Betony

Full sun to light shade

Coarse, well-drained loams

Masses of bright green foliage (not silver as in
   most ground-covering *Stachys*) foil small
   pink flowers

Zones 5 to 9

P. 332

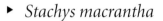

▲ *Stephanandra incisa* 'Crispa'

Dwarf Cut-leaf Stephanandra

Full sun to partial shade

Not particular about soil

Mounding to cascading small shrub with cut leaves billows down slopes and over walls; small white flowers in spring

Zones 4 to 8

P. 333

▼ *Symphoricarpos × chenaultii* 'Hancock'

Chenault Coralberry

Partial shade

Not particular about soil

Low, wide-spreading, and suckering deciduous shrub with pink fruits in fall

Zones 4 to 8

P. 334

▲ *Symphoricarpos orbiculatus*
Coralberry

Partial shade

Not particular about soil

Low-growing, suckering, deciduous shrub with red to purple fruits in fall

Zones 3 to 7

P. 334

▼ *Taxus baccata* 'Repandens'
Spreading English Yew

Partial shade

Well-drained, fertile soil

Elegantly spreading, needled, evergreen shrub to only 3 feet tall; plants grow slowly, so masses must be large enough when first planted

Zones 5 to 8

P. 335

▲ *Tellima grandiflora*
(Inset: The small flowers are an attractive, pale greenish-white.)

Fringecups
Partial shade

Moist, organic, acidic soil

Mass in woodland and shade gardens to complement companion ground covers such as *Tiarella* and *Heuchera*

Zones 4 to 7

P. 337

◄ *Teucrium chamaedrys*
Ground Germander
Full sun to light shade

Well-drained, slightly alkaline soil

The prostrate form makes dense, spreading, low mats several feet across; flowers small, pink

Zones 4 to 9

P. 338

▲ *Thymus pseudolanuginosus*
Woolly Thyme
Full sun

Well-drained, dry, infertile soil

Creeping, dense mats with woolly gray leaves
and pink flowers in summer

Zones 5 to 8

P. 339

▶ *Thymus serpyllum* var. *coccineus*
(Inset: Close-up)

Mother-of-thyme, Creeping Thyme
Full sun

Well-drained, dry, infertile soil

Creeping, dense mats with handsome green foliage; crimson flowers in summer

Zones 4 to 10

P. 339

◀ *Tiarella cordifolia*

Foamflower

(Inset: Pale white flowers cover the flowering
spikes and add a vertical dimension to extensive mass plantings.)

Partial shade

Moist, fertile soil

Colonizing, attractive, low deciduous perennial
covers large areas; flowers creamy white in
spring

Zones 4 to 8

P. 340

▼ *Tiarella wherryi*

Foamflower

Partial shade

Moist, fertile soil

Nonrunning species forms thick patches; pale
pinkish white flowers in spring

Zones 4 to 8

P. 340

▶ *Tolmiea menziesii*
Piggyback Plant

Partial shade

Constantly moist, fertile soil

Companion ground cover to *Heuchera* and *Tiarella* where sites are damp; leaves produce plantlets in contact with soil

Zones 7 to 10

P. 341

▼ *Trachelospermum jasminoides*
Confederate Jasmine

Partial shade

Moist, fertile soil

Mat-forming, low-growing, evergreen vine with extremely fragrant white flowers; not a strong climber but climbing stems often bloom best

Zones 8 to 10

P. 342

▲ *Vaccinium crassifolium*

Creeping Blueberry

Partial shade to full sun

Moist, well-drained, humus-rich, acidic soil

Carpeting mats with small, evergreen leaves;
  flowers pinkish or red

Zones 7 to 9

P. 344

◄ *Vancouveria hexandra*

Inside-out Flower, American Barren-wort

Partial shade

Moist, fertile, acidic soil

Slowly spreading, deciduous perennial with elegantly dissected foliage; best suited as a
  small-scale ground cover or companion
  ground cover

Zones 5 to 8

P. 345

▲ *Verbena canadensis* 'Alba'
Rose Verbena

Full sun

Well-drained, average soil

Loose, vigorously spreading perennial; flowers
  white

Zones 7 (hardy to 5, but not reliable as a ground
  cover) to 9

P. 346

▼ *Verbena* 'Homestead Purple'

Full sun

Well-drained, average soil

Vigorously spreading, low-growing perennial
  with hot-purple flowers throughout the
  growing season

Zones 8 to 10

P. 347

▲ *Veronica peduncularis*
'Georgia Blue'
Full sun to light shade
Well-drained, fertile soil
Low, dark green foliage spreads into tight mats;
small blue flowers in spring
Zones 6 to 8
P. 348

◄ *Veronica* 'Waterperry Blue'
Full sun to light shade
Well-drained, fertile soil
Trailing stems form low mats; can be evergreen
in warm climates
Zones 6 to 8
P. 349

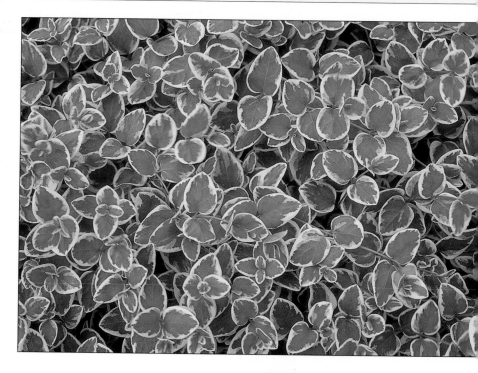

▲ *Vinca minor*
'Argenteovariegata'
Myrtle, Periwinkle, Graveyard Grass
Partial sun to deep shade

Not particular about soil

Variegated, dense, low evergreen mats spread
indefinitely; flowers light blue

Zones 4 to 8

P. 351

▶ *Vinca minor*
Myrtle, Periwinkle, Graveyard Grass
Partial sun to deep shade

Not particular about soil

Dense, low evergreen mats spread indefinitely;
flowers light blue

Zones 4 to 8

P. 351

▲ *Vinca minor* f. *alba*

Myrtle, Periwinkle, Graveyard Grass

Partial sun to deep shade

Not particular about soil

White flowered; not as vigorous a spreader as the typical form, but otherwise similar

Zones 4 to 8

P. 351

◄ *Viola labradorica*

Labrador Violet

Partial shade

Moist fertile soil

Best suited to temperate zones; low masses of deep green to purplish green deciduous leaves; flowers violet but scentless

Zones 2 to 7

P. 352

▲ *Waldsteinia ternata*
Barren Strawberry

Partial to full shade

Moist to nearly dry soil

Vigorously spreading, low perennial with
  glossy, evergreen foliage (deciduous at
  northern limits); flowers bright yellow in
  spring

Zones 4 to 8

P. 354

▼ *Zauschneria californica*
California Fuchsia

Full sun

Warm, well-drained, mineral soils

Lax, rhizomatous and cascading stems with
  green to gray-green foliage and tubular
  scarlet flowers—a favorite of hummingbirds

Zones 8 to 10

P. 355

▲ *Zauschneria* 'Dublin'

California Fuchsia

Full sun

Warm, well-drained, mineral soils

Masses of small, bright green leaves; scarlet
   flowers held well above foliage

Zones 8 to 10

P. 355

Encyclopedia of Plants

🐿 Encyclopedia of Plants

🌾 *Acanthus*

a-KAN-thus. Acanthus family, Acanthaceae.

From southern Europe comes a plant immortalized on many civic buildings and carved stone pediments—*Acanthus mollis*—one of the nearly 20 species native from the Mediterranean region to Asia. *Acanthus* species are long-lived perennials with coarsely toothed and often spiny evergreen to semideciduous leaves measuring 2 feet or more long. The showy, two-lipped flowers are arranged on dramatic elongated spikes (with leaflike hoods—bracts to botanists) that look like enormous foxgloves. These spikes are often 3 feet or more tall and long lasting, both in the garden and as cut flowers. The flowers themselves are pale lavender to white, often with purplish veining. The scientific name is very descriptive and means "thorny" or "spiny."

HOW TO GROW

A. mollis and *A. spinosus* are both excellent ground covers with similar cultural requirements. *A. mollis* makes a handsome large-scale ground cover for moist, partially shaded sites with a wide range of soils in Zones 7 to 9. Soil should retain moisture but be well drained. In Portugal, where it is native, great stands of *A. mollis* carpet woodland areas and shaded town gardens, where established plants are 3 to 4 feet tall and spread 4 to 5 feet. *A. spinosus* is shorter and grows in sun to partial shade.

HOW TO USE

A. mollis is one of the finest choices for a sculptural effect. Plant it in bold drifts—10 or more at a time—in shaded woodland areas or as a magnificent foundation planting around a building that recalls southern European architecture. It looks especially stunning when used in settings where the building architecture is on a grand scale—such as an art museum or on a college campus. In the home garden, the space needs to be appropriate to the scale of the plant. Whereas *A. mollis* is a plant for shade, moist soils, and warm Mediterranean climates (Zones 7 to 9), other *Acanthus* species are more commonly found in gravel gardens, where their spiny leaves blend well with other jagged textures.

A. hungaricus (A. balcanicus, A. longifolius)

a. hun-GAH-ri-cus. This species resembles *A. spinosus* but has paler foliage. It makes a handsome, slowly spreading mass and appears to be one of the hardiest selections for northern gardeners, as it is reliably hardy in most areas of Zone 6. Useful in zones 7 to 9.

A. mollis   P. 28

a. MOL-liss. Bear's Breeches. Lustrous, evergreen foliage (deciduous at the species' northern limit) makes a classic ground cover for shaded sites in Mediterranean climates. Hardy in Zone 8 (Zone 7 if well sited) and warmer. *A. mollis* may go dormant in hot, humid weather such as that found in the southeastern United States. *A. mollis* is reported invasive in the Pacific Northwest.

A. spinosus (Latifolius and Spinosus Groups)   P. 28

a. spy-NO-sis. Native to southern Europe, this handsome, spreading perennial has dark green, dissected foliage that is somewhat spiny. The hooded, mauve flowers appear in early summer. Hardy in Zone 6 if well sited (deciduous), reliable farther south. It is tolerant of more sun than *A. mollis*, but it does not tolerate full afternoon sun. Most useful in Zones 7 to 9.

❦ Achillea

ah-KIL-e-uh or ak-il-E-uh. Aster family, Asteraceae.

Achillea species are vibrantly colored, summer-flowering perennials with distinctive, fernlike, dissected foliage. The genus contains more than 100 species native to North America, Europe, and Asia. It is related to *Tanacetum* (garden tansies) and does well in similar garden conditions. Leaves are deeply dissected into narrow, featherlike sections that are often covered with silvery hairs. They are alternate and clustered into a tight basal rosette, from which the strong flowering stems emerge. Depending on the species, the stems can be 6 inches to nearly 3 feet tall. The individual flowers are small but clustered together into flat or gently mounded, eye-catching masses (corymbs to botanists) that measure up to 4 inches or more across. Flower colors range from ivory or white to bright yellows and reds. A. *millefolium*, the common yarrow, is native to both North America and Eurasia and is considered by some a wildflower in sunny fields. The genus is named for Achilles, the tragic hero of the Trojan War, and his medicinal use of the plant to stanch bleeding. Ironically, Achilles bled to death after being pierced in his heel.

HOW TO GROW
Achilleas are hardy in Zones 3 to 8 and in warmer Mediterranean climates. They require full sun to thrive and perform poorly in partial shade. Soil should be well drained and not overly fertile. Achilleas grow from rosettes that gradually increase in bulk, but they do not vegetatively spread with any speed. Their success as a ground cover requires using an adequate number of plants to provide coverage from the beginning. Even given this restriction, they are perfect for sunny, exposed sites and make stunning masses in bloom.

HOW TO USE
The apparently relaxed planting styles of contemporary landscape parks in Germany—those at Westpark and Weihenstephan are among the best known—celebrate the growing of perennials in naturalized "plant communities" based on their habitat needs. These large-scale demonstration gardens are vibrant proof of the ways in which many perennials, more commonly planted in ones and twos in perennial borders, can achieve a whole different dimension when displayed in large masses. Achilleas can be planted this way in broad, dramatic sweeps of at least 15 to 20 plants. When grown in lean soil with good drainage, especially in regions where hot summers are followed by crisp falls and early frosts, they can remain attractive for weeks, with the added bonus of pleasing winter seed heads. Mulch them with gravel and back them up with the upright stems of some of the shorter ornamental grasses such as *Calamagrostis, Molinia,* or *Helictotrichon,* and they will be effective for three seasons.

A. ageratifolia
aj-er-ah-tih-FO-lee-uh. This tufted perennial species from Greece has deeply toothed, silvery leaves and white flowers on 6-to 8-inch stems. Useful in Zones 3 to 8.

A. × lewisii

x lou-WISS-ee-eye. 'King Edward' is 6 to 8 inches tall and has soft yellow flowers. In northern gardens, it blooms in mid- to late summer.

A. millefolium

mil-leh-FO-lee-um. Yarrow. This is the most commonly offered species, and all cultivars require similar conditions to grow well. They bloom in early to midsummer. Many American nurseries list cultivars under this species; see the *Achillea* hybrids section below.

A. 'Taygetea'

tay-JEE-tee-uh. This cultivar has silvery foliage and grows to 12 inches tall. The yellow flowers are carried on stems reaching 2 feet tall.

A. tomentosa

toe-men-TOE-suh. Woolly Yarrow, Dwarf Yarrow. As implied by the common names, this species is smaller (to 8 inches tall) and has fernlike foliage with woolly white hairs. It requires full sun and sandy soil and performs well in seaside conditions. It can also be mown occasionally. Flowers are yellow. 'Aurea' (similar to 'Maynard's Gold') has strong yellow flowers.

A. hybrids   P. 29

Included here are numerous hybrids not associated with one species. Multiple new cultivars and hybrids have increased the available color range and blooming season. These are only a few of the named hybrids available but are particularly useful as ground covers.

'Appleblossom' ('Apfelblüte') has pale pink flowers that mature to cream on stems to 2 feet tall.

'Coronation Gold' has bright yellow flowers on 2- to 3- foot stems. Leaves are gray and finely cut. Plants mass particularly well.

'Fireland' ('Feuerland') has finely dissected, green foliage and bright red flowers that fade to pale yellow.

'Maynard's Gold' has bright yellow flowers on 12-inch stems and silvery, fernlike foliage.

'Moonshine' has pale lemon yellow flowers that play with the silver foliage.

'Terra Cotta' has flowers that open the color of smoked salmon and then age to the color of Italian clay pots—thus the name. These are carried on stems to 2 feet tall.

The Galaxy Series are hybrids between *A. millefolium* and *A.* 'Taygetea'. These plants have leaves resembling those of *A. millefolium* but a much wider range of flower colors. 'Heidi' has flowers that open deep pink and fade to lighter pink. 'Paprika' has burnt orange flowers. 'Salmon Beauty' has flowers that open pale salmon and fade to creamy yellow.

❦ Acorus

ak-OR-us. Arum family, Araceae.

Acorus has only two species: *A. gramineus* (Japanese sweet flag) is native to Japan, and *A. calamus*, (sweet flag or calamus) is widespread in Europe, Asia, and North America. Both species are long-lived perennials in moist to wet habitats such as streambanks and pond edges. *A. gramineus* is useful as a grasslike ground cover, whereas *A. calamus* is more typically found as a vigorous perennial in shallow water, with foliage growing to 3 feet tall. *Acorus* is related to, but without the dramatic flowers or seeds of, woodland and moisture-loving stalwarts such as *Arum* (arums), *Arisaema* (Jack-in-the-pulpits), and *Symplocarpus* (skunk cabbage). Leaves are alternate, arising from the horizontal rootstock in an overlapping pattern much like slender iris leaves. Flowers are insignificant. The name is thought to be of ancient Greek origin, referring to the pupil of the eye, possibly in reference to a former medicinal use.

HOW TO GROW

A. gramineus is hardy in Zones 7 to 9 and does best in full sun to partial shade. It requires moist, damp, or even wet soil. Plants are intolerant of dry soil for even short periods. Soil should be fertile, with a high organic content. Propagation is by division, and plants form clumps that are slow to spread. Accordingly, massing this species as a ground cover for immediate effect is best done with numerous plants.

HOW TO USE

Use the grassy foliage of *Acorus* to develop a transition zone between land and water, whether that land is a traditional lawn, a structured planting, or a connection to a man-made water garden. Plant *Acorus* in broad drifts—usually a minimum of 3 feet wide at installation—and allow the plants to spread. For a dramatic accent, use variegated *Acorus* as a broad stripe of color near more muted, all-green foliage. Interesting contrasts come with plant compositions involving the large foliage of moisture-loving plants such as *Darmera peltata*, *Hosta*, and *Gunnera*.

A. gramineus   P. 30

gra-MIN-ee-us. Japanese Sweet Flag. The leaves of *A. gramineus* are narrow and grasslike — usually ¼ inch or less wide and up to 18 inches long. Plants form clumps that slowly enlarge. Several variegated cultivars exist and are distinguished by color and location of variegation. 'Variegatus' has 10- to 18-inch-long leaves edged with cream and is hardier than the typical forms. It is semievergreen in Zone 6. 'Masamume' is similar to 'Variegatus', but the leaves have a stronger color contrast from the center to the edge. 'Ogon' has shorter leaves with narrow yellow stripes that rise only to about 10 inches. Other dwarf, variegated, or slow-growing forms are used for special effects rather than as ground covers.

❦ Aegopodium

e-go-PO-di-um. Carrot family, Apiaceae.

Thugs compete well with other thugs, so in situations where the ground is already occupied by plants with aggressive, close-to-the-surface roots (think of Norway maples, hemlocks, and beeches), the best companion may be this plant, with a well-deserved reputation for aggression. *Aegopodium* includes seven perennial species native to Europe and temperate Asia. As the mild foliage scent indicates, it is related to celery *(Apium)* and dill *(Anethum)*. Only one species, *A. podagraria* (goutweed), is commonly grown as a foliage ground cover — both the typical green-leaved plants and the white-variegated ones. Both foliage forms are useful for difficult, dry, shady sites where little else will grow. The deciduous leaves are often complexly dissected, with five to nine leaflets that arise from subterranean stems. The whitish flowers are individually tiny but are presented in flat-topped umbels that rise on strong stems above the foliage in early summer. The name means "goat foot," and the plant was once believed to be useful in treating gout.

HOW TO GROW

Grow goutweed in any fertile to marginally fertile soil, provided it is not waterlogged or severely dry. Plants thrive and spread to form nearly weed-free masses in moderately moist soil and partial shade. In full sun, consistent soil moisture is essential for good growth. Plants will tolerate dry shade, but the masses will be less vigorous and not as thick or weed-free. Due to the aggressive and vigorous growth of the rhizomes, it is difficult to restrain the plant in moist, partly shaded sites. It is these vigorously growing rhizomes that make the plant so successful as a ground cover for difficult sites. Hardy in Zones 3 to 9.

HOW TO USE

Although few gardeners would consider intentionally introducing these dreaded invaders, there are times when *Aegopodium,* especially in its variegated form, may be just the right plant. The cool, gray-green and white foliage makes an attractive mass beneath large trees or dark-leaved shrubs and effectively forms an edge around the woodland garden. *Aegopodium* is also an effective plant in urban situations, where tall buildings often result in deep, dry shade. Here paths or sidewalks can offer good barriers to the roving roots of both the species and the variegated forms. To prevent seeding, mow the foliage to the ground in early summer—it will quickly refresh.

A. podagraria P. 30

po-duh-GRAIR-ee-uh. Goutweed, Bishop's Weed. This perennial herb's leaves reach 4 to 8 inches or more tall if thriving. Smaller leaves may be found on the outer edges of expanding colonies, and they indicate the presence of rapidly growing rhizomes. Flowering stems rise to 12 inches or more tall. The name means "gouty" and refers to swellings at the base, as is the case with gout in the feet. 'Variegatum' has white-margined or white-streaked leaves and shows particularly well in damp, shady sites.

❦ *Ajania*

a-JAN-e-a. Aster family, Asteraceae.

The two dozen species of *Ajania* are native from central Asia to the Pacific coast of Siberia. The genus is very closely related to *Chrysanthemum* and *Tanacetum,* and the species listed here is often listed under *Chrysanthemum.* Ajanias are herbaceous perennials, and some species become woody at the base. Foliage is deciduous and lobed or toothed. When crushed, the leaves are fragrant to malodorous, depending on one's interpretation of the complex aromatics. Flowers are usually white or yellow and daisylike. The name commemorates a site in Siberia.

HOW TO GROW

Grow ajanias in full sun to very light shade, or their stems will become leggy and lax. Ajanias form sprawling masses up to 3 feet across and in time will form multiple crowns without spreading significantly. Plants will benefit from being severely pruned back in early spring, thus becoming bushier. Flowers bloom in mid- to late fall and help close the season in the garden. They are very tolerant of maritime conditions. Hardiness depends on the species but ranges from Zone 5 to warmer zones. The one species treated here is hardy in Zone 7 and up.

HOW TO USE
Despite their easy-care appearance, these plants need maintenance. *A. pacifica* is a popular foliage plant, mimicking the appearance of the shade-loving Japanese pachysandra, but in sunny sites. Remember that these daisies do not thrive in drought or shade, but instead prefer good drainage, adequate moisture, and fertilization.

A. pacifica (Dendranthema pacificum) P. 31

pah-SIF-i-kuh. This daisy was introduced from Japan by Maryland nurseryman Kurt Bluemel and is grown for its choice, variegated foliage. The tiny yellow flowers are a late-summer bonus. Plants grow into cushiony hummocks 8 to 10 inches tall and spreading to about 3 feet. The gray-green leaves are edged with a neat border of creamy white, and the overall effect is bright and attractive. Hardy in Zones 7 (warm Zone 6 with protection) to 10. Best in temperate maritime climates.

❦ Ajuga

a-JOO-ga. Mint family, Lamiaceae.

Ajuga is among the most familiar hardy ground covers grown for foliage color and includes about 40 species of annuals and perennials native to Eurasia and Australia. It is related to *Teucrium,* the garden germander. Leaves are opposite, as is typical of the mint family, and form a dense basal rosette. Leaf colors range from green to bronze to purple, with additional variegated combinations. Ajugas are deciduous ground covers at the northern limit of their range and semievergreen farther south. Flower colors are predominantly blue or purple, but rose and white selections exist. Flowers are small, and although their blooming season is short, they make a striking addition to the spring garden.

HOW TO GROW
Ajugas are hardy in Zones 4 to 9. They prefer light to moderate shade and, being relatively shallow rooted, are intolerant of drought. Plants

grown in dense shade are less vigorous, form weaker mats, and often do not bloom. They tolerate a great range of soil types (such as gravelly or silty loam), provided the soil is moist but relatively well drained. Propagation is by division or transplanting of the new rosettes that form along the stolons throughout the season. Plants spread vigorously by stolons and are persistent in lawns once established, as they withstand mowing. The appearance of masses will be improved by deadheading after flowering.

HOW TO USE

Do you like strong color contrasts? Abstract paintings? Would you like to emulate the work of the great Brazilian landscape architect Roberto Burle Marx? If so, you can introduce broad stripes of perennial color into your landscape with the use of ajugas. Far from being weeds that invade lawns, these spreading ground covers offer many possibilities for gardeners. For a tropical look, use bronze-leaved selections such as 'Gaiety', 'Bronze Improved', or 'Catlin's Giant' to contrast with equally tough masses of hostas, *Iris pseudacorus,* or shrubs such as variegated dogwoods. The silver highlights of 'Silver Carpet'—an altogether more demure plant—make for an attractive edging in perennial borders, while the glossy, green leaves of 'Rosea' or *A. reptans* are excellent at the edges of woodland gardens. Ajugas are compatible ground covers for permanently planted, strong-growing, medium to tall, spring-flowering bulbs such as *Galanthus* (snowdrops).

A. genevensis P. 31

jen-eh-VEN-sis. Usually considered to be a separate species, but listed as a cultivar of *A. reptans* by some nurseries, *A. genevensis* tolerates drier and more alkaline soils that *A. reptans.* The green leaves may appear wilted, especially when in flower. Flowers are typically dark blue. 'Robusta' is larger than the species. 'Tottenham' has lilac-pink flowers.

A. reptans Pp. 32, 33

REP-tanz. Once established, plants form dense, spreading mats that are capable of excluding most weeds. Leaves are deciduous, and if the plants become dry, the leaves will shrivel and not recover fully. Many cultivars are in the trade—all have blue flowers unless noted. 'Burgundy Glow' has silvery green leaves accented with pink flushes and pale cream edges. 'Bronze Beauty' has lustrous, bronze to bronzy green leaves. 'Catlin's Giant' ('Macrophylla') has dramatically large, burgundy foliage with 12-inch-tall flower spikes in midspring. 'Gaiety' ('Bronze Improved') has purple to bronze-green foliage and lilac flowers. 'Jungle Beauty'

('Jumbo') is just slightly smaller than 'Catlin's Giant' and has bronze-purple foliage; its flower stalks are only 10 inches high. 'Purple Brocade' has purple foliage and is a fast spreader. 'Pink Beauty' has light pink flowers carried above green leaves. 'Rosea' is similar, with normal foliage and pink flowers. 'Silver Carpet' has olive green foliage with silver highlights. 'Variegata' ('Argentea') has green leaves marked with creamy white.

❦ *Alchemilla*

al-ka-MIL-uh. Rose family, Rosaceae.

Alchemilla mollis (lady's mantle) is a mainstay of the perennial border, but it and several of the more than 250 other species in the genus are equally at home as ground covers in sunny gardens and bright woodlands. The genus also includes some remarkably hardy species, such as *A. alpina,* native to subarctic Greenland (Zone 2), that are useful garden plants. Most of the species are clumpers, but several are vigorous self-seeders that perform admirably as ground covers. *Alchemilla* leaves range from less than 1 inch across to larger than a hand, but the leaves are almost always shallowly to deeply lobed and covered with soft hairs, although these hairs may be limited to the leaf margin. Leaves rise from a strong, woody crown and range in color from dark green to the well-known light green of *A. mollis.* Flowers are tiny and without petals, but the pale green to chartreuse sepals (depending on the species) are carried above the foliage in open, cloudlike masses as if inspired by a pointillist painter. The name is taken directly from Arabic and alludes to the use of the plant by alchemists, who were inspired by the droplets of water at the edges of the leaves—even if there had been no dew or rainfall. To these alchemists, water and gold were both elemental, and if *Alchemilla* could exude water, might not some other plant exude drops of gold?

HOW TO GROW

In general, *Alchemilla* species do well in sunny sites with well-drained soils that are high in organic matter and thus moisture retentive. If the leaf edges dry out, the plants are getting too much sun for the moisture content of the soil, and either they need to be relocated to a shadier site or water must be added to the soil. *A. mollis* does well in climates with cool, moist summers when given morning sun. It appreciates partial to nearly full shade in warmer areas. To refresh after flowering, cut the flower stalks to the ground, top-dress with compost, and fertilize with an organic material such as fish emulsion, used as a foliar feed. Continue to fertilize every few days as long as the temperature remains under 80°F, and the plants will reflush with new growth in about 2 weeks. Although *A. mollis* is a clump-forming plant, it seeds readily and benefits from frequent division. Each division will grow to 1 foot tall and spread at least 2 feet. Hardy in Zones 4 to 8.

HOW TO USE

Repeating masses of *A. mollis* planted along a path leading into a woodland garden or as broad sweeps edging a partially shaded perennial border provide a classic ground cover in Zones 4 to 8. The bold foliage is a dramatic foil to more delicate woodland textures, and the striking lime green color (less intense in woodland settings) draws the eye ahead in anticipation of the next sight. Flower arrangers harvest both the lime green blossoms and the charmingly pleated leaves, so be certain to have large enough masses.

A. alpina

al-PIE-nuh. One of the smallest species, *A. alpina* grows only 6 to 8 inches tall and forms clumps that spread modestly. Foliage is a deeper green than that of *A. mollis.* According to some botanists, most of the plants offered under this name are mislabeled, as the true *A. alpina* is rare in cultivation.

A. erythropoda

air-ith-ro-PO-duh. This charming species looks like a miniature *A. mollis* and makes a fine, small-scale ground cover. It prefers morning sun and partial shade.

A. mollis (A. vulgaris) P. 34

MOL-iss. *A. mollis* is one of the classic plants in perennial borders and is also appropriate for massing as a ground cover. The softly pleated, green leaves look their best in early morning when catching drops of dew (or irrigation). This species' clouds of tiny, chartreuse flowers in early summer are popular with flower arrangers.

Anemone

an-EM-o-nee. Buttercup family, Ranunculaceae.

Could you make a garden from selections of just one herbaceous genus? If you consider the wide range of anemones, it is possibile. The 250 species of anemones, also called windflowers, are native throughout the Northern Hemisphere and have diversified to be denizens of habitats as divergent as open woodlands, alpine meadows, heath, moist prairies, and steppes. Consequently, their cultural conditions are quite variable. In most cases, windflowers do not grow as single plants, but instead form groups or extensive colonies—in other words, they are natural ground covers. Leaves are deciduous, alternate (sometimes opposite on the flowering stalks), and usually deeply cleft or divided into distinct leaflets. Flowers are five to many petaled and usually only ½ to 2 inches across, in colors ranging from white to pink, red, purple, and blue. According to some authorities, the name means "windflower" in Greek, possibly in reference to some of the wild species growing in rocky, windy sites.

HOW TO GROW

Wild windflower species grow in a wide range of environments and thus span a range of hardiness and cultural requirements, but the species most frequently used in gardens and woodlands as ground covers prefer light, loamy, well-drained soil and partial shade. Many of them go dormant before frost and are thus interplanted with other ground covers or perennials. They are also useful following naturalized bulbs. Propagation is by seed or division. Hardy in Zones 3 to 9, depending on the species.

HOW TO USE

Grow windflowers in large groups to extensive masses for the best effect. Consider using several species in adjacent areas so that the effect is carried through the season. In late spring, the white flowers of *A. sylvestris* bring patches of light into dark woodlands. Plant it as a companion to midspring bulbs or to cover the disappearing foliage of early-flowering ephemerals, such as spring wildflowers. As a transition from naturalized daffodils in a sunny meadow to a shadier woodland, it is superb. Be certain to plant it where you can enjoy its delicate fragrance. Though vigorous in light soils, it is generally regarded as an attractive nuisance, since it is easy to remove and share with friends. A later-flowering species that could be used in the same site is *A. tomentosa* 'Robustissima'. This vigorously spreading, mid- to late-summer perennial is sometimes planted in perennial borders. Consider growing it in naturalized situations at the edge of a woodland or in the shade (north side) of a building. It makes an excellent cover plant to follow spring bulbs. The clean, grapelike leaves are attractive from late spring to fall, and the rich pink flowers generally appear in late summer, when few other perennials offer this color.

A. *blanda*

BLAN-duh. Grecian Windflower. This small, spring-flowering ephemeral blooms in shades of blue, pink, and white. It is generally planted from small, dried tubers, which should be soaked overnight before planting. It does best in organic soil and light shade, making a charming but brief spring display that should be followed by complementary plantings. Useful in Zones 4 to 8.

A. *canadensis*

can-ah-DEN-sis. Meadow Anemone. This species will spread vigorously and quickly take over a moist meadow or other large area. Attractive white blossoms rise above light green foliage in spring. It may go dormant in summer in dry sites. Useful in Zones 3 to 7.

A. *sylvestris*

sil-VES-tris. Snowdrop Anemone. This fast-spreading woodland ground cover grows to 18 inches tall and has lightly fragrant, white flowers in spring. Foliage looks like grape leaves. When planted in moist, organic, light soils, this is one of those "stand back and watch it spread" plants. Heavier soils will slow it down, and it will tolerate slightly alkaline soils. Often dormant in summer, it is useful in Zones 4 to 7.

A. *tomentosa* 'Robustissima'   P. 34

toe-men-TOE-suh. Grape-leaf Anemone. Well known as a bully in perennial borders—where it quickly stakes its claim to all the territory in sight— 'Robustissima' makes an effective woodland edge. It has rich pink flowers in late summer and attractive foliage throughout the growing season. It does best in moist, organic soils and partial shade, but it will tolerate less-than-ideal situations and spread happily. Useful in Zones 5 to 8.

🌟 *Antennaria*

an-ten-NAR-e-a. Aster family, Asteraceae.

Who wouldn't love a plant called pussytoes? That name perfectly describes the soft, fuzzy flower heads in this genus of perhaps 100 species native to northern regions. *Antennaria* species are creeping, nearly prostrate perennials with deciduous, alternate leaves. Leaves are usually hairy, sometimes so felted with downy hairs as to be silvery over the entire leaf surface. Flower are inconspicuous and clustered into small, tight heads, as is typical of the aster family. These "pussytoes" are carried on flower stalks up to several inches above the foliage. Unlike many of their relatives, *Antennaria* flowers do not have showy, petal-like ray flowers. Instead, think of an aster without the colorful rays. This inconspicuous flower head is enclosed in a fuzzy ball. Even the scientific name refers to the hairs. It comes from the same Latin word as "antenna" (as in insects) and refers to the appearance of these hairs.

HOW TO GROW

To select a site for pussytoes, think of a kitten basking on a sunny stone bench — full sun, good drainage, and a light, gravelly soil. Given those conditions and bright but cool summers (the humid part of Zone 8 is about the southern limit for these plants), antennarias will thrive. Moist, rich, organic soils and partial shade will lead to weak plants that will ultimately rot out. Useful in Zones 3 to 8.

HOW TO USE

Plant *A. dioica* in well-drained, gravelly soil or between steppingstones. It makes a spreading carpet that effectively fills in between the stones. Or use it to create swirls of soft, touchable foliage at the edges of gravel gardens. It is an excellent foil for the harsher lines of spiky plants such as *Yucca, Kniphofia,* and *Liatris.* It is not suitable for humid growing conditions, such as in the Southeast.

A. dioica   P. 35

die-OH-ih-kuh. Pussytoes. The small, white (sometimes pink) flowers, which really do look like a cat's toes, are carried above gray-green foliage, which makes a slowly spreading carpet (think of a throw rug) in summer. This species is useful in Zones 3 to 8, but not in the humid South. 'Nyewoods' has bright pink or cherry red flowers.

❦ Arabis

AR-a-bis. Mustard family, Brassicaceae.

The 120 or so species of rock cress are native to temperate Europe, Asia, and the Mediterranean, with several species found in North America and the mountains of tropical Africa. Most are low-growing, sometimes creeping, perennials and annuals. Plants typically form basal rosettes, and depending on the species, leaves may be green or covered with silvery white hairs. Flowers are individually small, white to pink, and presented in eye-catching abundance during a short but dramatic blooming period in spring. The name refers to Arabia, since several species are native there.

HOW TO GROW

Arabis thrives in good garden soil and full sun to partial shade. Good drainage is critical to its long-term success, as it will rot if the soil is too moist or water retentive. Commonly used in rock gardens in calcareous to acid soil, several species are useful as ground covers if their soil needs are met.

HOW TO USE

Rock cress is a "cascader," or wall plant, that shows best when seen in association with stones, walls, or gravel. It can also be used as an attractive stabilizer for loose gravel on moderate slopes. The small, silvery gray foliage is a charming backdrop for the snow-white flowers in midspring. Cut back hard after flowering, it remains attractive from spring to fall. It does best in slightly alkaline soils that are well drained and does not survive excessive humidity. Hardiness depends on the species.

A. ferdinandi-coburgi   P. 35

fer-deh-NAN-dee-KO-burg-ee. A low, tidy perennial. 'Old Gold' has golden variegation and is useful in Zones 7 (Zone 6 with protection) to 9.

A. procurrens (*A. ferdinandi-coburgi* 'Variegata')

pro-CUR-ens. This species has gray foliage with cream edges. It is a slight, creeping plant that makes an almost flat mat and is charming among pavers. The white flowers are borne on slender stalks that grow to only 6 inches high. Useful in Zones 5 to 8.

❦ *Arctostaphylos*

ark-toe-STAF-il-os. Heath family, Ericaceae.

The words *arctostaphylos, uva-ursi,* and "bearberry" all mean the same thing in Greek, Latin, and English, respectively. The name accurately reflects the role of the berries of one species in the diet of bears. There are about 70 species in the genus, and all but two are entirely restricted to western North and Central America. All are long-lived, woody shrubs from less than 1 foot to more than 5 feet tall. Most of the species are native to California. The two species that naturally extend to Eurasia are *Arctostaphylos alpina* (sometimes placed in the genus *Arctous*) and *A. uva-ursi*. *A. uva-ursi* is native throughout the Northern Hemisphere in the boreal to cool temperate forest zones. Only *A. alpina* is deciduous. All the other species are evergreen shrubs with small, alternate, ovate, thick, glossy leaves. Flowers are shaped like small, pale urns and displayed in tight clusters. Fruits are attractive, pulpy or dry berries, often brown or bright red. *Arctostaphylos* is closely related to *Arbutus,* the strawberry tree of the Mediterranean and western North America, and *Vaccinium,* the blueberries of the Americas.

HOW TO GROW

Arctostaphylos species require nearly full sun, good drainage, and acidic soil. They are intolerant of lime and as a result may not perform well against concrete, where leaching modifies soil pH. Hardiness depends on the species or parentage of cultivars, as some are hardy to Zones 2 and 3, whereas others are hardy in Zone 8 and warmer. The numerous species native to western North America and their cultivars are usually not tolerant of the humid summers east of the Rocky Mountains, even in equivalent hardiness zones. In all cases, low and spreading selections of *Arctostaphylos* may root along stem nodes that come in contact with the ground.

HOW TO USE

Plant bearberry as an evergreen ground cover in sunny, well-drained, acidic, sandy to gravelly soils. It makes an excellent transitional plant in naturalistic areas, spreading moderately fast to form glossy carpets and rolling mounds. Bearberry works well in association with rocky outcroppings in thin, fast-draining soils, or near spring-flowering shrubs with light canopies, such as high- and lowbush blueberries, witch hazels, and shrubby dogwoods. It does well in seaside conditions, but it should not be planted where it is exposed to direct salt. Instead, plant it back from the shore, where it will scramble over rocks and thrive in the strong light. Bearberry does not tolerate humidity or boggy soils.

A. densiflora 'Howard McMinn'   P. 36

den-sih-FLOR-uh. Vine Hill Manzanita, Sonoma Manzanita. This is the only cultivar of this California native commonly seen in gardens as a ground cover. It has a mounding shape usually less than 5 feet tall, but it may spread to 6 feet wide. It is excellent for massing, since stem tips root when they touch the ground. It does best in sunny, dry sites with fast drainage. The abundant flowers are light pink. Plants take well to both pruning and shearing. This is one of the most tolerant of all western *Arctostaphylos* selections. Useful in Zone 7 and warmer.

A. 'Emerald Carpet'   P. 36

This is a low-growing shrub with bright, evergreen leaves and small, white flowers. Is it thought to be a hybrid of coastal California species. Use in Zone 8 and warmer.

A. *hookeri*

HOOK-ur-eye. Monterey Manzanita. Useful in Zone 7 and warmer, this West Coast species has bright red fruits. 'Monterey Carpet' is compact, maturing at 12 inches tall but spreading to more than 6 feet due to the rooting branches. This is one of the traditional ground-cover selections for western gardeners.

A. *nummularia* 'Pacific Mist'

num-yoo-LAI-ree-uh. Fort Bragg Manzanita. This selection is a broad shrub mounding to 2 feet tall and spreading to more than 10 feet. Leaves are grayish green and measure up to 2 inches long. Small, white flowers bloom in late winter. Useful in Zone 8 and warmer.

A. *uva-ursi*   P. 37

OO-vuh-UR-see. Bearberry, Kinnikinnick. Useful in Zones 2 to 7 (depending on the cultivar), this species is increasingly used where it is native and its cultural conditions can be met. It spreads quickly, and the small, olive green leaves turn bronze-red in winter. Selections vary in foliage gloss, density, and hardiness. All the listed cultivars are useful in the Pacific Northwest but decline in summer heat or humidity elsewhere. 'Big Bear' is a quick-growing cultivar from the Pacific Northwest with glossy, green foliage and good fall fruits. 'Massachusetts' is useful in Zones 4 to 7 on the Atlantic Coast and has glossy, dense foliage. The vigorous growth makes this a top choice for sunny, sandy soils, especially in maritime conditions. 'Microphylla' is a selection from the Pacific Northwest with tiny foliage. It does not perform well along the Atlantic Coast. 'Radiant' has shiny foliage and is used on the West Coast. 'Vancouver Jade' is a fast-growing, low shrub with large, red berries and larger and glossier foliage than the species. 'Point Reyes' is one of the most popular of the western selections, as it is relatively heat tolerant in the West.

❦ *Ardisia*

ar-DIS-e-a. Myrsine family, Myrsinaceae.

Ardisia is a large genus with more than 250 species of evergreen shrubs and trees of the tropics and subtropics, with most species native to Asia or the Americas. This genus is the only member of the family found in the temperate zones. The related *Myrsine africana* is grown in tropical regions for its attractive fruits. Several of the tropical *Ardisia* species have medicinal or culinary uses. Only a few species are seen in gardens or conservatories in North America. Leaves are evergreen, typically alternate, acuminate, and several inches long. Individual flowers are small and borne in many-flowered panicles. Depending on the species, flowers are white or reddish, and fruits are red or black and very ornamental. The name is based on the word ardis, which refers to the head of a spear and reflects the shape of the plants' anthers.

HOW TO GROW

The only species included here, *A. japonica,* is hardy from Zone 7 south. It is useful as a ground cover because of its tight, low massing of evergreen leaves. It requires partial shade, or the leaves may be sunscorched. Ardisias require moist but not saturated soils that are at least moderately fertile and well drained.

HOW TO USE

A glossy, evergreen ground cover for shaded situations in the humid South, *Ardisia* is an elegant choice for a transition from a formal garden to a wilder area or for planting in an otherwise dank and dark shaded area near a tall building. *Ardisia* is intolerant of drought and alkaline soils. It is especially attractive when occasional shafts of sunlight can reflect off the glossy, dark green, leathery foliage.

A. japonica   P. 38

juh-PON-ih-kuh. Marlberry. An evergreen, spreading shrub that can form colonies by underground runners, from which leafy stems rise 6 to 18 inches. Leaves are dark green and clustered into terminal whorls. *A. japonica* prefers moist shade and an acid loamy soil. Flowers are small and white, with the ornamental feature being the red fruits in winter. *A. japonica* prefers moist shade and an acid, loamy soil. It will not tolerate even moderately dry soils.

❦ *Arenaria*

ar-en-AR-e-a. Pink family, Caryophyllaceae.

Arenarias, or sandworts, are often thought of as rock-garden plants, but one in particular is useful as a ground cover for well-drained, sunny sites. The genus *Arenaria* includes more than 250 species native throughout the north temperate regions of the world. The closely related genus *Moehringia* is often included in *Arenaria*. *Arenaria* is also related to *Cerastium* (chickweeds) and is in the same family as *Dianthus* (carnations). The wild species are annuals or perennials, with some being subshrubs, whereas species grown in gardens are usually perennials. Foliage is green, with the opposite leaves being lanceolate or oblong lanceolate, often awl tipped and slightly prickly. Flowers are typically small and white, creating attractive sprays of bloom. The name is based on the Latin *arena*, or sand, and refers to the plants' native soils.

HOW TO GROW

Arenarias are hardy to Zone 4 and thrive in sunny, well-drained sites. They prefer gritty, sandy, poor soils. Planting in rich or moist soils will lead to short-lived plants rather than dense growth. Outside the rock garden, only a few species of *Arenaria* serve as ground covers, due to their lax, mat-forming stems. They do not spread far beyond their initial planting, so adequate numbers of plants must be used to create an effective ground cover.

HOW TO USE

The tufted forms lend themselves to massing along the edges of sandy, gravelly slopes, where they are naturally at home. *A. montana* is often found in Mediterranean gardens in France, where it blends nicely with rosemary, oregano, and thyme. Because arenarias spread slowly, they are best used in small-scale applications and are an attractive choice to fill between steppingstones, especially in terraces or patios.

A. montana   P. 38

mon-TAHN-uh. European Sandwort, Mountain Sandwort. The grassy, matlike foliage reaches only 4 inches tall and spreads only about 12 inches on lax, trailing stems. The small, white flowers appear in spring. Plants need alkaline soil, full sun, and very good drainage to thrive. Useful in Zones 4 to 8.

❦ *Artemisia*

are-te-MIS-e-a. Aster family, Asteraceae.

Artemisia species, commonly called wormwoods, grow on all the northern continents, especially in arid regions. They are rather closely related to sunflowers. The 400 species include annuals, perennials, and weak-wooded shrubs. Foliage is green to silvery green, depending on the abundance of silver hairs on the leaves. Leaves are typically dissected into broadly cut segments or even lacerated into delicate filigrees. Most species have fragrant essential oils, which accounts for part of the plants' popularity. Absinthe, an addictive and toxic narcotic beverage popular in certain artistic circles at the end of the 19th century, is derived from one species. Flowers are rather insignificant, greenish, wind-pollinated structures that are quite elegant when inspected with a magnifying glass. The name commemorates Artemis, the virgin Greek goddess of the hunt, who supposedly became this plant when pursued by an overly amorous divine suitor.

HOW TO GROW

Wormwoods like gravelly, lean, dry soils with little retained moisture and excellent drainage. If grown in moist, shady, or constantly humid conditions, they may decline or "melt" into a slimy mess. Wormwoods prefer full sun and can withstand a good deal of wind.

HOW TO USE

Choose artemisias to create spreading swaths of silver in thin, dry soils. When planted in richer conditions, they will quickly become rank and weak stemmed. Although *A. ludoviciana* is sometimes seen in perennial gardens, its thuggish nature is unsuitable for all but the largest plantings. 'Valerie Finnis' is more attractive and easily controlled. *A. stelleriana* does well in naturalistic seaside or cool desert conditions, where its intensely silver foliage reflects the bright light. 'Silver Brocade' flowers shyly, and with its low-spreading characteristics and silvery arching leaves, it is an easy-care choice. Cut it back anytime during the growing season to refresh the foliage. Plants may perform poorly in hot, muggy conditions.

A. californica 'Canyon Grey'

kal-if-OR-nih-cuh. This selection is a prostrate form of the native California species. It forms an airy mat spreading 4 feet or more. Useful in Zones 8 to 10.

A. *ludoviciana* 'Valerie Finnis'

loo-doe-vish-ee-AH-nuh. Named for the great English plantswoman, this selection has gray-white to nearly pure white leaves and stems rising 2 to 3 feet. Useful in Zones 4 to 8.

A. *stelleriana* 'Silver Brocade' P. 39

steh-LAIR-ee-AH-nuh. Beach Wormwood. This selection (also known as 'Mori' and 'Boughton Silver'; all three appear to be the same plant) was created at the University of British Columbia for the beauty of its cut foliage and compact growth habit. It makes a good, slow-spreading edger and ground cover for well-drained, sunny, slightly alkaline sites. Useful in Zones 4 to 8.

❦ *Asarum*

as-AR-um. Birthwort family, Aristolochiaceae.

The genus *Asarum* (commonly known as wild gingers) contains more than 20 species of rhizomatous perennials native to North America, Asia, and Europe. It is closely related to *Saruma* and in the same family as *Aristolochia* (pipe vines). The sometimes separate genus *Hexastylis* is treated here as part of *Asarum*. (Obviously, there is disagreement among taxonomists over the definition of the genus.) Leaves are long stalked; kidney, heart, or spear shaped; and deciduous or evergreen. Evergreen leaves often are attractively mottled. Flowers are fascinating to botanists but inconspicuous. Borne at ground level, they are brown and supposedly pollinated by flies, but without the bad odor, typical of fly-pollinated flowers. Wild gingers spread slowly by rhizomes or, if well sited, by seeds. The name *Asarum* appears to come from the common name of an ancient Greek herb. These plants have aromatic oils that are reminiscent of the totally unrelated edible ginger of Asia *(Zingiber officinale).*

HOW TO GROW

Asarums like rich, moist, well-drained, organic soil and partial shade. They are intolerant of full sun, wind, and excessive moisture (which may cause fungal diseases). Use wild gingers as attractive ground covers in naturalistic or woodland settings. Due to their slow-spreading habit, numerous plants are required to establish a mass. The evergreen species develop sunscald easily and need careful placement. Hardiness varies by species.

HOW TO USE

Choice, well-behaved, beautiful asarums are among the most elegant and sought-after ground covers. Plant them in nearly full to full shade in a woodland garden and allow them to spread, which they will do at a modest rate. Asarums can be planted as a contrast to tall, high-branched, deciduous trees, where they will present a gleaming carpet for the forest giants; in combination with wildflowers such as trilliums, columbines, or dicentras; or with flowering shrubs such as camellias, rhododendrons, and glossy hollies. Or think of them as companions to massed astilbes, ferns, and hostas. They look elegant and refined in formal, shaded entrance plantings, surviving dense shade. Be aware that overwatering or waterlogged soil will make them vulnerable to botrytis and other fungal diseases.

A. arifolium

air-eh-FO-lee-um. This species is noteworthy for its evergreen leaves with silvery markings. Useful in Zone 5 (where it may be semievergreen) and warmer, it quickly forms good clumps in woodland conditions.

A. canadense

can-ah-DEN-see. Wild Ginger. Useful in Zones 4 to 8, this deciduous East Coast native has heart-shaped, green, hairy leaves. The common name refers to the pungently aromatic roots. Plant it in full to partial shade. It is quite tolerant of some alkalinity.

A. caudatum ◆ P. 39

caw-DAY-tum. Western Wild Ginger. This western North American native hails from the redwood forests and needs shade and loose-leaf mold to thrive. Foliage is larger than that of *A. europaeum*. Useful in Zones 6 to 9, it spreads by rhizomes to form a rich carpet.

A. europaeum ◆ P. 40

your-o-PEE-um. European Wild Ginger. This evergreen perennial is useful in Zones 5 to 8. It has glossy, heart-shaped leaves and tiny, brown flowers in spring. It is excellent in shade, prefers well-drained but moist soil, and is vulnerable to botrytis when too wet.

A. shuttleworthii (Hexastylis shuttleworthii)

shut-ul-WORTH-ee-eye. Little Brown Jugs. This native of the southern Appalachians, which has leaves marked with silvery speckles, is useful in

Zones 6 to 8. Though hard to find, it is well worth the search to use in naturalistic garden areas. 'Callaway' is rhizomatous.

A. splendens

SPLEN-dens. This Japanese species, useful in Zones 6 to 8, forms clumps of striking, arrow-shaped foliage with silvery markings. It needs shade, some summer heat, and moist conditions.

A. takaoi

tay-KAY-oh-ee. This Japanese species is relatively new to North American gardens. It is reported as useful in Zone 5 and warmer. It has tiny, evergreen leaves (deciduous in northern areas) and is a good spreader.

☙ Aspidistra

as-pi-DIS-tra. Lily-of-the-valley family, Convallariaceae.

Aspidistra is a small genus of about five Asian species native from the Himalayas into China and east to Japan. It is closely related to *Convallaria* (lily-of-the-valley) and is in the same family as *Liriope*. All aspidistras are attractive evergreen herbs with subterranean stems. Leaves are usually 12 to 18 inches long, several inches wide, and rather rigid. Flowers and fruits are inconspicuous. *A. elatior* (cast-iron plant) is the most frequently encountered species, and the only one commonly used as a ground cover. The other species and their named cultivars are usually treated as specimen plants. The name *Aspidistra* comes from the word for small, round shield, apparently in reference to the shape of the flower's stigma.

HOW TO GROW

Grow aspidistras in partial to deep shade and any moist garden soil, provided it is acid to neutral. They thrive in moist, well-drained, humus-rich soil and will grow there for years with minimal attention. Aspidistras spread slowly by their underground to surface-level stems, from which the roots arise. Propagation is by division, but offsets may be slow to establish, let alone spread. Once established, aspidistras are persistent and tolerate considerable neglect. Naturalizing spring bulbs among them is not feasible due to competition from the roots and the low light requirements. Useful from Zone 8 (warm Zone 7 with protection) south, provided the site has ample summer moisture.

HOW TO USE

Along deeply shaded walkways, in the dank back corners of old gardens, and from city lots to woodlands, cast-iron plant lives up to its name, surviving neglect and poor conditions. To thrive, it needs well-drained, organic soil with adequate moisture. Feed it in late winter, and you will be rewarded with lush, gleaming foliage. The spreading roots make it an excellent choice for slopes and to prevent erosion.

A. elatior   P. 40

ee-LAY-tee-or. Cast-iron Plant. If you live in the Deep South, along the Gulf Coast, or in sheltered parts of the West, you'll find cast-iron plant a valued addition to your garden. The broad leaves of this evergreen perennial can create a 2-foot-high, slowly spreading mass where little else will grow. It is an excellent choice for dim, shaded areas. 'Akebono' is a Japanese selection with leaves marked with a narrow, vertical, white stripe. 'Variegata' has leaves with irregular, green and white, vertical bands.

❦ Aster

AS-ter. Aster family, Asteraceae.

The 250 species of asters are native to the Northern Hemisphere, with the vast majority native to North America. A few species are native to South America. Most asters are perennials, but a few are annuals or shrubs. *Aster* is closely related to *Solidago* (goldenrods). It has small flowers arranged into showy heads. Each head has ray flowers, which are commonly referred to as petals, and a central disk, which is composed of numerous tiny flowers with very short petals that are not individually noted by the casual observer. Asters are familiar garden, prairie, and woodland perennials with great diversity in flower color, plant habit, and growing conditions. Only one species, *A. divaricatus,* is normally used as a ground cover, although other species can be effectively massed. The name *Aster* comes from the Latin word for "star" (related words are "astronomy" and "astronaut"), in reference to the shape and brightness of the flower heads.

HOW TO GROW

Grow *A. divaricatus* in bright, well-drained, woodland sites, woodland margins, and like areas where its proclivity to run will be an advantage. This species is not fussy as to soil, provided it is not constantly moist. Planting in moist or rich conditions leads to a floppy, weedy appearance.

Plants will form spreading colonies within several years of planting, but they are easy to control. This species is useful in Zones 3 south.

HOW TO USE

Choose *A. divaricatus* for its long-flowering, white blooms in fall, and plant it in high to dense shade. Though often seen in the wild along roadside verges and ditches, it accepts dry growing conditions and does well in impoverished soils.

A. divaricatus   P. 41

dih-vair-ih-KAH-tus. White Wood Aster. This species has few competitors when it comes to lighting up partly shaded, dry corners of northern woodland gardens. Thriving in heavy to light shade and thin, dry soils, plants quickly spread by rhizomes and seed. The starry white flowers bloom in early fall on stalks 1 foot to nearly 3 feet tall. Leaves are oval or lance shaped, toothed, and moderately coarse.

❦ Astilbe

as-TIL-be. Saxifrage family, Saxifragaceae.

The ferny foliage and cotton candy flowers of *Astilbe* make it deservedly popular in damp, lightly shaded situations. The dozen species of *Astilbe* are native only to Asia and eastern North America. From these species and their numerous hybrids have come the ornamental garden cultivars so widely treasured throughout the north temperate regions of the world. Many astilbes are tall, dramatic accents, but some make effective small-scale ground covers. *Astilbe* is closely related to *Rodgersia*. Leaves are doubly or triply compound, giving the effective but false appearance of numerous small leaves on small branching stems. In reality, the stems are only slightly branched or unbranched, and there are relatively few leaves on each plant. Foliage height ranges from only a few inches in *A. chinensis* var. *pumila* to well over 3 feet in larger species and cultivars. Leaf color ranges from apple green to bronzy green and is an important consideration in making pleasing foliage compositions with other perennials. The tiny flowers are individually insignificant but are massed into very bright and showy inflorescences held well above the foliage, thus increasing the effective height of the plant. Peak bloom is in early summer. Ironically, the scientific name means "not brilliant," in reference to the individual flowers' display rather than the overall floral effect.

HOW TO GROW

Astilbes are intolerant of drought and perform best beside streams, pools, or in partial to light shade where there is sufficient soil moisture. Grow them where there is adequate open space above the plants so that their floral display can be admired rather than obscured by low-branching shrubs and trees. Astilbes prefer rich, loamy garden soil and will not tolerate strong root competition from greedy, shallow-rooted trees such as Norway maples and beeches, even if these trees are pruned high. Astilbes are slow to spread but can be propagated by division. Effective use as a ground cover requires planting sufficient numbers to provide a good cover in the first season. For nonspreading species, masses are made by complete planting of the area from the beginning. Useful in Zones 4 to 8.

HOW TO USE

Plant astilbes in drifts alongside watercourses or streams, beside ponds, or where bright ribbons of color are wanted in mid- to late summer. Astilbes are often grown as broad masses in contemporary European landscape parks and in transition zones for water gardens. They look especially attractive when paired with the shade-loving Japanese perennial *Kirengeshoma*, with its pale yellow, shuttlecock flowers. *A. chinensis* var. *pumila* and *A. simplicifolia* 'Sprite' make effective masses in woodland gardens and at the edges of perennial borders. *A. chinensis* var. *pumila* is among the most drought tolerant and one of the latest flowering. Its spreading characteristic and strong, bottlebrush, mauve flower spikes are prominent in late summer. The glossy, dark foliage of *A. simplicifolia* 'Sprite' is a nice foil to its pale pink flowers, although it is most valued for its finely cut foliage, which looks like a ruffle on an antique dress. *A. chinensis* var. *pumila* spreads better than *A. simplicifolia* 'Sprite'.

A. chinensis
P. 41

chi-NEN-sis. There is a great deal of natural and horticultural variation in size and hardiness in this species. *A. chinensis* var. *pumila* (often listed as 'Pumila') is most commonly used as a ground cover. When planted in moist, shaded sites with little root competition, it spreads moderately quickly into a low, weed-suppressing mat only 8 inches tall. The light lavender flower spikes appear in late summer. It tolerates heat and does better in the South than other astilbes. Plant *A. chinensis* at the edge of a walk or the front of a bed.

A. simplicifolia 'Sprite' P. 42

sim-pli-si-FO-lee-uh. This selection has dark, deeply cut foliage and pale pink flowers. It is popular for planting in large drifts, where it makes impressive foliage and floral displays.

Athyrium

a-THY-re-um. Wood fern family, Dryopteridaceae.

Athyrium is a widespread genus of ferns whose 200-plus species are found on all continents, although they are most abundant in tropical regions. Several species are native to the north temperate regions of the Americas, Asia, and Europe, but the majority used in gardens are from Japan. Athyrium is related to Woodsia (cliff ferns). As with most terrestrial ferns, the stems, also called rhizomes, emerge at ground level, and from them arise a crown of deciduous leaves, or fronds. The athyriums that spread (not all the species) do so by runners, but under suitable conditions, all may be propagated by spores. The name means "to sport," in the sense of to change or mutate, and refers to the diversity of the spore-bearing structures on the fertile fronds.

HOW TO GROW

Athyriums thrive in moist, organic soils that never dry out, especially along streambanks or in moist woods. They require partial to full shade and should be kept mulched with an organic material such as shredded leaves, rotted wood chips, or compost. Athyriums, especially A. filix-femina, spread vigorously by lateral stems in sites that are to their liking. Control is by digging up excess plants. Hardiness depends on the species and ranges from Zones 4 or 5 south.

HOW TO USE

Athyriums add rich texture to shaded garden areas. The bright green fronds of A. filix-femina make strongly spreading masses at the base of high-pruned shrubs. Low-branching shrubs look incongruous with athyriums, since the ferns seem to become tangled in the shrubs' lower branches. It is best to plant athyriums away from well-traveled footpaths and to avoid sites prone to strong winds, since the fronds are easily broken or damaged. The foliage of A. japonicum and A. niponicum look good in combination with massed perennials, both in woodland gardens and in semishaded streamside or pondside situations.

A. filix-femina   P. 42

FEE-lix FEM-in-uh. Lady Fern. With bright green fronds reaching 3 feet or
more tall, this is an impressive ground cover for cool, moist sites. Both
normal and red-petioled forms are useful in the garden. In the Victorian
period, more than 200 named selections were cultivated. 'Cristata' (part
of the Cristatum Group of crested forms) is a fast-growing, clumping
form with forked and fringed frond segments (pinnae) that blends well
with other ground covers in a woodland garden. Several distinct forms
may be sold under this name. Useful from Zones 5 south.

A. japonicum

juh-PON-i-kum. Black Lady Fern. Dr. J.C. Raulston introduced this fern to
American gardens after his 1985 expedition to Korea. The upright, triangular fronds grow to approximately 18 inches and spread slowly in woodland conditions to form a dense mass. Useful from Zones 5 south.

A. niponicum (A. goeringianum)   P. 43

ni-PON-i-kum. Japanese Painted Fern. 'Metallicum' and 'Pictum' are equivalent names for the plant properly listed as *A. niponicum* var. *pictum*. The
names describe one of the most attractive and eye-catching ferns. The iri-
descent silver markings and streaks of purple and green make for distinctive clumps. This form does not run but can be effectively massed. Grow
in full to partial shade with adequate moisture. In very cool climates, this
species will tolerate some sun. Useful from Zone 4 south.

🌿 Aubrieta

au-BREE-shuh. Mustard family, Brassicaceae.

Aubrieta is a small genus of about 12 species native from the Mediterranean to Iran and Afghanistan. Sometimes called rock cress, it is related
to *Alyssum*. Species include small, evergreen perennials and subshrubs.
Their hairy leaves are alternate, ovate or oblong, and entire or toothed,
giving the foliage a silvery green cast. These trailing plants cascade readily
over rocks, walls, and irregularities in the ground. The showy purple or
violet flowers are in lax terminal racemes. Seedpods are not considered
ornamental by fastidious gardeners. The name commemorates Claude
Aubriet (1665–1742), a French botanical artist.

HOW TO GROW

Grow aubrietias in sites with full sun and perfect drainage. They are not
fussy about soil pH and tolerate a wide range of soils, from acid to alka-

line. Plants will perform best in soils of moderate to above-average fertility, as in well-drained loams, but they will become excessively lax and prone to rot in too-rich soils. Aubretias are inherently lax-stemmed plants, and these stems are likely to root when they come in contact with the soil. New stems, however, come primarily from the established crown rather than the rooting stems. Aubrietias are not vigorous spreaders, so effective use as a ground cover is obtained by planting enough of them in the beginning rather than expecting the plants to creep into each other. Cutting the plants back immediately after they flower will promote denser growth. Hardy to Zone 4 with proper drainage.

HOW TO USE
The delight of aubretias comes from the brilliant colors of their spring flowers. In the cooler growing conditions necessary for success (the plants tend to "melt" in warmer East Coast zones—from Zone 7 south), aubretias are a spring highlight trailing over a stone wall or down a rocky slope, or planted between boulders. They must be cut back to prevent weediness and kept on a lean diet in well-drained, gritty soil.

A. deltoidea
del-TOY-dee-uh. Rock Cress. This spreading, herbaceous ground cover announces spring with its bright carpets of mostly purple flowers. Familiar to many as it creeps over walls in full sun, *A. deltoidea* looks best if sheared back hard after flowering.

A. hybrids   P. 44
A number of garden hybrids provide a range of colors. 'Argenteovariegata' ('Albomarginata') has cream-edged gray-green foliage and bright blue spring flowers. It is evergreen in milder climates. 'Purple Gem' spreads to approximately 2 feet and bears rich purple flowers. 'Red Carpet' has rich red flowers. 'Royal Blue' blooms in varying shades of blue and purple.

Aurinia
au-RI-nee-uh. Mustard family, Brassicaceae.

Only the well-known basket-of-gold, *A. saxatilis*, is commonly grown in gardens. Ranging from central Europe to Asia Minor, the seven *Aurinia* species are found in habitats such as dry, sunny rock ledges, cliff faces, and rocky plains. These perennials grow to at most 2 feet tall and are often woody at the base. The basal leaves are clustered into rosettes and are gray-green underneath because of silvery hairs. Flowers are individually small but displayed in showy masses. The name comes from the Latin word for "gold," a reference to the bright, colorful flowers. *Aurinia* is very closely related to *Alyssum* and is sometimes merged with it.

HOW TO GROW

Grow aurinias in sunny, well-drained, mineral soils. They prefer slightly acid soils and will not perform well on alkaline rocks, such as limestone or dolomite. Propagation is by seed or purchased plants. Use basket-of-gold where the bold yellow flowers can spill over ledges, rocks, or other well-drained surface features. Winter hardy to Zone 4, aurinias generally decline in the heat and humidity of Zone 7 and south.

HOW TO USE

The classic spring trio — *Aurinia, Aubrieta,* and *Alyssum* — are all excellent when planted as cascade or wall plants. *Aurinia* and *Aubrieta* are chosen for their brilliant colors and Joseph's coat effect after the dull gray winters that many northern gardeners endure. Use them in sunny rock gardens, along pathways, and in areas where annuals can be used to continue the color throughout the season.

A. saxatilis (Alyssum saxatile)   P. 44

sax-ah-TIL-iss. Basket-of-gold. Easily grown and showy, provided it has full sun and perfect drainage, this species does best among rocks or covering the top of a warm wall. The normal form has bright golden yellow flowers, thus the common name. 'Citrina' (very similar to 'Sulphurea') has pale sulphur yellow flowers that cover the spreading mat of grayish foliage in midspring. 'Compacta' has bright yellow flowers and a denser growth habit than the species. Other cultivars may be of particular interest to rock garden enthusiasts.

❦ Baccharis

BAK-kar-is. Aster family, Asteraceae.

There are more than 300 *Baccharis* species, and all are native to the Americas, from coastal Virginia and California all the way south to the Straits of Magellan. *Baccharis* is closely related to *Aster,* but unlike that well-known genus of garden perennials, *Baccharis* comprises trees, shrubs, and perennials, with most of the diversity in the American tropics. Only a few of the shrubby species are used as ornamentals in warm temperate gardens, and these are highly tolerant of salty soils. Leaves are evergreen, small, alternate, and oblong or lanceolate. Flowers are inconspicuous, with plants being entirely male or female. In contrast to the flowers, the tiny seeds are produced in conspicuous masses of cottony fibers that are carried in the wind and may make an ephemeral mess, which either delights those who enjoy such outbursts of natural phenomena or frustrates gardeners who pride themselves on a neat and tidy appearance. Fortunately, cutting-grown plants from nurseries are usually selected from seedless male plants. The name fancifully commemorates Bacchus, god of wine, and relates to the spicy fragrance of the roots of some species.

HOW TO GROW

Grow *Baccharis* in exposed sites with full sun. The plants are extremely useful in coastal and desert soil conditions. Amazingly, they are tolerant of a wide range of soils, from almost soggy to extremely dry, which reflects their adaptation to coastal environments. Being densely branched, *Baccharis* also is quite tolerant of strong winds. Use *Baccharis* on banks and slopes where access is difficult. The species that are useful as ground covers create billowy, mounded masses that spread by horizontal branches to 6 feet or more. They do not increase by runners or strongly rooting branches, so the initial planting must be dense enough to create the desired cover in a reasonable period of time. Hardiness depends on the species.

HOW TO USE

Baccharis will grow in average or dry conditions and in acid to neutral to alkaline soils. It is reputed to be both deer and fire resistant and demands only full sun to perform up to expectations. Plant *Baccharis* in masses to achieve an effective ground cover, use it on banks for stabilization, at the shore, or near buildings. Its natural form and late-season white flowers are a bonus. Whereas female plants release clouds of seeds and fluff, male plants are seedless. Some cultivars are available by sex. Selections of *B. pilularis* are considered appropriate choices for areas where fire retardance is a concern, and 'Twin Peaks' is recognized as one of the best species for desert landscaping.

B. 'Centennial'

This evergreen shrub grows to 18 inches tall and several feet wide and is particularly useful in warm, dry climates. It produces few, if any, seeds. Reported to be hardy in Zones 8 to 10.

B. halimifolia

hal-i-mi-FO-lee-uh. Bush Groundsel. This fast-growing shrub is appropriate for massing in warm maritime climates. Useful in Zones 6 to 9 but grows to be a large shrub in the South.

B. magellanica

mah-jel-AHN-ni-cuh. The male forms of this South American shrub are low-growing, fast-spreading evergreens. They remain less than a foot tall and spread to several feet across. They require full sun and well-drained soil. Useful from Zone 7 south.

B. pilularis   P. 45

pil-yule-LAIR-is. Coyote Bush. Native to dry areas of Oregon and California, this low-spreading shrub is an excellent and reliable ground cover in dry to desert regions of the West. Growing 2 to 3 feet tall and spreading to 10 feet or more, it is often used as a bank stabilizer and a fire-retardant cover for large areas. It is also resistant to salt spray. 'Pigeon Point' is larger in all respects, with bright green leaves and a fast-spreading habit. 'Twin Peaks' is also called dwarf coyote bush and spreads quickly into a low (6 to 12 inches tall), wide (6 feet), fire-resistant, drought-tolerant mound. This is a male selection, so there is no seed fluff. Useful in dry areas of Zone 7 and warmer.

❧ Berberis

BER-ber-is. Barberry family, Berberidaceae.

Berberis is a huge and complex genus of more than 450 species of shrubs, with most of the species diversity in Asia and South America. Only a few species are native to Africa, Europe, and North America. The genus is closely related to *Mahonia*. Shrubs range from about 12 inches tall to more than 12 feet, but only a few are useful as ground covers. The others are best used as specimens or for virtually impenetrable hedges. Leaves are simple and either evergreen or deciduous. Deciduous leaves often display spectacular fall colors. The spiny teeth on the leaves and the spines on the branches make these plants unfriendly to people but preferred sanctuaries for wildlife that can navigate the sharp points. Flowers are sharp yellow or orange and usually clustered. Fruits are attractive blue or black berries. Barberries provide a full year of interest but are primarily limited in use by their sharp nature. The name is a transliteration from Arabic of a term for the fruits.

HOW TO GROW

Barberries are tough plants that adapt to a wide range of situations, provided they are not subject to drying winter winds or prolonged summer desiccation. The species used as ground covers require full sun to light shade and are not especially particular regarding soil type or pH. Soil should be well drained but not subject to prolonged dryness. Barberries can be cut back, often quite severely, and regrow prolifically. Hardiness depends on the species.

HOW TO USE

Grow barberries where people will not come in regular contact with the thorns. They make excellent barrier plantings. Their spiny, arching branches and often brilliant fall color make them a popular choice as well. Some barberries, such as *B. verruculosa* and *B. thunbergii* 'Kobold', are used as hedges, although they also function well as massed ground covers. Note that in public plantings, their merits as thorny barriers may be offset by the certainty that some of the thorns will act as litter catchers.

B. thunbergii   P. 45

thun-BERJ-ee-eye. Japanese Barberry. Though often thought of as a hedging plant, *B. thunbergii* can work well as a ground cover. 'Kobold' is among the lowest-growing cultivars, reaching less than 3 feet high at maturity. It has attractive dark green foliage and yellow flowers. Useful in Zones 4 to 8.

B. verruculosa

veh-roo-kew-LOH-suh. Warty Barberry. This evergreen shrub grows 3 to 5 feet tall and masses well. Fruits are black and glossy. Useful in Zones 7 (Zone 6 with protection, but not evergreen) to 9.

❦ *Bergenia*

ber-GE-ni-a. Saxifrage family, Saxifragaceae.

Bergenia species are native to the mountains of Nepal, China, and Japan and north into the rugged Russian Far East. About eight species are familiar to Western gardeners, with various taxonomists recognizing additional species and varieties. *Bergenia* is closely related to *Saxifraga* (saxifrages) and is sometimes merged into that genus. Plants are herbaceous perennials that develop significant crowns, from which the large, alternate leaves rise. Leaves are strong, quite thick (almost like cardboard), and deciduous or semievergreen, depending on the species and garden situation. Flowers are showy, in various shades of pink and occasionally white, and are held on strong stalks high above the foliage. Garden hybrids of *Bergenia* species have led to numerous forms in the trade. These differ in flower color, leaf shape, and massing qualities. The genus commemorates the German botanist and doctor Karl von Bergen (1704–1759).

HOW TO GROW
Grow bergenias in partial shade and out of drying winds. They prefer woodsy, organic soils that are well drained but not dry. Most prefer acid soils but will tolerate circumneutral to marginally alkaline soils. In nature, they are found in rock fields above the timberline in the Russian Far East, as well as beneath rhododendrons in deciduous forests. Bergenias are useful in the garden for their bold, almost leathery foliage. They are hardy in Zones 4 to 9 and remain evergreen from Zone 6 south given adequate moisture, shade, and protection from wind.

HOW TO USE
The shiny foliage of bergenias provides a lush appearance in northern gardens. Though perfectly at home massed in woodland gardens, they are also seen in cooler Mediterranean plantings in full sun to partial shade, depending on summer temperature ranges. The English plantswoman Beth Chatto displays them beautifully in her gravel garden. They also have been used in perennial beds and were a signature plant of the legendary English gardener Gertrude Jekyll. Selections of *B. cordifolia* are noted for their good fall and winter color and make fine additions to areas designed for winter viewing, such as patios and terraces close to building entrances.

B. ciliata   P. 46
sil-ee-AH-tuh. This beautiful species from Nepal requires a sheltered site for dramatic performance and is stunning either as a small-scale ground cover or as an accent within a larger foliage composition. Leaves are rich green and hairy on both sides and may die back during cold winters. *B. ciliata* performs best in medium to heavy soils. Useful in Zone 7 and warmer.

B. cordifolia
PP. 46, 47

cor-di-FO-lee-uh. Heart-leaved Bergenia. This East Asian native is currently popular as an edger for beds and borders, but it works equally well massed as a ground cover. Gertrude Jekyll used this species in her designs so frequently that it was said to be one of her signature plants. It has large, leathery leaves and pink, white, or rose flowers in spring. Though root hardy to Zone 3 (in which case the leaves are deciduous), it performs best in Zones 6 to 9, provided it has ample water. 'Profusion' has pinkish-white flowers. 'Rotblum' has rose-red or magenta flowers. 'Silberlicht' has pure white flowers.

❧ Brunnera

BRUN-ne-ra. Borage family, Boraginaceae.

Brunnera is a small genus with three species from southwestern Asia. Only one, B. macrophylla, is useful as a ground cover. Brunnera is closely related to Symphytum (comfrey) and in the same family as Myosotis (forget-me-nots). When in bloom in spring, brunneras may be mistaken for perennial forget-me-nots. They have bold, heart-shaped, dark green leaves and clouds of tiny, blue flowers. Leaves are rough to the touch due to numerous stout hairs. Plants are usually less than 2 feet tall and do best in partial shade or woodland settings. The name commemorates Samuel Brunner, a Swiss botanist active in the early 1800s.

HOW TO GROW

B. macrophylla grows in any fertile garden soil, provided it is not allowed to dry out. It thrives in full shade to partial shade, where its blue flowers are a welcome spring addition. It will grow in full sun in cool climates, provided the site is constantly moist, such as a streambank. This species will seed freely if growing conditions are to its liking. Useful in Zones 3 to 9.

HOW TO USE

The tiny, delicate, intense blue flowers are in startling contrast to the rough, hairy leaves, making brunneras an interesting challenge for gardeners. Is this a thug or a delicate specimen? Plant the green-leaved species in sunnier areas, and use the variegated 'Langtrees' in partial shade. Both require moisture to survive. The coarse texture is an interesting contrast to more delicate woodland plants. Suitable companion plants include Epimedium, Geum, and Waldsteinia.

B. macrophylla P. 47

mak-ro-FIL-uh. Brunnera, Alkanet, Siberian Bugloss, Dwarf Anchusa. This species makes a dense, mounding ground cover. The large, textured leaves are a nice foil to the tiny, blue flowers in spring. In woodland areas with some moisture, the leaves can grow to 8 inches wide. This species will tolerate some drought and thin soil. 'Langtrees' is a popular selection with silvery white markings on the leaf margins.

❧ Calamintha

kal-a-MIN-thuh. Mint family, Lamiaceae.

Calamintha comprises six or seven species of perennials native to open forests from central Europe to central Asia. It is closely related to *Scutellaria* (skullcaps) and *Lavandula* (lavender). Calaminths are long-lived, aromatic perennials that may become woody at the base. Leaves are opposite, ovate, soft, and fragrant to the touch. Lavender-blue, pink, or white flowers are produced in midsummer. The lax-stemmed plants make thick masses up to 15 inches tall. Hardy in Zones 4 to 8. The name means "beautiful mint."

HOW TO GROW

Grow calaminths in dry, well-drained, sunny locations. Although native to forest openings and thriving in barely but evenly moist woodsy soils, calaminths are not overly particular about soil pH. Stems may root where they come in contact with the ground. Named selections must be vegetatively propagated.

HOW TO USE

Are you landscaping with herbs? The aromatic qualities of calaminths make them preferred choices for planting near structures in sunny to partly sunny informal landscapes. Think of them as the foam on a cappuccino — the tiny, white flowers in midsummer are a bonus to the sturdy stems and minty foliage. Plants spread by rhizomes but are easily controlled. You can also plant calaminths as a low-growing, informal hedge or a spreading edger for a bed. They are especially pretty when combined with some of the smaller buddleias, such as *Buddleja davidii* 'Nanho Purple', or in drifts in front of grasses such as *Pennisetum alopecuroides*.

C. nepeta (C. nepetoides) P. 48

NEP-eh-tuh ssp. NEP-eh-tuh. Delicate in every respect, with finely textured foliage, tiny blue flowers, and a deliciously minty fragrance, this species makes a charming planting in dry, well-drained, sunny spots. It blooms throughout summer and into fall, although it does not do well in high humidity. 'Grandiflora' has pink flowers. 'Grandiflora Variegata' has pink flowers and leaves with cream markings. 'White Cloud' has small, white flowers and normal foliage.

☙ *Callirhoe*

kal-ir-HO-e. Mallow family, Malvaceae.

The nine species that make up *Callirhoe* are North American perennials most common in the central and southwestern United States. They range from Florida and Illinois west to Texas and Wyoming. They are related to hollyhocks (*Alcea* and *Althaea*). All are low growing with very showy flowers. Leaves are alternate and typically deeply cleft. Flowers seem to be inordinately large for the plant size, are visible at a considerable distance, and are brilliant wine red, rose, pink, or occasionally white. The name commemorates a minor Greek deity who was the daughter of Achelous, a river god.

HOW TO GROW

Grow *Callirhoe* in sites with full sun and good drainage. Soil should be more mineral than organic, especially in regions with humid, wet summers, or the plants will rot. The spreading stems do not root (although they carry profuse blooms), so coverage is dependent on establishing numerous perennial crowns. Useful in Zones 6 to 9, provided summer sogginess is avoided.

HOW TO USE

These species are valued ground covers in the south central United States, as they thrive on high summer heat. Their brilliant color is dramatic when planted near ornamental and grasslike plants such as *Miscanthus, Molinia,* or *Nolina,* or choose them to face down massed shrubs such as *Weigela* or *Vitex* or taller perennials such as *Liatris.* Among the boldest splashes of color in the summer landscape, they are perfect for larger gardens, where their brilliant hues have an impact.

C. involucrata   P. 48

in-vol-yoo-CRAY-tuh. Wine Cups. In hot, dry, sunny sites, the sprawling stems display cherry red blossoms that cascade happily through borders and over walls. This deciduous hollyhock relative does best in full sun and dry situations. Native from Texas to Utah and Wyoming, it performs well in Zones 6 to 9, especially where summers are dry rather than humid.

❦ *Calluna*

kal-LOO-nuh. Heath family, Ericaceae.

Calluna is a genus with only one species, best known to all as heather. It is closely related to *Erica* (heaths). Heather is a semievergreen shrub that grows to 18 inches tall. The small, needlelike leaves are paired, often over-lapping, and range in color from bright green to yellow and purple, thus giving the entire plant a distinctive hue. Flowers are small, urn shaped, and pinkish or white. The name means "to cleanse," in reference to the use of the plants as brooms.

HOW TO GROW

Grow heather in full sun and well-drained, organic-rich, acid soil. Although it will adapt to salt air and low-fertility, acid soils, it will burn in cold, drying winter winds and is recommended for coastal locations with moderate winters and mild summers. Heather grows more slowly than the heaths and should be planted on approximately 1-foot centers, since the plants will not typically spread beyond their initial planting. It does not do well in areas of high summer humidity and hot nights. Hardy in Zones 5 (with protection) to 8.

HOW TO USE

Although heather was used in Europe in the mid-twentieth century for island beds and front yard plantings, it looks and does best when grown in conditions as close as possible to those of its native moorlands. Massed in sweeps where it can grow naturally to its full size, heather makes a beautiful and evocative landscape statement.

C. vulgaris   P. 49

vul-GAIR-iss. Scotch Heather. Summer-flowering species are considered hardier than the closely related heaths. 'Blazeaway' has yellow new foliage in spring that turns light green in summer and red in fall. Flowers are modest and lavender, blooming in late summer. 'County Wicklow' has double, light pink flowers in summer and evergreen foliage. 'Robert Chapman' is nearly prostrate, with golden yellow foliage that develops orange or scarlet tones as the season progresses. Flowers are purplish pink. 'Silver Knight' has ever-gray foliage and lavender flowers in late summer. 'Tib' is a well-known selection with pink flowers, evergreen foliage, and a spreading habit.

❦ Campanula

kam-PAN-yoo-luh. Bellflower family, Campanulaceae.

Campanulas are one of the great treasures of the gardening world because of their diverse habit and bold blue flowers, with every shade of blue imaginable. There are more than 300 species of *Campanula*, all restricted to the Northern Hemisphere. Centers of diversity are in the Mediterranean and Balkans, through the Caucasus and mountains of western Asia. Relatively few garden species hail from East Asia or North America. They are closely related to the Asiatic balloon flower *(Platycodon)*. Campanulas range from low, mat-forming perennials to stately, tall garden plants nearly 4 feet tall. Flowers are bell shaped (thus the names bellflower, bluebells, and harebell). White and pink cultivars exist in several species. The Latin name means "little bell."

HOW TO GROW

Grow the ground-covering campanulas where their creeping nature can be controlled or is desired. They are not fussy as to soil, provided it is friable and well drained without being droughty. All species will suffer from excessive moisture around the roots. Several of the more aggressive species spread vigorously by underground stems. Control them by digging up excess offshoots. Useful in Zones 4 to 8, unless otherwise noted.

HOW TO USE

The deceptively innocent air of the bellflowers masks a tough plant that makes a useful spring- and early-summer-blooming herbaceous ground cover. Bellflowers are excellent as edgers to walkways and walls where their growth is contained and the plants are placed in good viewing positions. Use them in partial sun to light shade to bring glowing patches of blue and white to the edges of woods, or plant them in cottage gardens beneath perennials such as Siberian iris.

C. carpatica   P. 49
car-PAH-ti-kuh. Carpathian Bellflower. This is one of the most popular species, and named selections are available with flowers from white to blue. It grows in low tufts that spread to about 18 inches. 'Blue Clips' and

'White Clips' are among the selections most often grown. 'Deep Blue Clips' is a rich, deep blue.

C. garganica
gar-GAH-ni-kuh. This small, mat-forming species has tufted foliage and pale blue, starlike flowers. It performs well planted in a wall or as a ground cover for small areas.

C. portenschlagiana (C. muralis)   P. 50
por-ten-schlag-ee-AH-nuh. Dalmatian Bellflower. A vigorous, evergreen spreader (deciduous in its northern limits), this species has clusters of deep blue flowers in summer. 'Aurea' has bright gold foliage in spring that greens as the season progresses.

C. poscharskyana
pa-shar-skee-AH-nuh. Serbian Bellflower. This well-known, ground-covering bellflower has trailing shoots that form a dense carpet. The lavender-blue bells are presented in spring. Selections include 'Alba' (not quite white), 'Blue Gown' (light blue), and 'Lisduggan' (lavender-pink).

C. takesimana (C. punctata var. takesimana)   P. 50
tak-iss-eh-MAH-nuh. A strong, invasive ground cover from temperate Asia, this species has deciduous, heart-shaped leaves up to 6 inches long that grow thickly from the profuse and shallowly running (and rooting) stems to produce a dense, bright carpet that chokes out weeds and everything else. The pendent flowers are off-white or pink, speckled with purple. The vigorous growth is advantageous for massing but requires careful siting.

❦ Carex
KAR-eks. Sedge family, Cyperaceae.

"Sedges have edges" is the rhyme for identifying members of the sedge family. Indeed, sedge stems are usually triangular in cross section, and thus have three edges, whereas grass stems are round in cross section. Sedges are related to bulrushes *(Scirpus)* and papyrus *(Cyperus papyrus)*. Sedge identification is usually considered to be difficult, as there are 1,500 to 2,000 species native to marshy and wet sites throughout the world. Gardeners encounter very few species, although many more will undoubtedly be discovered to make fine ornamentals, since this has become a "hot" genus for cutting-edge gardeners. *Carex* species, as is true of grasses, have a subtle beauty of foliage and fruit stalks that is overlooked by those insistent on color alone. Of the species in intentional cultivation, only a few are considered ground covers. The name is an ancient Latin word that was applied to some sort of sedgelike plant.

HOW TO GROW

Grow most sedges in sites with constantly moist to wet soil and partial shade, as are found along forested streams or pools. Soil should be of high fertility and organic content. Sedges can be extremely hardy, depending on their native range, as different species are native from the Arctic to tropical mountains.

HOW TO USE

Carex species do not spread aggressively, but rather make massive clumps, so their effective use as a ground cover is derived from planting adequate numbers from the beginning. They bring a unique grassy texture to shaded woodland and marsh conditions, where most ornamental grasses will not survive. Plant them where the linear quality of their foliage can contrast with larger, bolder leaves, such as those of *Hosta*, *Darmera peltata*, *Petasites*, and ferns.

C. caryophyllea

ker-ee-oh-FIL-ee-uh, commonly ker-ee-oh-fil-EE-uh. 'The Beatles', sporting a texture that resembles the famous four's haircuts, is a low, evergreen sedge that creeps politely along steppingstones and walkways. It grows 3 to 4 inches or more tall. Useful in Zones 7 to 9.

C. glauca   P. 51

GLAW-ka. Blue Sedge. This species is a hardy, vigorous, long-lived ground cover that is especially suited for erosion control. It grows 8 to 10 inches tall and spreads in dry to moist soils. Useful in Zones 5 to 9.

C. muskingumensis   P. 51

muk-ing-um-EN-sis. Palm Sedge. This species is native to Michigan (Muskegon County, thus the botanical name). It gives a tropical, slightly rakish look to the garden, with its tufted foliage and spreading habit, much like some strange, miniature palm tree. It grows 2 to 2½ feet tall in moist soils, requires partial shade to sun, and will not tolerate drought. Useful in Zones 4 to 8.

C. nigra
P. 52

NIE-gruh. Black Sedge. This one is noted for its glossy green foliage and black flower spikes. It prefers moist soils and partial to full shade. Useful in Zones 6 to 9.

C. pennsylvanica

pen-sil-VAN-ih-kuh. This eastern North American native is another shade-loving ground cover that reaches 6 to 10 inches tall. Native to acid woodlands, such as those consisting of oaks and tulip poplars, it will tolerate average to dry soils. Useful in Zones 4 to 8.

C. tumulicola

too-muh-LIH-koh-luh. This West Coast native has very narrow, dark green leaves. It forms spreading hummocks that reach about 12 inches tall and mass well to form a ground cover. Useful in Zone 7 and warmer.

❧ Ceanothus

see-an-O-thus. Buckthorn family, Rhamnaceae.

Ceanothus, or California lilacs, are endemic to the Americas, with the greatest diversity in California itself. *C. americanus* (New Jersey tea) is the only species native to eastern North America, but it is not useful as a ground cover. *Ceanothus* is closely related to *Rhamnus* (buckthorn) and is the only genus in the entire buckthorn family prized for its ornamental flowers. As implied by the common name, the flowers cover the same color range as *Syringa* (true lilacs) — light to deep blues, with additional purple and rose tones. Flowers are individually quite small but are clustered into very showy cymes. Plants are woody, long-lived shrubs that grow from only a few feet to more than 12 feet tall. All *Ceanothus* species have tough, small, often toothed, evergreen leaves. Those useful as ground covers form dense, low, nearly impenetrable masses that sprout clouds of flowers in spring. The name is an ancient Greek one formerly used for a very different genus by the philosopher Theophrastus.

HOW TO GROW

Grow *Ceanothus* in full sun to very light shade where its intolerance of summer water and humidity can be met. Avoid summer watering from automatic irrigation systems. Soils of normal fertility are adequate and should be well drained without being unstable when dry, as can occur with some clayey or very sandy soils. Use as a ground-cover plant from nursery stock known to be reliable in your region, primarily in western North America. *Ceanothus* will quickly decline, however, with summer humidity. Hardy in Zones 7 to 9.

HOW TO USE

Ceanothus is a spectacular ground cover on the Pacific Coast and in warm, arid parts of the Southwest. It adds glorious blue color to the landscape in spring and evergreen, lustrous foliage throughout the year. Remember that *Ceanothus* species are vulnerable to root rot if overwatered. They also resent summer humidity and consequently perform poorly if used outside their preferred region. They are not particular as to soil, provided it is well drained. Mass them on banks and slopes or in places where a genuine carpet is called for. Only a few species or their cultivars serve well as ground covers.

C. gloriosus
glo-ree-O-sus. Point Reyes Ceanothus. This species has small, glossy, dark green foliage and lavender-blue flowers in spring. It does well in acid, well-drained soil and full sun, especially on banks, where its mounding habit creates a pleasantly undulating cover. In interior California, these plants require well-drained soil and light shade to survive hotter conditions. 'Heart's Desire' has small, glossy leaves and a low, dense form.

C. griseus var. horizontalis   P. 52
GRIS-ee-us var. hor-i-zon-TAL-iss. Carmel Creeper. This is a low-spreading, evergreen shrub that reaches approximately 2 to 3 feet in height and can spread 10 to 15 feet. It makes an excellent ground cover for slopes and rough ground, with its glossy, leathery leaves and pale blue flowers in late winter. 'Yankee Point' and 'Hurricane Point' are selections for landscape use. Carmel creeper requires well-drained soil and can be pruned successfully. It does not tolerate the extreme heat of interior southern California.

C. maritimus
mah-RIT-i-mus. 'Point Sierra' and 'Frosty Dawn' are recently introduced creeping shrubs with bluish to lavender flowers. Both are compact, creeping shrubs with grayish green leaves covered with white felt underneath. Useful in Zones 8 to 10.

❦ Cerastium

ser-AS-te-um. Pink family, Caryophyllaceae.

The 60-plus species of *Cerastium* are found throughout the world, but only a few are intentionally cultivated as garden perennials. They are related to *Arenaria* and more distantly to *Dianthus*. Cerastiums are low, ground-hugging and mat-forming perennials with opposite, simple leaves. Leaves are typically covered with white hairs that give an overall gray or white cast to the foliage mats. The small, white flowers are borne in abundance in cloudlike cymes and account for the common name snow-in-summer. The scientific name refers to an animal's horn, and if you look closely, the seed capsules do indeed look like horns.

HOW TO GROW

Grow cerastiums in sunny, well-drained sites where the soil is friable and of modest fertility. Cerastiums are native to the poor soils of rock slopes and similar habitats, so growing them in a rich organic soil will lead to weak plants prone to rot. Note that cerastiums are not as long-lived as other ground covers and may die out over time unless periodically reinforced with new divisions. Cerastiums spread vigorously and are easily propagated by division. Useful in Zones 3 to 8, but not reliably perennial in hot, humid regions such as the Southeast.

HOW TO USE

The silvery foliage of cerastiums makes them traditional cottage garden plants, often attractively displayed along old stone walls and cascading down steps. As a ground cover, they make a carpet of tiny gray leaves, highlighted in midspring with ivory flowers. Use cerastiums to soften high walls, spill over corners, and creep among rocks. They look out of place in humid climates and thrive in low humidity and ample sunshine, without in any sense enjoying desert or hot conditions. They spread persistently, so one plant may cover up to 10 square feet over time.

C. tomentosum   P. 53

toe-men-TOE-sum. Snow-in-summer. The woolly, gray foliage and tiny, white flowers of snow-in-summer make it one of the most familiar plants for sunny northern gardens. It forms a matlike ground cover in full sun and sandy soils of low fertility. Prune after flowering to neaten the appearance of the plant and control spread.

❦ *Ceratostigma*

ser-at-o-STIG-muh. Sea lavender family, Plumbaginaceae.

The seven or eight species of *Ceratostigma* range from tropical Africa through India and into Tibet and China. They are shrubs and perennials with alternate, thin leaves. Only one perennial species, *C. plumbaginoides*, is useful as a ground cover in North America. The stems of this species zigzag at each node, giving the plant a distinctive posture. Young leaves are reddish green in spring, green in summer, and reddish bronze in fall.

Like the related *Plumbago* (leadwort) and *Limonium* (sea lavender), *Ceratostigma* has beautiful, small flowers and is a tough plant given the proper conditions. The name refers to the hornlike projections on the stigma at the center of the flower.

HOW TO GROW

Only one species, *C. plumbaginoides* (plumbago), is widely grown throughout North America. Grow this species in warm climates (it is marginally useful as a ground cover in Zone 6) where it has bright shade to full sun, as this allows the best development of foliage color. Alkaline to neutral soils are preferred. Ceratostigmas are intolerant of wet soils but can stabilize hot, dry slopes either by themselves or in combination with other ground covers through which they can weave. Plants spread by underground runners to make dense mats. Useful in Zones 7 to 9.

HOW TO USE

Among elegant and underused ground covers, plumbago rates as one of the top choices. Use it as a follow-up to spring bulbs and under trees, perhaps where *Doronicum* or *Dicentra* has gone dormant in summer. In colder climates, ceratostigmas may remain in underground retreat until summer finally arrives around Fourth of July. Plant it as a lush base for spring- and summer-blooming shrubs and trees. It spreads steadily and brings two marvelous bonuses—blue flowers of a sweet and heavenly color, combining the richness of lapis with the purity of sapphires, and neat foliage that turns an arresting burgundy as nighttime temperatures begin to plunge. *Ceratostigma* deserves careful placement—perhaps as an arresting accent under the coppery bark of *Prunus maackii* or as a foil to the rough textures of *Koelreuteria paniculata*.

C. plumbaginoides (Plumbago larpentiae)   P. 53

plum-baig-in-OY-deez. Plumbago. This species brings true blue into the late-summer garden. Its distinctive green leaves and stems are slow to appear in spring, but the wait is rewarded with the development of the striking blue flowers. The plants spread rapidly by underground stolons. Fall foliage colors are striking and make plumbago worth planting even if it never bloomed.

ᴡ *Chamaemelum*

kam-eh-MEL-um. Aster family, Asteraceae.

Chamaemelum is better known as chamomile. Only two or three species are native to Europe and the Mediterranean, and the genus is sometimes merged into its larger relative, *Anthemis*. True chamomile tea is made from this species, but sweeter and stronger chamomile teas are made from *Matricaria recutita* (also known as *M. chamomilla*). *Chamaemelum* is an almost prostrate evergreen perennial with finely cut, aromatic leaves. Plants form mats, eventually up to 1 foot across. The small, yellow, buttonlike flowers appear in midsummer. The name comes from Greek and literally means "ground apple," although this allusion is obscure.

HOW TO GROW
Grow chamomile in full sun to very light shade and well-drained soil with only moderate water retention. It does not withstand more than rare foot traffic when used as a lawn substitute. Useful in Zones 5 to 9, but it is unsuitable where summers are hot and muggy.

HOW TO USE
Use chamomile as a ground cover for small areas, for pathways, or among steppingstones. It will form mats over time, but the mats will not spread farther. It has also been planted as the "seats" of stone benches—as anyone who has visited Sissinghurst in England will attest. Chamomile is an acceptable lawn alternative for small areas, provided it is subjected to very little foot traffic and is mowed or sheared occasionally.

C. nobile (Anthemis nobilis)   P. 54
no-BIL-ee. Chamomile. Perennial chamomile is the low-growing, fragrant herb used in teas to lull one to sleep. The small, daisylike flowers and bright green foliage can be planted as an aromatic carpet between steppingstones, in herb gardens, and as a delicate lawn substitute in sunny areas. Grow chamomile in sites with excellent drainage, light sandy soil, and full sun. It will tolerate a little shade and, being deep rooted, requires

only moderate water once established. If left untrimmed, it will reach about 9 inches tall.

❧ *Chrysogonum*

kris-OG-o-num. Aster family, Asteraceae.

Chrysogonum is a genus with only one species, *C. virginianum* (green and gold). It is native from Florida to Pennsylvania and thrives in the foothills and lower elevations of the Appalachians, where it grows in moist, open woodlands. It has heart-shaped leaves that are deciduous and coarsely toothed. Plants spread by runners. The yellow flowers (not the whole plants) are reminiscent of a small zinnia. The name means "golden joints" and refers to the flowers, which grow from prominent swellings along the stem.

HOW TO GROW

Grow green and gold in a bright woodland setting or partly shaded garden where it will not dry out for prolonged periods. It is not particular regarding soil type, but it will perform best in organic soils. When the plant is in flower, the stems may reach 15 to 18 inches tall, although they are only about half that height during the rest of the growing season. *Chrysogonum* is best used in informal masses and settings. Useful as a ground cover in Zones 6 to 8.

HOW TO USE

Green and gold brings a sunny splash of color to shaded woods and woodland edges. Imagine finding a tiny, yellow, spring-flowering daisy in the deep woods, and you get the idea. This southeastern native flowers in moist shade in midspring and then sporadically into early summer. In the hot summers of the Southeast, it comes to a standstill, but it is likely to continue with occasional flowers in cooler northern gardens. Plant it in drifts, where the dark green foliage and yellow flowers will shine — perhaps near hollies *(Ilex opaca)* — or carpeting the ground around moosewood *(Acer pensylvanicum)* to draw attention to the striped bark of the trees. To continue the golden theme, plant leopard's bane *(Doronicum)* at the dry edge of a woodland garden or golden groundsel *(Senecio aureus)* in a moist meadow.

C. virginianum P. 54

ver-jin-ee-AH-num. Green and Gold. This low-growing, matlike ground cover has showy, yellow flowers that appear in spring and last until warm weather. It grows in full sun to partial shade, but it requires ample water when grown in full sun and needs afternoon shade in the South. Mature height is 4 to 6 inches. 'Eco-lacquered Spider' is a vigorous, running form from Georgia nurseryman Don Jacobs. The gleaming foliage looks almost wet, and the plant grows best in moist shade.

❦ *Cistus*

SIS-tus. Rock rose family, Cistaceae.

The 20 species of *Cistus* are shrubs native to the Canary Islands, off the Atlantic coast of Africa, through the Mediterranean and the Caucasus. *Cistus* is related to *Helianthemum,* the sun roses. The evergreen leaves are opposite (rarely alternate) and may have enough hairs to give them a gray or felted appearance. The large flowers have five petals, which are usually crinkled when opening, and range in color from white to rose, red, and magenta (excluding the often large and dark markings on the petals). Plants are remarkably tough once established and have a well-earned reputation for being fire resistant. This is the ancient name of a shrub in the Mediterranean region.

HOW TO GROW

These rugged and reliable shrubs do exceptionally well in western North America where summers are dry and winters are relatively warm. They require full sun and well-drained soil. They do not seem to be overly particular about soil pH, but they do not survive in humid or cold climates. Useful in Zone 8 and warmer; may tolerate Zone 7 with careful siting.

HOW TO USE

If you've traveled in arid areas of southern Europe in spring, you have seen masses of *Cistus* carpeting the roadsides with their glossy foliage and crepe paper–like flowers. These Mediterranean rock roses give the same sense of healthy growth and disease resistance that one finds with rugosa roses in cold climates. The informal white and pink flowers are generous in their display, making this an excellent choice for sites near driveways and houses, especially when the plant's fire-retardant qualities are considered. Be prepared to water deeply to establish the plants. Thereafter, they are highly drought resistant and also adapt to desert and coastal situations with saline soils. They are useful planted in masses to bind soil to banks and terraces.

C. salviifolius (*C. villosus* 'Prostratus') P. 55
sal-vi-FOL-ee-us. Sage-leaf Rock Rose. This low shrub, 1 to 2 feet tall and up to 6 feet across, has white flowers with yellow markings at the base. Leaves are fuzzy gray-green and about 1 inch long. It makes a very effective ground cover.

C. 'Sunset'
This spreading shrub, usually less than 3 feet tall but much broader, is useful when massed on banks or in drifts. Leaves are soft green and make an attractive background for the magenta flowers.

❦ *Comptonia*
comp-TON-ee-uh. Myrica family, Myricaceae.

The single species of *Comptonia* is native to impoverished soils in eastern North America. *Comptonia* is closely related to the wax myrtles and bayberries of candle fame *(Myrica)* and is merged with that genus by some botanists. It is a small, open shrub that rarely exceeds 2 feet tall. Its alternate leaves vary from wavy to incised. The deciduous to semievergreen foliage has a distinctive olive-bronze cast that is all the more remarkable for its delicious fragrance, which makes it so useful in natural potpourris. The insignificant flowers are borne in small, birchlike catkins in spring. The rosin on these catkins is also fragrant. Comptonias naturalize by underground stems to form sizable colonies. The name commemorates a patron of English botany, the Reverend Henry Compton (1632–1713), bishop of London and zealous Protestant, who was one of the aristocrats who invited William of Orange to invade England.

HOW TO GROW
Grow comptonias in poor, sandy, or peaty soil and full sun. They despise being disturbed after planting but tolerate intermingling with nonaggressive woodland-edge perennials and ground covers (such as some ferns, *Gaultheria* or *Vaccinium*) to make charming mosaics. Hardy from Zone 3 south, but it performs best in regions with cool summers.

HOW TO USE

Northern and cool-climate gardeners find *Comptonia* useful for naturalizing on and stabilizing slopes and construction cuts in full sun. They do not accept clipping, so they are best used in a naturalistic or rustic design or where a bold mass is desired. The thin, dark stems and ferny foliage are a demure disguise for this tenacious, rhizomatous plant, which seems mostly to find its own place in a planting scheme. Growing in moist, acid meadows and in dry, thin soils on steep hillsides, *Comptonia* thrives in full sun to partial shade. It does not seem to work well in small domestic areas, but its irresistible, vanilla-like fragrance makes it a sought-after ground cover for larger gardens. It is difficult to propagate and transplant since it resents competition, except from some wilder natives, such as sumacs, blueberries, and witch hazels.

C. peregrina   P. 55

pair-eh-GREEN-uh. Sweet Fern. Use this low-growing shrub to form aromatic mats in sites where it can colonize banks and naturalistic areas. Its extensive spreading roots make it an excellent soil binder and erosion preventer. It seems to do best in thin, acid soils of low fertility and requires little water once established. Sweet fern is quite resistant to salt and is frequently found growing near the beach. It does not transplant well.

❦ *Convallaria*

con-val-AIR-ee-uh. Lily-of-the-valley family, Convallariaceae.

The fragrant, creamy bells of this much-loved genus signify the romance of spring in cool climates. Most authorities consider there to be only one species, *Convallaria majalis,* ranging across the Northern Hemisphere, with a single variety (var. *keiskei*) restricted to Japan. Others raise the Japanese variety to species status and claim there are two species in the world. Equally unclear is whether lily-of-the valley is native to the eastern United States. Some botanists believe that the remote populations represent natural stands, whereas others contend that these plants escaped from gardens. *Convallaria* is related to *Aspidistra* and *Liriope,* both fine ground covers in their own right. *Convallaria* has dark green, upright, entire leaves that measure up 8 inches long and are carried on stout petioles. Stems are subterranean, so as the leaves emerge, they create Lilliputian fantasy forests. Flowers are fragrant, ivory bells that hang individually from a graceful stalk. To see the flowers best, try gathering a bunch and displaying them in a small vase set on a mirror. The red berries mature in late summer to fall and are toxic to humans. They have been known to be too attractive to infants, resulting in many visits to the emergency room. Berries are also attractive to birds, which disperse the seeds. The scientific name means "lily of the valley."

HOW TO GROW

Grow lily-of-the-valley in normal garden soils. It prefers partial shade and will develop sunscald or leaf scorch in too bright or dry a location. Hardy in Zones 4 to 9, lily-of-the-valley spreads rapidly in cool climates but only creeps in warmer areas from Zone 7 south, where additional shade and moisture are required to coax it into growth.

HOW TO USE

One of the traditional "pass-along plants," lily-of-the-valley can be divided in spring or fall, planted from pips, or propagated by seed. Once established, it is very tolerant of neglect and will persist and slowly spread for decades. Although it thrives in moist, well-drained soils, it also will grow in droughty conditions. It can be used as a ground cover under large shrubs, near walkways in the shade, and near foundations—keeping in mind the toxicity of the berries and their allure to infants.

C. majalis P. 56

mah-JAH-liss. Lily-of-the-valley. This is one of the most nostalgic spring flowers, and the delicate fragrance captures the ephemeral nature of the season. Though easy to grow, the plants can take time to become established and form substantial colonies. Birds then spread their seeds to unexpected places. Lily-of-the-valley prefers full to partial shade, well-drained soil, and a cool climate. 'Aureovariegata' ('Striata') has cream and green, longitudinal stripes on the leaves. 'Flore Pleno' has double, creamy flowers that are larger than the species. 'Fortin's Giant' ('Fortin's Variety') grows 12 to 15 inches tall and has larger flowers than the species. The var. *rosea* is a pink-flowered form that in all respects is more delicate than the species.

Convolvulus

kon-VOL-vu-lus. Morning glory family, Convolvulaceae.

Convolvulus and the closely related *Ipomoea* (morning glories) are best known to gardeners as annual, ornamental or weedy vines grown for their spectacular but ephemeral flowers. Yet among the 250 species of

Convolvulus around the world are several low shrubs that are useful as ground covers in warm temperate climates. *Convolvulus* species are annual or perennial herbs, vines, and low shrubs. Leaves are alternate and linear or heart shaped. In the species listed here, leaves are evergreen. In some species, the foliage is covered with soft gray or white hairs, giving the plants a dramatic, silvery appearance. Flowers are funnel shaped and vary from less than an inch to several inches across. Colors range from off-white to blue to rose-pink. In all cases, the flowers last only 1 day and then collapse — a mechanism that promotes cross-pollination. The name means "to entwine" and refers to the plant's vining growth.

HOW TO GROW

Convolvulus needs atmospheric and soil warmth and good drainage, such as in gravelly soils. Plants will tolerate clayey soils, provided the soil is allowed to dry out and never becomes waterlogged, or else the roots will rot. The species listed here become woody at the base or even shrubby. They should be rejuvenated by severe pruning if they become leggy. Useful in Zones 8 to 10.

HOW TO USE

Grow these ground-covering perennials and shrubs in full sun in Mediterranean Zone 7 and south. On warm slopes, they will create a living mosaic less than 2 feet tall. They can be interplanted with companion ground covers such as *Cerastium* and *Helianthemum*. *Convolvulus cneorum* is reputed to be fire resistant once established.

C. cneorum   P. 56

ne-OR-um. Silverbush. The silky white flowers of this species make it delightfully decorative. It forms low mounds in sunny, hot, well-drained spots. Foliage is narrow and appears almost silky. This distinguished plant grows to 3 feet tall and wider.

C. sabatius (C. mauritanicus)   P. 57

suh-BAY-tee-us. Ground Morning Glory. This trailing perennial is grown extensively in Mediterranean climates, where it is excellent for banks, rocky slopes, and draping over walls in full sun. It reaches a height of approximately 6 to 8 inches and spreads about 2 to 3 feet. Flowers are lavender-blue.

❦ *Cornus*

KOR-nus. Dogwood family, Cornaceae.

Mention dogwoods, and most gardeners imagine either flowering trees or suckering shrubs with attractive stems. The genus includes more than 60 woody species native to the north temperate region and is related to *Aucuba*. One species, *C. canadensis*, is a dwarf, colonizing shrub that makes a fine ground cover for cold northern gardens. Leaves are usually simple and alternate, although they may be in false whorls due to short stem internodes. Flowers are inconspicuous, typically surrounded by four white bracts that are commonly mistaken as petals. Fruits are red (as in *C. canadensis*), blue, or black and are eaten by birds and other small animals. The wood is very hard and can be sharpened into knives used for butchering animals. The Latin name means "horn," which is also hard and useful for sharp instruments. The English name is a corruption of "dag wood," the "dag" being short for "dagger," a type of knife used for stabbing and scraping.

HOW TO GROW

Grow *C. canadensis* in Zones 2 to 4 in sites with rich, moist, organic, strongly acid soil and partial shade. Plants spread by creeping rhizomes, from which new aerial stems and leaves arise. Note that established clumps resent being divided. *C. canadensis* is intolerant of hot, dry situations, although it grows at high elevations in states far to the south of its contiguous northern range, which runs from Greenland across northern North America to Kamchatka and down to Japan, Korea, and northernmost China.

HOW TO USE

C. canadensis is a choice selection for woodland edges beneath large trees and among acid-loving shrubs such as *Kalmia* and *Rhododendron*. Whether naturalized in wild gardens or planted in more formal settings, this tiny, perfectly formed dogwood seems to carry with it the scent of the cool north woods. Difficult to establish in warmer climates, it is sufficiently ubiquitous in northern New England and the Pacific Northwest to be sold as "sod." It will shrivel or "melt out" in areas with hot summers, whether humid or dry.

C. canadensis (Chamaepericlymenum canadensis)   P. 57

can-ah-DEN-sis. Bunchberry. This much-prized, low-growing dogwood is native to cool northern climates in the United States and Canada, where it grows in acid soils and woodland shade. The showy, white flowers are followed by red fruits and dramatic, red foliage in fall.

Coronilla

kor-o-NIL-uh. Pea family, Fabaceae.

The 20-plus species of *Coronilla* are native to Europe and the Mediterranean region. They include annuals, perennials, subshrubs, and low shrubs. *Coronilla* is related to *Trifolium* (true clover) and *Lathyrus* (vetches). As with all legumes, the plants host nitrifying bacteria and thus enrich the soil. Leaves are alternate and compound and typically have a bluish green cast. The pealike flowers are rose, pink, violet, white, or bicolored and are clustered into open, cloverlike heads. Crown vetch *(C. varia)* is native from southern Europe to Syria and has been widely planted in eastern North America as a ground cover in poor, dry soils. It is now an invasive exotic there. The name means "little crown," in reference to the flower heads.

HOW TO GROW

Grow crown vetch only after carefully considering its dramatically invasive habit and the consequences to the environment. Conditions to its liking are poor, dry, well-drained soils and full sun—a perfect description of road banks, highway cuts, and unstable slopes related both to mining and new home construction. Under these conditions, crown vetch will establish and grow vigorously, precluding further garden work (not usually a consideration for rights of ways or industrial sites). Note that seeds and flowers are poisonous if eaten.

HOW TO USE

Gardener beware! Crown vetch has irregular spreading and clambering branches that can climb to nearly 4 feet. It overruns and smothers all vegetation and low fences within its reach and is difficult to eradicate. Thus what seems to be an attractive and effective means of erosion control may be the harbinger of an ecological disaster. Crown vetch should be introduced with great care and full knowledge of the consequences to the native plant community.

C. varia P. 58

VAR-ee-uh. Crown Vetch. This assertive ground cover is useful but overused for quick cover on banks that are prone to erosion. It has an extensive root system and fixes nitrogen. It can be a weed, but in highway situations it has some use as a cheap, tough ground cover. It grows best in neutral soil with good drainage and will survive drought once established. The attractive pink flowers appear in midspring. Hardy but invasive in Zones 4 to 8.

❦ *Cotoneaster*

ko-tone-ee-AS-ter. Rose family, Rosaceae.

New gardeners often mispronounce this genus name as "cotton-easter." The 50 *Cotoneaster* species are native to Eurasia, with the greatest diversity occurring in eastern Asia. They are closely related to hawthorns *(Crateagus)*, apples *(Malus)*, and pears *(Pyrus)*. All cotoneasters are long-lived, woody shrubs ranging from 20 feet tall down to prostrate, rock-hugging mats. The leaves are alternate, simple, and deciduous or evergreen, depending on the species. The deciduous species often have good fall foliage color. The small flowers are white or pink and resemble diminutive apple blossoms. Fruits are very attractive, red or black "berries" that are often devoured by birds. The name is corrupted Latin and means "quincelike." The genus is botanically complex and horticulturally nuanced, with the result being that the species assignments of some plants seem ever in flux.

HOW TO GROW
Cotoneasters are very effective ground covers that thrive on neglect once established. They should be grown in full sun to light shade and any well-drained soil of average fertility. The ground-covering species naturally spread horizontally and will look much better if left untrimmed rather than shorn or clipped. They also are less likely to get diseases from unsterilized clippers if left alone. The only serious disease is fire blight, but it can be devastating and require removal of plants or entire plantings. Hardiness depends on the species.

HOW TO USE
Cotoneasters are one of the best choices for sunny foundation plantings. Think of the herringbone winter branching of *C. horizontalis* as it apparently climbs at the base of a house, or the winter-persistent red fruits of *C. apiculatus* (some dogs love to eat these frozen red treats). Cotoneasters can be used on dry or rocky slopes and banks, or you can train them as espaliers on rocks or against walls. It is best to avoid planting them where

they will encroach on walkways and driveways, however, as their clipped stems will become stubby and unattractive.

C. adpressus
ad-PRES-sus. Creeping Cotoneaster. This deciduous species has a short, rigid, branching form and is clad with small, tidy, mid-green foliage. Mature plants reach about 18 inches tall and often spread to about 6 feet. Useful in Zones 4 to 8. *C. adpressus* var. *praecox (C. nanshan)* has slightly larger foliage and fruits than the species and is more vigorous in growth, reaching 2 to 3 feet tall.

C. apiculatus
P. 58

ah-pik-ew-LAY-tus. Cranberry Cotoneaster. This species holds its red fruits during the winter but is otherwise similar to *C. adpressus.*

C. dammeri (C. humifusus; some cultivars are treated as C. procumbens or C. × suecicus)
DAM-er-eye. Bearberry Cotoneaster. An excellent carpeting ground cover, this species spreads more than 10 feet while reaching only 2 to 3 feet in height. It is evergreen in milder areas and marginally evergreen in colder climates. Useful in Zones 5 to 8. Many of the plants sold as the species are possibly the cultivar 'Major', which has more vigorous growth and slightly larger leaves (more than 1 inch long).

C. horizontalis
P. 59

hor-i-zon-TAL-iss. Rockspray Cotoneaster. This species is low growing (to 2 feet tall) and spreads more than 8 feet, with delicate, finely textured branches. Makes a fine ground cover in Zones 5 (Zone 4 with good siting) to 8.

C. linearifolius (C. microphyllus var. thymifolius and 'Thymifolia')
lin-air-e-FOL-ee-us. Thyme-leaf Cotoneaster. As implied by the common name, this dwarf to prostrate Himalayan cotoneaster has small, gray-green leaves and pinkish gray twigs, making it a valuable addition to a mixed ground-cover planting or where a change in scale is needed. Useful in Zones 5 to 8.

C. perpusillus (C. horizontalis var. perpusillus)
pur-PEW-sil-us. This low, ground-hugging plant is striking for its red leaf color in fall and orange fruits, as well as the distinctive fish-bone pattern of its branching. Useful in Zones 5 to 8, but very susceptible to fire blight.

C. procumbens (C. dammeri 'Streibs Findling')   P. 59
pro-KUM-bens. This ground-hugging shrub is only a few inches tall and has attractive, glossy, evergreen foliage. Useful in Zones 7 to 8.

C. salicifolius
sal-iss-i-FO-lee-us. Willowleaf Cotoneaster. As implied by the common name, this species has long, narrow leaves that are semievergreen or evergreen. The scarlet fruits last into winter. Useful in Zones 6 to 8. 'Repens' is an excellent ground cover selected for its small, narrow leaves and attractive fruits.

C. × suecicus
x SWEE-see-us. These selections are often treated as part of C. dammeri and share its hardiness. 'Coral Beauty' has coral-colored fruits and is very dense but not fast growing. Spring-flowering 'Skogholm' is also noted for its vigorous growth, but its fruiting is sparse.

❧ Cyrtomium
seer-TOE-mee-um. Wood fern family, Dryopteridaceae.

Long used as a houseplant with a tropical look, Cyrtomium is becoming more widely used as a shade-loving ground cover in warm climates. The 10 to 12 species are native to warm regions of Asia, Africa, Hawaii, and the Americas. Cyrtomiums, or holly ferns, are related to Christmas ferns (Polystichum). They are erect, with fronds reaching 2 to 3 feet tall. The individual pinnae (sections of the fronds) are relatively large, leathery, and often more than an inch long and nearly as wide. The pinnae are responsible for the common name—they remind observers of holly leaves. The fronds are deciduous at the northern limit of the ferns' growth and evergreen farther south. The name is based on a Greek word meaning "arch" and refers to the curving venation pattern.

HOW TO GROW
Grow cyrtomiums in light to deep shade and an organic soil that does not dry out. Provision of ample moisture is essential to good growth, or the fronds will not survive. Once established and thriving, cyrtomiums spread by spores. Unwanted young plants are easily removed. Hardiness varies by species.

HOW TO USE

Use cyrtomiums as ground covers where their olive green foliage can be appreciated. Although they will stand more sun than many ferns, they thrive in deeply shaded, moist areas. Plant them in drifts alongside bold-leaved perennials, such as hardy gingers (*Curcuma*), aspidistras, or selections of crinums or hippeastrums. Shrubs such as camellias, magnolias, and many hollies are among the woody plants that benefit from the attractive foil of holly ferns. Flower arrangers are also among the biggest fans of these fast-spreading ground covers.

C. falcatum

P. 60

fal-KAY-tum. Holly Fern. A stalwart in southern gardens, this species makes a handsome, glossy, evergreen ground cover. It will tolerate drier air and more light than many ferns. Place plants about 18 inches apart and not too deep, and they will quickly fill in. Useful in Zones 8 to 10. 'Rochfordianum' has coarsely fringed frond segments.

C. fortunei var. intermedia

for-TOON-ee-eye var. in-ter-MEE-dee-uh. This variety is said to be hardier than *C. falcatum*. It makes a nicely textured ground cover in a woodland garden. Hardy in warm Zone 7 to 10.

❦ Daboecia

da-bo-E-see-a. Heath family, Ericaceae.

Daboecia is among the very few genera whose scientific names commemorate Catholic or Orthodox Christian references. (Others include *Hypericum* ["above the icon"] and *Veronica* [the "true image"].) *Daboecia* commemorates St. Daboec of ancient Ireland and is related to *Ledum* and *Kalmia* (mountain laurel). Of the two species in this genus, one, *D. cantabrica*, is native to Atlantic Europe from Ireland to Spain, and the other is endemic to the Azores off the coast of Africa. *D. cantabrica* is a small, evergreen, heathlike shrub that reaches 20 inches tall and 2 feet across. It has attractive, bell- or urn-shaped flowers, which are produced in summer in colors from white to purple and mauve. *Daboecia* is useful as a ground cover only where heaths and heathers are reliably grown.

HOW TO GROW

Grow daboecias in full sun and organic, acid soils, such as those required for heaths and heathers. They require winter protection with a covering of salt hay or evergreen boughs to avoid sunscald. In North America, these plants are best suited to gardens in cool maritime climates on both coasts, in warm Zones 6 to 8.

HOW TO USE
So you've visited Ireland or Scotland and brought back the memory of walking among wild heaths. If you live in a cool maritime climate, perhaps the Pacific Northwest or southern New England, you could try planting *D. cantabrica.* This species looks best when used as a ground cover to complement and mass with heaths and heathers when making a living mosaic, or to break up larger groups of single species. Its slightly unkempt appearance lends itself well to naturalistic drifts and romantic compositions.

D. cantabrica (Menziesia polifolia) P. 60
kan-TAH-bri-kuh. Irish Heath. This native of Atlantic southwestern Europe and Ireland thrives in maritime climates. It does not do well in harsh winter conditions, such as those found in the interior of North America. Where it can be protected, it grows into dense hummocks and can be used to face down larger shrubs in the border. If given good drainage; light, sandy, acid soil; and protection from harsh winter winds, it will flower well. Clip in midspring to encourage growth. *D. cantabrica* f. *alba* has delicate white flowers, while 'Pallida' has rose-pink flowers. 'William Buchanan' is a dense, prostrate selection with deep green leaves and purplish rose flowers. 'Buchanan Gold' has cream-variegated foliage.

❦ *Dalea*
DALE-ee-uh. Pea family, Fabaceae.

Dalea is a large genus of more than 250 species of annuals, perennials, and low shrubs native to the warmer regions of the Americas. Leaves are alternate and compound. The pealike flowers come in a range of colors. The dry fruits are one- or two-seeded pods and are not ornamental. Only one species, *D. greggii,* is used as a ground cover. The name honors Dr. Samuel Dale, a British botanist and apothecary of the late 1600s and early 1700s.

HOW TO GROW
D. greggii requires full sun and well-drained, alkaline soil. Low branches will root where they come in contact with the soil, so this plant needs

room to spread and make a thick mat. It prefers hot, dry summers and is drought tolerant once established in Zones 8 to 10 where summer humidity is low.

HOW TO USE

One of the best ground-covering shrubs for warm southwestern gardens, *D. greggii* should be planted in full sun in level or gently sloping areas. From an initial planting, it will spread to cover 10 feet or more. In spring, the amethyst flowers seem to float above the pearly gray foliage. Particularly well adapted to alkaline soils, it requires excellent drainage and low summer humidity, or it will rot.

D. greggii P. 61

GREG-ee-eye. Trailing Indigo Bush. This low, evergreen (really, ever-gray) shrub is native to Texas and northern Mexico, where it grows in rocky limestone areas. It is attractive and useful for erosion control on slopes and where its silvery gray foliage and pale purple flowers can be appreciated. Do not overwater, as might occur if you place it near a sprinkler system for other plantings.

❦ *Daphne*

DAF-nee. Leatherwood family, Thymeliaeaceae.

The 70 *Daphne* species are native to Europe, North Africa, and Asia. North American gardeners who treasure unusual native shrubs may be familiar with the related genus *Dirca,* whose two species are endemic to eastern and western North America. Daphnes are small, woody shrubs with deciduous or evergreen, simple, alternate leaves. The small, white flowers are borne in late winter to early spring in the leaf axils and have an intensely sweet fragrance. The brightly colored, succulent fruits are extremely toxic to lethal if eaten. The name is Greek and commemorates Daphne, the daughter of a river god. She was relentlessly pursued by Apollo, prayed for help, and was transformed into a shrub to escape him. Since this is the same myth for the bay tree, *Laurus nobilis,* it is likely that the linkage of the plant to the myth has shifted over the years.

HOW TO GROW

Grow daphnes in partial shade and perfectly drained soils, such as gravelly soils on slopes. Daphnes require good air circulation to the roots near the surface, but they resent hot soils and any type of disturbance. Poor drainage is lethal. If necessary, plant daphnes in slightly raised beds with circumneutral soils specially prepared for quick drainage. Use as a low, shrubby ground cover by planting it on 1½- to 2-foot centers and allowing the plants to fuse. Do not use daphnes in gardens where children will roam, due to the extremely toxic and attractive seeds. Propagation is by seed, and plants will self-seed in favorable conditions. These shrubs can be temperamental and short-lived, but they are worth the effort for their intense fragrance. Hardy in Zones 5 to 9, depending on the species.

HOW TO USE

The perfume is enticing, and the flowers are lovely, but daphnes have a reputation for being "difficult." Given appropriate growing conditions, however, they are also charming ground covers. Plant these temperamental prima donnas close to a path or doorway, where they will not be overlooked. The perfume from a modest mass of *D. cneorum* is guaranteed to draw you outdoors on a chilly spring day. Or try planting three to five of the larger-growing, variegated forms of *D. × burkwoodii* 'Carol Mackie' to add eye-catching appeal to the garden.

D. × burkwoodii   P. 61

This hybrid between *D. cneorum* and *D. caucasica* is a mounding shrublet growing to 3 feet tall and spreading 4 to 6 feet wide. Like all daphnes, it requires loose, well-drained soil. 'Carol Mackie' ('Variegata') is an excellent variegated form with cream-edged leaves and pink flowers. 'Somerset' has evergreen foliage and pale pink flowers.

D. cneorum   P. 62

nee-O-rum. Garland Daphne. Flowering carpets of garland daphnes, with their distinctive perfume, are one of the most sought-after spring effects. They are also one of the trickiest low shrubs to grow well. They prefer sunny sites with well-drained, neutral to alkaline soil, spread slowly, and die unexpectedly. Despite this, they are worth all the effort required. 'Ruby Glow' grows 6 to 12 inches tall and has dark, evergreen foliage and rich pink flowers. Useful in Zone 5 and warmer.

D. odora

o-DOR-uh. Winter Daphne. This species is considered the most fragrant of all the daphnes. Its deep pink flowers show well against the evergreen foliage. The shrubs grow 3 to 4 feet tall and wider. This species does best in partial shade and well-drained, porous soil. Plant it in masses for the best effect and intoxicating fragrance. Useful in Zone 7 and warmer.

❦ *Dennstaedtia*

den-STED-tee-uh. Dennstaedtiaceae.

Of the 70 species of *Dennstaedtia,* most are found in the tropics throughout the world. The genus is related to *Pteridium* (common bracken fern). One species, *D. punctiloba* (hay-scented fern), is a superb ground cover for north temperate woodland gardens. Hay-scented fern is native to open, dry woods and stony forests in eastern and central North America, where it often forms extensive carpets on the forest floor. The slender rhizomes creep just below the soil surface, and from them arise the individual fronds, which can reach 2 feet tall. The fronds are deciduous, soft green, bipinnate, and relatively resistant to breakage. The dry fronds are delightfully aromatic and smell like new-mown hay, thus the common name. The scientific name commemorates the German botanist August Dennstedt (1776–1826).

HOW TO GROW
Grow hay-scented fern in bright shade, such as found beneath trees with no lower branches or in parklike openings in the woods or landscape. Soil should be slightly dry; more mineral than organic; and rocky, stony, or otherwise tending to poor from a garden perspective. Useful in Zones 3 to 8.

HOW TO USE
Hay-scented ferns will spread over several acres or more if conditions are to their liking. They make an ideal ground cover for naturalized meadow edges that run into woods. Few other plants give such a "been there forever" appearance so quickly to a new planting of shrubs and trees. You can successfully weave these ferns between blueberries, maples, oaks, hollies, and native species in larger landscapes. When they are used in smaller spaces, control may be more of a problem than establishment, although they can be managed by digging out the advancing rhizomes or blocking them with barriers. Avoid placing hay-scented ferns where their fronds will be broken by constant foot traffic or pets, since broken fronds will not be replaced until the following year.

D. punctilobula

P. 62

punk-tuh-LAW-buh-luh. Hay-scented Fern. This creeping, deciduous perennial has light green fronds that grow 1 to 2 feet tall. The distinctive aroma, often compared to that of new-mown hay, is released when the foliage is crushed and persists in the dry foliage at the end of the season. Plants thrive in dry, partly sunny woodlands, where they spread to form extensive colonies.

❦ Dianthus

dy-AN-thus. Pink family, Caryophyllaceae.

Carnations, garden pinks, and sweet Williams are among the 250 to 300 species of *Dianthus*. The center of diversity is the Mediterranean and extends through the Balkans to Asia Minor. Within the pink family, *Dianthus* is closely related to *Gypsophila* (baby's breath), *Saponaria* (bouncing Bet), *Lychnis* (Maltese cross), and *Silene* (campions). *Dianthus* species span the range of annuals, biennials, and perennials, but the ground-covering species are all perennials. Leaves are opposite, sometimes mostly basal on the stems. In the case of *D. gratianopolitanus,* they are grasslike and blue-green. Flowers are dramatically colorful and presented above the foliage on strong stems. The five petals are bent out to make a starlike landing platform for butterflies, which are their pollinators. Flower color ranges from white to pink and magenta to every imaginable shade of red. Some flowers also are fragrant. The name is Greek for either "divine flower" or "God's flower."

HOW TO GROW

Grow *Dianthus* species in full sun and fast-draining, calcareous to neutral soil. Plants and mats will succumb to rot if the soil retains water. *Dianthus* thrives in soils that are poor in organics but rich in minerals, as is typical of limestone soils. If the soil is acid, adjust the pH with lime. The plants will look better if deadheaded after bloom. Hardy from Zone 4 south, depending on the species.

HOW TO USE

An essential plant for the cottage garden and a species with a long history in horticulture, *Dianthus* should be used as a ground cover where both the grasslike foliage and flower colors can be appreciated. Place it next to a path or cascading over a wall — remembering that this is a hanging mat, *not* a ground-holding, stoloniferous plant. When *Dianthus* is planted on flat ground, the foliage and flowers should be trimmed back into a tight mound following bloom. In acid soil, plant it close to a wall where leaching from the plaster will help add lime to the soil. Mulch with gravel or grow in a gravel garden. Be aware that the center of the mound will likely die out after a couple of years, so the plants must be lifted and reset.

D. arenarius
air-en-AIR-ee-us. Sand Pink. This hardy perennial makes an attractive, tufted ground cover in rock gardens, edging situations, and small masses.

D. 'Bath's Pink'   P. 63
This selection has grayish foliage and clove-scented, pink flowers. It is widely considered the most heat- and humidity-tolerant selection.

D. deltoides   P. 63
del-TOY-deez. Maiden Pink. This well-known perennial forms a carpet of blue-gray, grasslike leaves. Flowers can be white, pink, or dark red, depending on the selection.

D. gratianopolitanus (D. caesius)   P. 64
grah-tee-an-oh-po-lee-TAY-nus. Pink, Cheddar Pink. Like all pinks, this species does best in full sun and well-drained, calcareous to neutral soil. It forms grassy, dwarf, narrow-leaved mounds. 'Tiny Rubies' is covered with bright rose-pink flowers in spring. It spreads well and is grown widely, but it is especially popular in northern New Mexico, Colorado, and nearby areas.

❧ Dicentra
dy-SEN-truh. Poppy family, Papaveraceae.

Few other flowers are considered to give such a romantic tone to a spring shade garden. There are nearly 20 *Dicentra* (bleeding heart) species, all of them perennials native to woodlands in eastern Asia and North America. Most of the species spread slowly by rootstocks and stubby runners, making dramatic colonies. Leaves grow up to 2 feet tall and are dissected into such small segments that they are sometimes mistaken for fern foliage by new gardeners. The pendent, heart-shaped flowers come in red, pink, white, or combinations of all three. All the flowers are freely suspended from the flower stalks, where they wave in the breeze and capture the fancy of those who can imagine woodland spirits playing joyfully with these as children do with toys. Fruits are inconsequential, if produced at all. The name means "two spurs," a totally unsentimental description of the flowers.

HOW TO GROW
Bleeding hearts are denizens of woodlands and forest openings, so they thrive best in garden situations that replicate those conditions. Provide them with rich, loamy soil and partial shade. Full sun and soil dryness will lead to premature dormancy in the heat of summer. Hardiness varies by species (or, for the hybrids, their parentage); the ones listed here are useful in Zones 4 to 9.

HOW TO USE
The delicate foliage and nodding flowers of *Dicentra* species mass attractively in woodland gardens, along shaded paths, and in shrub plantings where a soft ground layer is appropriate. Group them in masses where they will receive adequate moisture and not be troubled by harsh, drying winds. They look especially appropriate as a ground cover near kalmias and evergreen rhododendrons. Also try to plant some bleeding hearts in an elevated bed or along a wall so that they are visible at or above eye level. Some bleeding hearts, such as *D. spectabilis,* die down too early to be successful ground covers. Others perform well all summer in full to partial shade and adequately moist, acid soil.

D. eximia
ex-EEM-ee-uh. 'Snowdrift' ('Alba') has ferny foliage and white flowers over a long season.

D. formosa   P. 65
for-MO-suh. This western North American species spreads by runners better than *D. eximia.* Under optimal conditions, the pale to deep rose flowers bloom almost throughout the growing season. 'Sweetheart' has white flowers. 'Zestful' has two-tone pink flowers over a long season.

D. hybrids   P. 65
'Bountiful' has deep blue-green foliage and fuchsia flowers. 'Luxuriant' has blue-gray foliage and dark pink or purplish red, nodding flowers.

❧ *Dichondra*

dy-KON-druh. Morning Glory family, Convolvulaceae.

Looking at a *Dichondra* lawn when not in bloom, one would not expect it to be a relative of morning glories. In bloom, however, the small, white flowers reveal the relationship. *Dichondra* encompasses about 15 species native to warm temperate and tropical regions around the world. The plants are rooting or trailing perennials with rounded or heart-shaped leaves. Flowers are small to insignificant, white or creamy white, and funnel shaped—just like miniature morning glories. The dry fruits are ornamentally insignificant. The name means "two lumps" and refers to the fruit shape.

HOW TO GROW

Dichondra spreads at a moderate rate by surface runners and is planted from plugs, sods, or seeds. It is not successful in areas with winter temperatures cooler than those in warm Zone 8 and does best where winter temperatures never drop below 20°F. Walking on frozen *Dichondra* may kill it. With full sun and ample moisture, it is likely to remain almost totally prostrate. With partial shade and adequate moisture, it may grow to several inches tall. In warm climates, *Dichondra* may perform well between steppingstones.

HOW TO USE

In gardens of the Deep South, especially in Florida and parts of Texas, *Dichondra* is a popular choice as a ground cover between steppingstones or for large areas. Though not really a perfect lawn substitute, it provides a carpetlike effect that combines attractively with trees and shrubs. Yes, you can walk on it, though not on those mornings when a rare frost chills it —footsteps then mean death to the plants.

D. micrantha (D. carolinensis, D. repens)   P. 66

my-CRAN-thuh. Pony-foot. This species is planted as a lawn substitute in parts of the United States with high summer temperatures, rare frosts, and abundant water. The tiny leaves have the outline of a water lily leaf— only miniaturized. The small flowers, when produced, are pale white or greenish.

🌿 *Dryopteris*

dry-OP-ter-iss. Wood fern family, Dryopteridaceae.

Dryopteris (wood or shield fern) includes about 150 species from throughout the world, with a great number of them native to the north temperate zone. *Dryopteris* is related to *Thelypteris* and *Gymnocarpium*. It establishes short, erect or ascending rhizomes, from which the fronds develop. When the rhizomes are nearly erect, the leaves give the appearance of forming a ring, or crown, of foliage. Fronds are deciduous or evergreen, lanceolate or triangular in outline, and up to tripinnate. They range from 15 to 30 inches or more long. The name comes from the Greek for "oak" and "fern," possibly in reference to the type of woodlands where some of the temperate species originated.

HOW TO GROW

Grow shield ferns in moist, organic, enriched soil of average to above-average fertility. They prefer partial shade, but some species may be grown in nearly full sun with additional moisture. Once established, several species are surprisingly drought tolerant. Plants spread very slowly, so effective massing results by establishing numerous plants from the beginning. Useful from Zone 4 (some species) south.

HOW TO USE

Many species are useful in woodland and shade gardens. The few presented here mass well as ground covers, but knowledgeable gardeners may wish to use additional species as well. Shield ferns work nicely as ground covers in moist, shaded woods where their bold foliage is not obscured by low branches or competing shrubs. Their sturdy fronds can be beautifully contrasted with summer-flowering lilies (*Lilium canadense*) or Asian perennials such as *Kirengeshoma palmata*, which can assume shrublike size. Or think of them as textural complements to rhododendrons or hollies, or as the understory for spring-flowering *Halesia* and *Styrax*.

D. erythrosora

ee-rith-ro-SOR-uh. Autumn Fern. This is a perennial, clump-forming favorite that can be effectively massed. The bronzy fiddleheads unfurl to produce leathery fronds about 2 feet long. Autumn fern is evergreen in mild climates, with rich fall color when frosted. It makes an excellent companion planting to hostas. Useful in Zones 5 to 9.

D. filix-mas

FEE-lix-MAS. Male Fern. The slender, upward-arching, rich green fronds may reach 3 feet in length. Male fern masses well on a large scale. Useful in Zones 4 to 8.

D. intermedia

in-ter-MEE-dee-uh. Intermediate Shield Fern. This attractive species spreads quickly, with fronds reaching 1½ to 2 feet tall. Useful in Zones 4 to 8.

D. marginalis   P. 66

mar-jin-AL-iss. Marginal Wood Fern. This eastern North American native spreads slowly while creating dramatic clusters. Fronds are less than 2 feet tall and do not recover well from drought. Useful in Zones 5 to 9.

❧ Duchesnea

doo-CHES-nee-uh. Rose family, Rosaceae.

Barren strawberries *(Duchesnea)* look remarkably like true strawberries *(Fragaria)*—enough so that people are often terribly disappointed with their meager crop of mealy fruits. The six species of *Duchesnea* are all native from India to East Asia. They are very closely related to true strawberries and are distinguished only by their yellow flowers and their grainy, unpalatable fruits. These perennial herbs spread by runners. The strawberry-like leaves are deciduous, flowers are small and have five yellow petals, and fruits look like strawberries but are dry and mealy. The name commemorates the French horticulturist Antoine Duchesne, who published a natural history of all known strawberries and their relatives in 1766.

HOW TO GROW

Barren strawberries form an effective, fast-spreading, weedy ground cover in partial to full shade. They prefer soil that is well drained but not dry. Useful in Zone 5 and warmer.

HOW TO USE

Plant this fast-moving ground cover only where you are certain you want the help of its aggressive horizontal stems. It tolerates occasional foot traffic and looks attractive as a green mulch ruffle around trees where its shallow root system finds little competition. Avoid overly soggy or droughty sites.

D. indica (D. chrysantha)   P. 67

IN-duh-kuh. Barren Strawberry, Mock Strawberry. This ground cover is native to India but hardy to Zone 5. Leaves are deciduous, and if the season
or area is extremely dry, the plants may go dormant by late summer.
Plants are seldom more than 8 inches tall, but because of the aggressive
runners, the colonies have an unlimited spread. *D. indica* is most useful as
a soil binder on very steep banks where there is some (though not abundant) moisture and excellent drainage.

❦ *Epigaea*

e-PIJ-ee-uh. Heath family, Ericaceae.

The three species of *Epigaea* are native to eastern North America, Japan,
and the Caucasus. The Caucasian species is sometimes separated into its
own genus, *Orphanidesia,* but all three species are related to *Gaultheria.*
Epigaeas are low shrublets that might be mistaken at first glance for
tough perennial herbs. The alternate, simple, evergreen leaves are tough
as cardboard, only 1 to 3 inches long, and held close to the ground, where
they often obscure the prostrate branches. Flowers are tiny, waxy, white
or pinkish, and cup shaped. Flowers of the American species are intensely
fragrant. The name means "upon the earth," in reference to the plants'
creeping habit.

HOW TO GROW

E. repens (Mayflower) has been driven nearly to extinction throughout
much of its former range, so it is important to obtain this species from
nursery-propagated stock. Epigaeas require soil that is highly acid, organic, well drained, and moist — not an impossible combination on
rocky faces and slopes in mixed deciduous and coniferous forests. They
prefer light shade to filtered sun and despise hot, humid summers, thriving instead in cool climates similar to those favored by *Cornus canadensis.*
Use epigaeas as a stunningly fragrant, low, naturalistic, evergreen ground
cover, provided you can emulate its natural growing conditions. Although it is native down to Zone 2, it is best used in Zones 3 to 6 (cool microsites).

HOW TO USE

If you long to re-create the beauty of an eastern woodland or are enhancing a naturalistic shade planting, mayflower adds a memorable and delicately fragrant note. It blends gently with ferns and wildflowers into a

picture that seems the essence of spring. Leaves are dark green and roughly textured, and the tiny white flowers seem to huddle under the shelter of the leaves. In moist, acid, well-drained, woodland conditions, it will spread ever so gradually into a low 6-to 9-inch-tall mass.

E. repens   P. 67

REE-penz. Mayflower, Trailing Arbutus. This evergreen, ground-hugging shrub has branches that root along the stems. The entire colony resents being disturbed, which is why it can be so difficult to transplant to a new site. The fragrant flowers appear in spring, thus giving the plant its name. Mayflower must have superb drainage and strongly acid soil.

❦ Epimedium

ep-im-EE-dee-um. Barberry family, Berberidaceae.

Epimediums, often known as barrenworts or bishop's hat, are choice, attractive ground covers for moist or dry sites with deciduous shade. The 20 species range from southeastern Europe and northern Africa, through the Caucasus, to China and Japan. Closely related to *Vancouveria*, a native of the Pacific Northwest, *Epimedium* is in the same family as *Berberis* (barberry) and *Nandina* (heavenly bamboo). The creeping, clump-forming rootstocks produce bi- and tri-ternately compound leaves that grow 1 to 2 feet tall. Foliage is leathery and deciduous or evergreen, and it matures to a dark, often bronzy, green. Emerging leaves often display other ephemeral colors. Just when the new leaves are appearing, the plant flowers, producing delicate, waxy-looking blooms that are held at or above the top of the leaves. These fragile, spurred flowers — which vary in color from yellow to white, pink to purple-red — are thought to be reminiscent of a bishop's hat. Fruits are not ornamental. The scientific name is an ancient Greek term for a different plant. The common name implies a connection to infertility — an interesting note, since practitioners of Chinese traditional medicine use particular parts of *Epimedium* for male impotence. Self-administrators beware — the barberry family is noted for toxic to deadly alkaloids.

HOW TO GROW

Gardeners have a rich selection of species, hybrids, and cultivars from which to choose. Species and cultivars based on the European and North African species *(E. alpinum, E. perralderianum,* and *E. pinnatum)* are in general more heat and drought tolerant than the moisture-loving species from China and Japan. The numerous hybrids are intermediate in many respects and offer a wide selection of foliage height, flower color, and hardiness. Epimediums are hardy, depending on their parentage, in Zones 4 to 8 and farther south. Foliage is evergreen or deciduous depending on the climate and exposure. Grow epimediums in light to moderate shade, such as is found under high-branched trees or caused by buildings. Epimediums do not thrive in deep shade. Most prefer acid soil, although they will tolerate circumneutral soil, as long as the soil is well drained but not nutrient poor. Provide a light organic mulch each year, as this encourages plants to spread. The current horticultural practice is to remove old leaves in late winter so that new growth and flowers can be enjoyed.

HOW TO USE
Epimediums are slow to get established, but once they are settled in, most move steadily onward. Several *Epimedium* species (*E. alpinum, E. perralderianum,* and hybrids involving either) make excellent ground covers for naturalizing in large areas, as they spread by creeping rootstocks. Many others, including numerous named cultivars, make excellent clumping masses that are perfect for smaller-scale gardens. Avoid sites with constant, drying winds or salt spray (including road salt).

E. alpinum   P. 68
al-PIE-num. This deciduous species from central Europe spreads up to a foot a year and reaches 12 to 15 inches tall. The creamy yellow, spurred petals makes for a lively spring display. Once established, it does better in dry shade than many others of the genus, although it does require watering during its first years. Useful in Zones 4 to 8.

E. diphyllum
die-FIL-um. The spurless white flowers rise less than 10 inches from the ground and are held above the compact, semievergreen mounds of foliage. This is a late-blooming species and requires moist, rich, partly shaded, woodland conditions. Useful in Zones 5 to 8.

E. grandiflorum
gran-di-FLOR-um. This large-flowered epimedium is native to Japan and Korea and is one of the showiest and most variable barrenworts. An ever-increasing number of named forms are available. These vary in color and height, but all are reliable in Zones 5 to 8. Two of the most useful for

massing are 'Rose Queen', a classic form with pink flowers and white-tipped spurs, and 'Lilafee', a deciduous selection with purple flowers from Germany's Ernst Pagels.

E. × perralchicum 'Frohnleiten'   P. 68
x per-AL-chee-cum. This selection comes from Heinz Klose's famous German nursery. The tall, evergreen, serrated foliage rises 12 to 15 inches. In spring, the acid yellow flowers are followed by coppery red foliage. Plants spread at up to 8 inches a year. Useful in Zones 5 to 8.

E. perralderianum 'Weihenstephan'
per-al-der-ee-AY-num. This mostly evergreen epimedium remains attractive even without a spring haircut. The dark green foliage seems almost spiny, and the flowers are bright yellow and appear in midspring. Useful in Zones 6 (with protection) to 8.

E. × versicolor   P. 69
x vers-i-COL-er. 'Neosulfureum' is not to be confused with the much more common 'Sulphureum'. The former is shorter and slower growing than the latter and has yellow flowers. Useful in Zones 5 to 8. 'Sulphureum' is one of the best ground-cover selections. It grows into a thick mass of foliage that chokes out all weeds. Flowers are lemon yellow. Useful in Zones 5 to 8.

☙ Erica

ER-i-cuh. Heath family, Ericaceae.

Mention heaths (the common name for *Erica* species), and the hills of Scotland or the moors of England often come to mind. Yet of the more than 500 *Erica* species, only a few are native to Europe and grown in North America. The vast number of named cultivars obscures the fact that relatively few species are involved. Most of the rest of the species are endemic to South Africa and its distinctive Mediterranean climate. These can be grown in roughly the same regions where *Fuchsia* is winter hardy. *Erica* is closely related to *Calluna* (heather). Ericas are evergreen shrubs with needled foliage. The winter-hardy ones are small, usually less than 18 inches tall, and have branches spreading about the same distance. Growth can be irregular, especially in windswept sites. The small, urn-shaped flowers appear in early summer and range in color from white to pink and magenta. Numerous cultivars have been selected for foliage color, plant height, plant habit, and flower color. The name comes from the Greek word for "heath."

HOW TO GROW

Grow ericas in full sun and well-drained soil that is never subjected to extended drought or dampness. They prefer acid soil (some exceptions for collectors) and do particularly well as ground covers in maritime regions with cool summers. Ericas can be clipped after flowering, but only to still-leafy stems. Protection from winter wind is essential for use as a ground cover. Mulch with salt hay, evergreen boughs (perhaps from your Christmas tree), or weed-free straw. Useful in Zones 5 to 8.

HOW TO USE

Winter- and early-spring-blooming heaths are prized in areas where they thrive. Use as ground covers where their bright foliage and attractive flowers can be seen but not walked on. Massed plants look best when treated naturalistically, either by themselves or mixed with compatible ground covers.

E. carnea   P. 69

KAR-nee-uh. Winter Heather. Winter Heath. This low, evergreen shrub is considered to be the most cold-tolerant species, blooming right through late snows. Leaves are short needles. Flowers are little bells that appear from late winter to early spring. Flower color varies by selection. 'Springwood White' has creamy buds that open to white flowers. It grows vigorously as a ground cover, remaining under 10 inches tall. 'Springwood Pink' is similar but with pink flowers. 'Vivellii' ('Urville') is one of the most striking ericas in the landscape and makes eye-catching masses with its deep red flowers and winter-bronzed foliage.

❦ Euonymus

yoo-ON-e-mus. Spindle tree family, Celastraceae.

Gardeners tend to either hate or love *Euonymus*, which indicates that it includes extremely versatile garden plants that have been inappropriately or excessively used in the mass market. The 175 or so species are native throughout the north temperate zones of the world, with the great majority native from the Himalayas to China, Korea, and Japan. *Euonymus* is related to *Celastrus* (bittersweet), and both genera have species that are now invasive exotic pests throughout North America. *Euonymus* species are woody plants ranging from prostrate, ground-covering shrubs to small trees. Several species develop corky "wings," or ridges, on the twigs and stems. Leaves are simple, alternate or opposite, usually lanceolate or ovate, and less than an inch to 4 inches or more long. The deciduous species typically have spectacular fall colors, as indicated by the common name burning bush for *E. alatus*. Evergreen species have thick, usually smooth and glossy leaves that may have additional mottling. Flowers are tiny, creamy white, and insignificant. By contrast, fruits are small, woody capsules that open to show suspended seeds covered by brilliantly colored flesh. The flesh is orange or red and contrasts strongly with the rest of the capsule. Birds eat these gaudy, suspended seeds, and the entire structure is responsible for one of the American regional names for *E. americana*—hearts a-busting with love. *Euonymus* is Greek and means "good name," as in a good family reputation. It also commemorates Euonyme, the mother of the ancient Furies. These meanings are likely linked, since the Furies descended and drove mad only those whose behaviors were so outrageous as to break all bonds of civilized people.

HOW TO GROW

Grow *Euonymus* in full sun to partial shade. Plants are not particular as to soil pH, texture, or composition, provided it is friable, of average fertility, and neither saturated nor excessively droughty. Scale may be a problem in some areas, in which case treat plants with dormant oils. Some species are serious invasive pests in parts of North America. Hardy in Zone 4 south, depending on the species.

HOW TO USE

A ubiquitous solution for many landscapes in search of a living "green mulch," *Euonymus* should be used as a ground cover where a dense mass is needed and where there will be no companion ground cover that is likely to become smothered. The creeping, mounding stems can become troublesome litter collectors in public places and have been known to form welcome cover for rodents. When clipped against a wall or planted on a bank or in a bed, however, they can be mowed regularly—as in early spring each year—and will provide handsome foliage and brilliant burgundy fall color. Variegated forms can be massed and maintained as hedges or high, shrubby ground covers, adding colorful accents to sites in cold climates.

E. fortunei P. 70

for-TOON-ee-eye. Wintercreeper. This much-used evergreen ground cover spreads rapidly to about 4 to 5 feet, or indefinitely if not pruned. It benefits from annual shearing in spring to control growth, enhance spread, and thicken the mat. This shearing can be done with a power mower. There are numerous selections in the trade, attesting to its wide adaptability. The named cultivars are usually based on foliage differences. 'Acutus' is vigorously prostrate and has narrow, dark green leaves. 'Coloratus', commonly known as purple wintercreeper, has dark green foliage during the growing season that turns purple or bronze in fall and winter. 'Emerald 'n Gold' has green leaves with yellow margins and some red tints in fall. 'Kewensis' has tiny leaves (about ¼ inch long) and forms a nearly flat mat. 'Minimus' has small leaves (slightly larger than 'Kewensis') and more vigorous growth overall. 'Silver Queen' has green leaves with white markings.

❦ *Euphorbia*

yoo-FOR-bee-uh. Spurge family, Euphorbiaceae.

Euphorbia includes about 2,000 species of trees, shrubs, perennials, and annuals, all related to poinsettias. Most euphorbias are found in warm temperate, tropical, or desert environments throughout the world. The number of species hardy in much of North America is more manageable. The vegetative features of the plants vary widely, so only a few general statements can be made with accuracy. First, all euphorbias have an irritating to toxic latex, or milky sap, which may be white, creamy, yellow, or orange and may turn darker upon exposure to air and drying. In all cases, keep this sap away from your eyes, nose, mouth, or cuts. Second, the "flowers" are extremely complex and are usually accompanied by colorful small leaves (bracts—an important word in the following entries), which may be white, red, yellow, orange, or some other attractive color. Leaves, too, are often brightly colored, especially in the fall. The name honors the ancient Greek healer Euphorbus, who was the physician of the king of Mauretania, in North Africa.

HOW TO GROW

Most often considered a Mediterranean plant, *Euphorbia* does include some species that thrive in cooler zones and even in moist or woodland conditions. Most euphorbias require well-drained soils with only average fertility. Rich soils will lead to leggy and weak growth, while moist soils will promote stem and root rot (there are exceptions to this rule—see the listings).

HOW TO USE
These species are gaining in popularity in the Midwest and on the East Coast. *E. polychroma* is among the best known and is an excellent choice for massed plantings in large landscapes, as well as use in smaller residential sites. The height of *E. griffithii* makes it most appropriate for use in large, dramatic plantings. *E. amygdaloides* var. *robbiae* adds an exotic note to shaded woodlands and quickly spreads into glossy masses that survive dry shade and relative neglect.

E. amygdaloides var. *robbiae* (*E. robbiae*)   P. 70
ah-mig-dal-OY-deez var. ROB-ee-eye. Wood Spurge. This classic evergreen ground cover thrives in woodlands or partial shade, spreading to form healthy masses less than 12 inches tall. Flowers and yellow bracts appear in spring and are held above the foliage. Useful in Zones 6 (warm Zone 5 with protection from winter sun) to 9.

E. cyparissias   P. 71
sy-par-ISS-ee-us. Cypress Spurge. This species must be carefully sited to prevent it from becoming weedy due to its running underground stems. It makes an effective mass in dry, gravelly gardens. Reaching just 10 to 18 inches tall, the plant's finely textured, blue-gray foliage makes it look like a tiny cypress. Yellow bracts appear in spring. 'Orange Man' has bracts that turn orange as they age. Useful in zones 6 to 8, especially in dry conditions.

E. griffithii 'Fireglow'   P. 71
grih-FITH-ee-eye. This vigorously spreading selection looks like a theatrical red asparagus as it emerges in spring. It has bronze foliage and brilliant orange bracts. Plants reach 3 to 4 feet tall and are reliable performers in Zones 6 to 8.

E. myrsinites   P. 72
mir-sin-EYE-tees. Spurge. This classic ground cover can be used to cascade over walls or spill across the ground in sites with very well drained soil and full sun. The fleshy, waxy, blue-green, oval leaves spiral around trailing stems that seldom rise more than six inches from the ground. Few

other ground covers add such a dramatic note to the garden. The chartreuse bracts appear in spring. Cut back after bloom to control vigorous self-seeding. Useful in Zones 6 to 9.

E. palustris

paw-LUS-tris. Swamp Spurge. Breaking all the rules, this euphorbia revels in wet to moist locations with full sun. As it matures, it may spread into drier and shadier areas nearby. Plants grow 3 to 4 feet or more tall and form extensive colonies. Use them in a grand-scale composition, where their size and acid yellow bracts will show to best advantage.

E. polychroma (E. epithymoides)   P. 72

pol-ee-CRO-muh. Cushion Spurge. This hardy, herbaceous perennial forms an eye-catching, mounding ground cover. The acid yellow bracts (they look like small out-of-season poinsettias) are attractive for weeks. In the fall, the plants become the center of attention as the light green foliage turns a brilliant orange-red. Cushion spurge prefers full sun to very light shade and soil with moderate moisture yet excellent drainage. Useful in Zones 4 to 7, as it does not do well in high heat and summer humidity.

❦ Ficus

FY-kus. Mulberry family, Moraceae.

Ficus contains more than 800 species, including the common fig (F. carica), the India rubber tree (F. elastica, not to be confused with the genus Hevea from Brazil), and the bo tree (F. religiosa), under which Buddha became enlightened. Ficus species are found in all warm regions of the world, with the greatest abundance from India to Polynesia. The genus is related to Morus (mulberries) and Maclura (Osage orange) — not so far-fetched a relationship if one thinks of mulberry and Osage orange fruits as figs turned inside out. Most Ficus species are shrubs to large forest trees with alternate leaves that are deciduous or evergreen. All parts of the plant are full of latex, which is often white and leaks from every broken or cut surface and then congeals. Flowers are individually almost microscopic but clustered together by the hundreds into specialized flowering and fruiting structures unique to figs, called syncomia. The fig species have coevolved with tiny wasps that perform the pollination in the synconium, and the plant and insect have intertwined life cycles. Only one species, F. pumila (creeping fig), is a ground cover for North American gardeners. It exhibits potentially unlimited growth in warm gardens. Its climbing habit and small, evergreen leaves make it most unlike a typical fig. *F. pumila* clings tenaciously, supposedly by secreting a tiny amount of latex from the aerial roots, which then dries and helps hold the root even on the smoothest of surfaces.

HOW TO GROW

Grow *F. pumila* where you want a tough, evergreen, apparently nonflowering, climbing ground cover. It is not particular as to soil type but will perform best in circumneutral to acid soils. Partial shade is preferred, and plants will not attach well to extremely hot (such as south- or west-facing) metal surfaces. Creeping fig rarely fruits in North American gardens, but if it does, the fruits are inedible. Useful in Zone 8 (with careful siting) and warmer.

HOW TO USE

Use *F. pumila* to cover a garage wall, a smooth concrete retaining wall, or an unsightly shed. If unchecked, it will grow 30 feet or more across constructed surfaces over time. Typical situations include beds at the base of a blank wall, which also is to be covered by the plant; beds beneath and on masonry features, such as arches and columns, where the plants can be clipped to give an immediate sense of antiquity; and garden beds where a low, woody mass is desired.

F. pumila (F. repens)   P. 73

PEW-muh-luh. Creeping Fig. This warm-climate ground cover makes a uniformly flat mat. It will plaster itself to vertical surfaces or carpet the ground. It does best in moist, well-drained, loamy soil and partial sun to light shade. It does not thrive in dry soils or under droughty conditions. Note that as the climbing stems mature, they develop many short, woody side branches. The cultivars differ by foliage features. 'Minima' has smaller than normal leaves. 'Variegata' has irregular white markings on the leaves.

ꙮ *Forsythia*

for-SITH-ee-uh. Olive family, Oleaceae.

Six of the seven *Forsythia* species are native to East Asia; the seventh is native to southeastern Europe. *Forsythia* is closely related to *Jasminum* (true jasmine) and is in the same family as *Syringa* (lilacs) and *Fraxinus* (ash trees). All forsythias are shrubs ranging from almost prostrate to more than 6 feet tall. Leaves are deciduous, opposite, simple, oval, and up to 3 inches long. Leaf edges are highly variable, even on the same plant, from entire to dramatically cut. The yellow, four-petaled flowers emerge in early spring before the leaves. Fruits are not ornamental.

HOW TO GROW
Grow ground-covering forsythias in full sun for best coverage. They are not at all particular as to soil, as long as it is not periodically desiccated or seasonally saturated. If pruning is desired, do so after flowering. Forsythias commonly suffer from "spring fever pruning" — the urge by gardeners to cut something back in early spring. Useful in Zones 3 to 8.

HOW TO USE
Forsythias are frequently planted as hedges and shrub masses in the East and Midwest, but low, ground-hugging selections also exist. Tough, resilient members of the olive family, they can survive in very difficult sites. Plant them as ground covers on steep banks, where the stems can root as they grow across the surface, or use them above retaining walls, where they can cascade down as a living screen. Low-growing forsythias are poor bloomers regardless of growing conditions, but they are useful in cold climates where a tough, rooting, woody ground cover that masses to about 2 feet tall is needed.

Low-Growing *Forsythia* Hybrids   Pp. 73, 74
'Arnold Dwarf' was named at Boston's Arnold Arboretum in 1941. It grows 2 to 3 feet tall and 6 to 7 feet wide, rooting where it touches. Foliage is dense, dark, and tough. It is sometimes listed as a cultivar of *F.* × *intermedia*. 'Bronxensis' grows only 12 inches tall and spreads quickly to many feet. It is often listed as a selection of *F. viridissima*.

❦ *Fragaria*

fra-GAR-ee-uh. Rose family, Rosaceae.

Fragaria species, the true strawberries, are noted for their delectable fruits. The 12 to 15 species are native to North America, Chile, and Eurasia, even into southern India — a geographic pattern strongly suggesting that the fruits are much beloved by birds. Numerous hybrids have been made in the past century for fruit production, but strawberries are also very versatile deciduous or evergreen ground covers. *Fragaria* is closely related to *Rubus* (blackberries and raspberries). Strawberries are perennial herbs that spread vigorously by aboveground runners. Plants usually grow to only 4 to 8 inches tall. The trifoliate leaves are evergreen (*F. chiloensis* and its hybrids) or deciduous and often have striking red hues as winter advances. Flowers are clear white and five petaled. Fruits are the well-known strawberries of jams, shortcakes, and seasonal desserts.

HOW TO GROW

Strawberries prefer humus-rich, loamy soil that is well drained but never totally dry. Soil pH is not critical, but an alkaline to circumneutral soil is preferred by some species. Grow strawberries in full sun, provided they can obtain adequate moisture, or in light shade. Hardiness varies by species.

HOW TO USE

Use strawberries as a ground cover, with a very different mindset than that for fruit production: leave them to themselves and enjoy the fruits you do obtain as a delightful bonus. Srawberries can be interplanted with other woodsy ground covers for a mosaic, but they may overrun the other species. In domestic gardens, think of planting them as a ground cover in a well-pruned apple orchard or as a delicious companion to species roses. They also lend themselves to planting near doorways and patios, where breakfast can be enjoyed on the run.

F. chiloensis   P. 74

chil-o-EN-siss. Chilean Strawberry. An important parent of our cultivated fruit, this species is also an excellent ground cover, with evergreen foliage that turns dark red in cold weather. It prefers full sun and sandy, well-drained soil with adequate water throughout the year. The white flowers bloom in spring, followed by small, red, rather tasteless fruits. Plants spread profusely by runners. Useful in Zones 5 to 10. 'Green Pastures' has smaller leaves but larger flowers and may not be as hardy as the species.

F. 'Pink Panda'   P. 75

This recent introduction by Blooms of Bressingham (England) has bright pink flowers, red stems, and shiny green leaves.

F. vesca (F. ananassa 'Fraise des Bois')
VES-kuh. European Wild Strawberry, Ever-bearing Strawberry. This species is less frequently grown as a ground cover but is useful as one in Zones 5 to 10, where its white flowers and small, edible fruits can be appreciated. 'Lipstick' has bright red flowers. 'Shades of Pink' has pink flowers. 'Variegata' is an excellent ground cover with white-variegated leaves. It likes partial shade.

F. virginiana
ver-jin-ee-AH-nuh. Wild Strawberry. This species is native from eastern Canada to Oklahoma and is useful as a ground cover in woodland gardens with companion plants (such as other native plants), since it does not usually make a truly tight carpet. The fragrant fruits are used in making preserves.

☙ *Galax*
GA-lax. Diapensia family, Diapensiaceae.

Galax consists of one species endemic to the southern Appalachians. It is related to another southern Appalachian native, *Shortia galacifolia* (Oconee bells), which has similar evergreen foliage. *Galax* is a long-lived perennial that grows from a slowly creeping, almost woody rootstock that is technically a stem. Leaves measure up to several inches across and are a dramatic, glossy dark green. The rounded, heart-shaped leaves are held on slender but wiry stalks several inches above the ground. Flowers are tiny, white, and clustered atop leafless racemes that rise well above the foliage. A stand of *Galax* in flower deep in shady woods is stunningly beautiful and not soon forgotten. The name is based on the Greek word for "milk" and probably refers to the appearance of the flowers.

HOW TO GROW
Galax has a reputation as being difficult to establish. It needs deep, organic, acid soil with good moisture and cool woodland conditions for the fibrous roots to become established and thrive. Once established, it will persist for decades, spreading to form a solid mass of stunning beauty. Useful in Zones 5 to 8.

HOW TO USE

This is one of the loveliest evergreen ground covers for use in cool, shaded gardens with acid soil. Not only are the spring flowers charming, but the fall color is a brilliant coppery red, reminiscent of bergenias, but in a smaller, hardier leaf. Plant *Galax* where you want to create a focal mass in deep shade, perhaps with native azaleas or rhododendrons. Drifts of jack-in-the-pulpits and trilliums are other attractive companions.

G. urceolata (G. aphylla)   P. 75

ur-see-oh-LAY-tuh. *Galax* is a highly desirable ground cover with dark, polished, evergreen foliage that turns coppery red in fall. Its spikes of white, veronica-like flowers light up deep, shady spaces in early summer. Once established, it will spread slowly and indefinitely. Be sure not to let it suffer from drought during its first few seasons.

❦ *Galium*

GAY-lee-um. Madder family, Rubiaceae.

Galium contains more than over 250 species, many of which are non-ornamental to weedy species of the temperate regions of Eurasia and North America. Several species also are native to Australia. *Galium* is sometimes separated into several genera, in which case, the one species listed here becomes *Asperula odorata*. *Galium* is related to *Pentas* and is in the same family as *Coffea* (coffee). Its leaves are opposite, with large, leaflike stipules that create an overall whorled appearance along the four-angled stems. Both the leaves and stems have small, rough hairs that make the plants unpleasant to handle. The small, white flowers are massed into clusters in early summer. Only one species, *G. odoratum*, is commonly grown as a ground cover, although others are prized in rock gardens and perennial beds. The common name, bedstraw, refers to a traditional use of the plants, while the scientific name comes from the Greek word for "milk," since one of the species was traditionally used to curdle milk.

HOW TO GROW

Grow bedstraws in partial shade and well-drained soil of average fertility. Bedstraws prefer a partly organic soil, as is found in open woodlands. They may not make a solid ground cover in compacted or too friable (such as overly sandy) soils, which will prevent the rooting stems from taking hold and spreading. Galiums are intolerant of wet and soggy soils. They may spread vigorously in ideal sites and are readily controlled by uprooting unwanted plants. Useful in Zones 4 to 8.

HOW TO USE

Galium can be planted to create a light, frothy effect among ferns, columbines, dicentras, and doronicums (leopard's bane). Its tiny, white flowers will enhance the showier blooms of other spring wildings, and since it is shallow rooted, its vigorous spreading tendency is easily controlled by light hand weeding. Galiums look best when mixed with plants with larger-textured foliage, such as viburnums or spring-flowering dogwoods. They grow happily in light shade (as under crabapples, hawthorns, or silverbells), as well as in deeper shade, and are even reported to be an effective ground cover under black walnuts.

G. odoratum (Asperula odorata)   P. 76

o-dor-AH-tum. Sweet Woodruff, Ladies' Bedstraw. This European native has been commonly grown as a ground cover in North America for more than a century. Its are leaves used to flavor the "May Wine" traditionally served in open bowls on May Day. The deciduous leaves are bright green at first, acquiring olive green or yellow overtones through the season. The tiny, starlike flowers are white. Fast spreading in moist, shady sites such as woodland settings, but easy to control, this species also tolerates dry sites, such as under maple trees.

❦ *Gaultheria*

gawl-THEE-ree-uh. Heath family, Ericaceae.

The 200-plus *Gaultheria* species imperfectly ring the Pacific. Species are native to the mountains of South America into Brazil, others to North America, and numerous species to China and the Himalayas of India. The species sometimes segregated as *Pernettya* (including *G. mucronata* here) are native to New Zealand and Tasmania, as well as to South America and Mexico. Gardeners in mild coastal climates can grow a selection of these evergreen relatives of huckleberries, which form low, trailing or spreading shrubs. Leaves are small, leathery, and evergreen. Flowers are pendent, white urns, much like those of blueberries and huckleberries. Fruits are white, bright red, or purple-black berries that may be retained on the plant into winter. Note that the leaves and nectar of some species are reported to be poisonous if eaten. The name commemorates the French botanist Jean Gaulthier, who lived in Quebec in the 1700s. A diminutive *Gaultheria* is native to that province.

HOW TO GROW

Gaultheria species require good moisture for the first few years so that the roots can settle in and start to spread. Although they will survive in dry, thin, acid forest soils, they will do much better in moist, acid woodland conditions. In a garden situation, the plants will tolerate more than half sun, but they must have additional water. Drying winds will cause the foliage to burn in both summer and winter. Plants do best in climates with relatively cool summers, such as maritime locations or northern latitudes. In all cases, they do well with afternoon shade. Depending on the species, they may be winter hardy in the far north or tolerant of only mild winters. Hardiness varies in Zones 4 to 9, depending on the species.

HOW TO USE

G. procumbens (wintergreen) is often used as a ground cover in woodland plantings. The tiny leaves, with their distinctive scent, look wonderfully at home in the company of native viburnums, blueberries, and witch hazels, as well as with rhododendrons, kalmias, and azaleas. Think of planting wintergreen as a carpet under spring-blooming dogwoods or shadbush, or interplanting it with Virginia bluebells, ferns, and late-summer cimicifugas. It has excellent fall color, winter fruits, and trustworthy cold hardiness to Zone 3 (selected species). *G. shallon* is a fine, shrubby native of the Pacific Northwest but is underused because of its ubiquity.

G. mucronata (Pernettya mucronata) P. 76

mew-cron-AH-tuh. Chilean Pernettya. This small, spreading, evergreen shrub grows to 18 inches tall. The tiny, urn-shaped flowers are followed by white or dark burgundy fruits. The shiny, dark green foliage turns bronze in winter. *G. mucronata* is a handsome shrub that forms large, spreading clumps, but it grows only on the West Coast. Plant it for its beautiful (though poisonous) berries. Place it near a driveway in a low, suckering mass, or perhaps use it as an informal hedge near an ornamental pool, facing the edge with shorter grasses or moisture-loving perennials. It likes full sun to very light shade. Useful in Zones 7 to 9, especially in the Pacific Northwest. 'Alba' has white, pink-tinged fruits. 'Rosea' has large, pale pink fruits. 'Rubra' has pink flowers and small, glossy leaves on red stems.

G. procumbens

pro-KUM-benz. Wintergreen, Checkerberry. This is a familiar ground cover in eastern woodlands. The glossy, round, evergreen leaves are held just off the forest floor. The bell-like, white flowers are followed by bright red fruits. Useful in Zones 3 to 8.

G. shallon   P. 77

SHAL-lon. Salal. This ubiquitous denizen of open woods in the Pacific Northwest grows in moist, acid soils. It makes a splendid, low, shrubby, rhizomatous ground cover. Plants grow up to 5 feet tall (often shorter) and form extensive colonies. They have attractive, bell-like flowers in spring, evergreen foliage that changes to hues of copper and scarlet in fall, and purple or black fruits that appear by late summer. Flower arrangers love salal throuhout the year. Useful in Zones 7 to 9.

❦ Gazania

gaz-A-nee-uh. Aster family, Asteraceae.

Gazanias are native to South Africa, where the 40-plus species range in color from white to yellow, orange, gold, bronze, and rosy pink. Peak bloom is in early summer, and the spectacular flowers, held well above the foliage can reach up to 3 inches across. Leaves are evergreen or semi-evergreen, often white underneath, and clustered into basal rosettes. They are simple or dissected, depending on the species. Gazanias are distantly related to thistles (*Carduus* and *Cirsium*). Two origins are given for the name. One is from the Latin *gaza*, meaning "treasure" or "riches," in reference to the gaudy flowers. The other is from Theodore of Gaza (c. 1398–1478), who translated the ancient botanical works of Theophrastus from Greek to Latin.

HOW TO GROW

Gazanias are popular perennials in southern California and the Southwest (Zones 9 and 10), where they bloom from spring through summer in shades of pink, yellow, orange, and white. Flowers are displayed against grayish green foliage. Cultivars based on *G. rigens* (trailing gazania) flower less prolifically than the commonly grown annuals, but they make effective, spreading ground covers for a variety of slopes and sites. Gazanias require well-drained soil, full sun, and moderate amounts of water on a regular basis.

HOW TO USE

It may be hard to believe that these attractive "daisies" are tough work-horses for difficult sites. Use *G. rigens* on slopes to bind soil, or plant it in large masses near heat-reflective buildings and parking areas, as well as in residential sites, where its elegant flowers can be appreciated. In the arid southwest plants require some water on a regular basis.

G. rigens   P. 77

RY-genz. Trailing Gazania. This is a long-lived perennial, with many new selections becoming available. Most are thought to have *G. rigens* var. *leucoleana* parentage, but they may be hybrids. 'Mitsuwa Orange' has bright orange flowers. 'Mitsuwa Yellow' has large yellow flowers. 'Sunburst' has orange flowers and gray foliage. 'Sunglow' has yellow blooms.

❦ Gelsemium

gel-SEM-ee-um. Buddleja family, Loganiaceae.

The few species of *Gelsemium* are native only to a small part of eastern North America and southeastern Asia—a geographic pattern found in many native plants and reflecting the preglacial vegetation of several million years ago. Our common native species, *G. sempervirens* (Carolina jessamine), is native from coastal North Carolina south to northern Mexico, while the Asian species *(G. rankinii)* ranges from China to Sumatra. *Gelsemium* is related to *Buddleja* (butterfly bush) and includes vines and twining shrubs with opposite, evergreen leaves. Flowers are funnel shaped, and fruits are not of ornamental importance. *Gelsemium* is a corrupted form of the Italian word for "jasmine."

HOW TO GROW

Carolina jessamine thrives in sunny to partially open sites, where it forms a mounding ground cover and climbing thicket with bright yellow flowers in early spring. It grows to about 3 feet tall and spreads indefinitely. Note that flowers and foliage are poisonous when eaten. Useful in Zones 8 to 10.

HOW TO USE

Plant Carolina jessamine, the official flower of South Carolina, where its sprawling evergreen canopy can spread and mound. For formal use as a ground cover, plant it where there are no objects to climb. It is ideal for naturalistic use, where its climbing and spreading proclivities help stabilize banks and cover disturbed areas.

G. rankinii

ran-KIN-ee-eye. This reblooming species is seen less frequently than G. sempervirens. It has the same vigorous growth and habit but reblooms well in fall. Flowers are almost scentless.

G. sempervirens   P. 78

sem-pur-VYE-renz. Carolina Jessamine. This twining vine and ground cover has glossy, evergreen, opposite, elliptical leaves that measure about 1 inch long. Flowers are funnel shaped and clustered into groups of three to five. The pale yellow, almost waxy-looking flowers bloom in late spring and early summer, but their fragrance does not carry far compared to that of true jasmines (Jasminum). 'Pride of Augusta' is a double-flowering form.

❦ Genista

jen-IS-tuh. Pea family, Fabaceae.

Genista encompasses about 75 usually shrubby species from the Mediterranean, North Africa, and West Asia. Known commonly as brooms and related to the genus Cytisus, these species are arching, branching shrubs formerly used for making dust brooms. They range from almost prostrate shrubs, which are useful as small-scale ground covers, to large shrubs reaching more than 15 feet tall. Leaves are deciduous or semievergreen, small, and with only one or three leaflets per leaf. The small leaves may be dropped during dry weather, and the shrub then continues to photosynthesize using its green stems. Flowers are pealike in size and shape but come in varying shades of yellow and are clustered into small heads. Fruits are not ornamental but are distinctive for their explosive rupture, thus flinging the seeds many feet away from the mother plant. Genista is the ancient Latin name for these plants, and the phrase planta genista was corrupted into Plantaginet, the family name of a line of English kings.

HOW TO GROW

Grow brooms in full sun, or they will sulk and weaken. Soil must be well drained, as brooms despise having even damp feet. Plants are not overly particular as to soil pH, but they do prefer a slightly alkaline condition and low to moderate fertility. Hardiness depends on the species.

HOW TO USE

Use the low-growing selections listed here as small-scale ground covers where they can spill over low structures or grow on the level just above foot traffic. They can be especially useful in dry Mediterranean climates to control bank erosion.

G. pilosa 'Vancouver Gold'   P. 78

pil-O-suh. This selection was introduced by the University of British Columbia Botanical Garden. It grows 4 to 6 inches tall and spreads to 3 feet. Bright yellow flowers cover the branches in spring. It makes a useful ground cover for banks.

G. sagittalis   P. 79

sag-it-TAH-liss. This broom is distinctive at a glance, as the low-lying branches look as if they have been flattened with a rolling pin. It grows to 12 inches tall and spreads modestly, making a small-scale ground cover that can be mixed with other compatible ground covers. Flowers are light yellow and sparse.

❦ *Geranium*

jer-A-nee-um. Geranium family, Geraniaceae.

Wild species of *Geranium* are found throughout the world, with the majority of the 400 species being native to the temperate regions. These "true" geraniums are in the same family as the houseplants and bedding annuals commonly called geraniums, which are actually in the genus *Pelargonium*. Geraniums are perennials with alternate, sometimes opposite, and sometimes basal leaves. Leaves are deciduous (rarely evergreen) and often divided like a hand. Flowers are white, pink, or reddish and have five identical petals. Given the enormous number of species, flower size ranges from insignificant to nearly 2 inches across. The slender fruits curl open as they dry and look like the bills of miniature cranes — thus the common name. *Geranium* is from the Greek word for "crane."

HOW TO GROW

Geraniums may be used effectively as reliable and attractive ground covers for woodland and naturalistic settings. The hundreds of species and their numerous cultivars means that there is a selection available for almost any type of garden setting and soil in Zones 4 to 9. In general, ground-covering species perform well in soil of at least average fertility and that never dries out. Hardiness depends on the species.

HOW TO USE

These attractive perennials are treasured for their many garden roles in temperate and Mediterranean climates. Delightful flowers and foliage, easy cultivation, and their ability to spread quickly and to smother weeds make them among the most desirable ground-cover plants. If you have a problem situation, there is probably a geranium to fix it.

G. × cantabrigiense (G. dalmaticum × G. macrorrhizum)   P. 79

x can-tah-bri-jee-EN-see. This variable hybrid has many named forms. The typical form grows to 8 inches tall and has fragrant foliage and masses of pink flowers in early summer. Useful in Zones 5 to 8, especially in the Southeast if grown in partial shade. 'Biokovo' has white flowers with pink centers in late spring to early summer. It grows to 12 inches tall and makes a vigorous ground cover once established. 'Karmina' has raspberry-pink flowers in early summer and grows only 6 to 8 inches tall. 'St. Ola' has glossy, evergreen foliage in warm climates.

G. endressii

en-DRES-ee-eye. This deciduous species reaches 12 to 15 inches tall and has pink flowers with dark stripes. Many cultivars traditionally listed here are treated as hybrids under G. × oxonianum, but the species is still useful in Zones 5 to 8.

G. himalayense   P. 80

him-ah-lay-EN-see. This spreading geranium grows to 12 inches tall. Flowers are violet-blue with a crimson eye and bloom in late spring to early summer. Useful in Zones 5 to 8. 'Gravetye' forms thick masses of low foliage that set off the large flowers. 'Johnson's Blue', a hybrid of this species, has very large, blue flowers that can be used to create broad sweeps of color among shrubs. It is one of the classic selections and is planted in a dramatic sweep at Sissinghurst (England).

G. macrorrhizum

Pp. 80, 81

mak-ro-RISE-um. This is one of the classic ground-covering geraniums, performing well even in dry shade. Touch the slightly sticky, green leaves to release the fragrance of ripe apples. Foliage is less than 12 inches tall. Useful in Zones 4 to 8. There are numerous selections, some with foliage markings, and with flowers ranging from white to pink to deep magenta. 'Album' has white flowers with a pale pink blush. 'Bevan's Variety' has deep magenta flowers. 'Czakor' is especially useful in woodland situations, where its shocking magenta-pink flowers seem to glow in the dark. 'Ingwersen's Variety' has pale pink flowers and light green foliage. 'Variegatum' has pinkish flowers and gray-green foliage with creamy splashes.

G. × magnificum (G. ibericum × G. platypetalum)

x mag-NIF-i-cum. This geranium is at its blooming peak in early summer, when the blue flowers are one of the most brilliant features in the garden, making it stunning in a mass planting. Plants spread well to make a fine ground cover less than 2 feet tall, with the added bonus of attractive fall color. Useful in Zones 4 to 8.

G. × oxonianum (G. endressii × G. versicolor)

P. 82

x ox-ohn-ee-AH-num. This hybrid group is extremely variable, but many of the larger selections make good ground covers. Useful in Zones 5 to 8. 'A.T. Johnson' has silvery pink flowers. 'Claridge Druce' is very vigorous and has magenta-pink flowers with darker veins. This is a good selection in the South because it tolerates heat once established. 'Wargrave Pink' is a classic workhorse, with clear pink flowers that peak in late spring and continue sporadically until frost.

G. phaeum (G. 'Mourning Widow')

P. 82

FAY-um. Mourning Widow Geranium. This is the best *Geranium* species for shade. It does well in dry areas, where it colonizes extensively and reaches 18 inches tall. In early spring, the wine red flowers are held above the foliage and add a distinctive note to the garden's spring display. Useful in Zones 5 to 8. 'Album' has white flowers. 'Samobor' has deep brown markings on the foliage and bronze-red flowers; it does well even in deep shade. 'Variegatum' has leaves marked with cream and touches of pink.

G. sanguineum

P. 83

san-GWIN-ee-um. Bloody Cranesbill. This species forms weed-proof mats up to 8 inches tall and several feet across. It has bold magenta flowers and is useful in Zones 4 to 9. 'Album' has white flowers and more open growth; it is less aggressive. *G. sanguineum* var. *striatum* ('Lancastrense') has shell pink flowers with red veins.

❦ *Gypsophila*

gip-SOF-il-luh. Pink family, Caryophyllaceae.

Gardeners know some of the *Gypsophila* species as baby's breath, but there is a great deal of diversity in the genus's 125 species, which are native from the eastern Mediterranean (including North Africa) to West Asia. Gypsophilas are closely related to pinks and carnations. They include annuals and perennials, although the species listed here are all perennials. Leaves are deciduous, opposite, lance shaped and usually bluish green. The small, white or rose pink flowers have five petals and are produced in cloudlike abundance in early summer. Fruits are insignificant. *Gypsophila* means "chalk lover" in Greek, in reference to its strong preference for limy soils.

HOW TO GROW

Gypsophilas require alkaline, well-drained, airy soil and full sun. Waterlogged, clayey, or compacted soils are lethal to these plants. Gypsophilas establish best as small plants. Once established, they should be deadheaded soon after flowering to promote thicker growth. Plants will not tolerate hot, muggy summers. Useful in Zones 3 to 9.

HOW TO USE

Use *G. repens* and its cultivars as a ground cover where the low mats of foliage can display their clouds of flowers in early to midsummer. Plant baby's breath in cutting gardens, along pathways, or as frothy masses on hillsides. Wherever they are planted, the tiny flowers will attract attention —and bees. Remember to dry some of the flowers for use in winter wreaths and other holiday arrangements.

G. repens P. 83

REE-penz. Creeping Baby's Breath. This is a classic for gravelly, light, limy soils. The grayish green foliage works well with the white flowers. 'Rosea' has pink flowers.

❦ *Hebe*

HEE-be. Figwort family, Scrophulariaceae.

Hebes have been described as woody veronicas, and indeed the two genera are very closely related. The 130 to 150 species of *Hebe* are native to New Guinea, Australia, New Zealand, and cool regions of South America, including the Falkland Islands. Most of the species, and indeed almost all of our garden selections, are from New Zealand. Hebes are evergreen shrubs that range in habit from low, creeping mats native to alpine zones to large shrubs more than 4 feet tall. Most frequently encountered are shrubs less than 2 feet tall, with opposite, often thick to almost fleshy, evergreen leaves ranging from less than 1 inch to 2 inches long. Flowers look very much like those of *Veronica* in shape, color, and floral display, although *Hebe* flowers may be clustered into heads rather than the spikelike racemes so typical of *Veronica*. Hebe flowers, though small, are strikingly beautiful, as they are presented against the dark backdrop of the evergreen shrub. Colors range from white to pale lilac to intensely deep violet and purple. The name commemorates a minor Greek deity, the goddess of youth and cupbearer (wine, of course) to the gods.

HOW TO GROW
Hebes need a cool maritime climate without bitterly cold winters. Such conditions are found throughout much of the Pacific Coast. Some species are tolerant of the more humid summer conditions along the Gulf and southern Atlantic coasts. Grow hebes in full sun and nutrient-rich, organic soil that never dries out yet drains well. Useful in Zones 8 to 10.

HOW TO USE
The shrubby hebes are more frequently seen in Europe than the United States, but they are well worth experimenting with as ground covers. Grow in masses to face down larger shrubs and trees. Plant on banks, along pathways, or in parking lot medians. They blend well with mass plantings of heaths and heathers and appreciate the same moderate maritime climates. Hebes require well-drained soil.

H. glaucophylla
glaw-co-FYE-luh. This low shrub tends to stay under 12 inches tall but spreads farther. It has dense, gray-green leaves and white flowers.

H. pinguifolia P. 84

pin-gwe-FO-lee-uh. 'Pagei' is a mounding shrublet that reaches 18 inches tall and is frequently planted in large landscapes but can be massed for smaller applications. The petite, blue-gray foliage shows off the white flowers in early summer. 'Sutherlandii' masses well and is a relatively new introduction from New Zealand.

H. 'Youngii' (*H.* 'Carl Teschner')

This exceptionally fine ground-covering *Hebe* has tiny, dark green leaves and is covered with small purple and white flowers in summer.

❦ *Hedera*

HED-er-uh. Ivy family, Araliaceae.

Most North American gardeners know the common ivy, *H. helix,* but it is only one of the 15 species native from western Europe to Japan. The other species are not nearly as hardy, and some are simply not seen in our gardens. *Hedera* is closely related to *Schefflera* (umbrella tree). These evergreen, woody vines have alternate, often lobed leaves. There are hundreds of named selections based on minor but attractive variations in leaf shape, size, mottling, and variegation. Hederas have contrasting juvenile and adult foliage. As long as the plant is vining, the leaves are juvenile. In mature plants, woody, nonclimbing branches grow out from the main vine mass. It is these branches that have the adult foliage, as well as the insignificant greenish white flowers and dark fruits. Fruits are very attractive to birds. Given the plants' ability to colonize large areas, they are invasive in the Pacific Northwest. The name is the classic Latin name for ivy, and the plant was important to the cults of Bacchus and Dionysus (the Roman and Greek gods of wine, respectively) for their secret revels.

HOW TO GROW

Ivy is not particular as to soil, site, or growing conditions, provided its very basic needs are met. Ivy prefers organic, moist soil and partial shade. Given those conditions, it will grow extensively onto adjacent walls, tree trunks, signs, or other stationary objects. Plants will tolerate very poor soils as long as they are not dry, especially if they are in full sun. Variegated plants need sun to develop their coloration fully. Ivy may not grow at all immediately after planting, but once established, it will form impenetrable colonies. In some regions, *H. helix* is so invasive that it should be planted with care, if at all. Useful in Zones 4 to 9.

HOW TO USE

In parts of the South and Northwest, ivies are out of control and weedy, but in other regions, they have an important role to play in the garden. Does your yard call for a "tree" that is guaranteed to stay at a certain height? If so, plant ivy on a metal support and keep it trimmed to size. Do you long to transform a modern statue or column into something that appears ancient? Ivy can add the look and texture of age in short order. On steep, shaded slopes—especially where the shade is derived from buildings rather than trees—ivy will make an effective ground cover as long as the soil is not baked dry or the plants walked on. Boston Ivy is in another genus, *Parthenocissus triscupidata.*

H. canariensis (H. algeriensis) P. 84
kan-ar-ee-EN-siss. Algerian Ivy. Native to the Canary Islands, off the coast of northern Africa, this species has large, glossy, evergreen foliage that creates a coarse texture and looks best at a distance. Plants can be mowed occasionally to maintain tidiness. This plant is very adaptable, as seen by its use along California freeways. Useful in Zones 8 to 10. 'Gloire de Marengo' ('Variegata') has elegant foliage with gray, green, and white markings.

H. colchica (including *H.* 'My Heart') P. 85
COAL-chi-cuh. Persian Ivy. This species is hardier than Algerian ivy and is useful in Zones 7 to 10. 'Dentata' has leaf petioles flushed with purple. 'Dentata Variegata' ('Dentata Aurea' and 'Variegata') has leaves with gray-green and primrose yellow markings. 'Sulphur Heart' ('Paddy's Pride') reverses the above patterns, with leaf veins and centers in creamy yellow.

H. helix
HE-liks. English Ivy. This is the hardiest ivy, being useful in Zones 4 to 9. At its northern limit, it should be grown on north-facing slopes, sides of buildings, and similar areas protected from winter sun. There are hundreds of named cultivars in the trade, distinguished by leaf shape, size, glossiness, and color. Those listed here are commonly offered as ground covers. *H. helix* var. *baltica* ('Baltica') is dark green with white veins and is the hardiest selection, having been found originally near the Baltic Sea. 'Buttercup' has small, yellow leaves and requires some sun for best color. 'Gold Heart' has green leaves with pale-colored centers. 'Needlepoint' has small, green, sharply pointed leaves and needs some shade; it is popular in

the South. 'Sagittifolia' has grayish green, arrow-shaped leaves. 'Spetchley' has tiny leaves and forms a dense cover; it is superb for small areas.

❦ Helianthemum

he-lee-AN-the-mum. Rock rose family, Cistaceae.

The 110 species of *Helianthemum* are native from Europe, the Mediterranean, and northern Africa to central Asia. They are shallow-rooted, dwarf or prostrate shrubs with evergreen or semievergreen leaves that usually measure less than 1 inch long. Leaves are elliptical and vary in grayness. Flowers measure up to an inch or more across, have five petals (double forms exist), and look like miniature wild roses—thus the common names sun rose and rock rose. Each flower lasts only 1 day, but numerous flowers are carried on each flower stalk, so the blooming period spans several weeks. Colors are in warm sunset shades of yellow, orange, copper, pink, and white. The name is Greek and means "sun flower."

HOW TO GROW
Helianthemums need a site with full sun and good, screelike drainage where they will not be subject to winter wet collecting around their stems and roots. They are not particular about soil pH, but they do dislike humidity and are adapted to the kind of dry summers typical of the American West and Mediterranean climates. For best growth as a ground cover, shear plants lightly after bloom to encourage spreading and branching. Useful in Zone 6 and warmer, unless noted.

HOW TO USE
Use sun roses as ground covers on sunny, dry banks where the plants can fuse into a colorful mass and provide brilliant floral sweeps when in bloom and pleasing green foliage blankets the rest of the season. Branches root as they spread, ultimately forming a thick mat. One of the classic images in twentieth-century horticulture is a photograph of sun roses in Rosemary Verey's garden at Barnsley House (England), where they made colorful drifts along an old stone path.

H. hybrids   P. 85
Most of the best selections are hybrids, commonly listed as *H. nummularium* hybrids. They differ in foliage grayness and flower color. 'Brunette' has green leaves and dark orange flowers. 'Mesa Wine' has dark green leaves and dark red flowers. 'Saint Mary's' has dark green leaves and white

flowers. 'Stoplight' has grayish green leaves and red flowers. 'Wisley Pink' has gray foliage and pink flowers. 'Wisley Primrose' has gray-green foliage and pale yellow flowers.

᭜ *Helleborus*

hel-LE-bor-us. Buttercup family, Ranunculaceae.

The 20 or so species of *Helleborus* are native from western Europe to China, with most of the species being native from the Mediterranean to the Caucasus. The various species are known by common names such as Lenten rose, Christmas rose, and hellebore. The genus is closely related to *Aquilegia* (columbines), *Delphinium* (delphiniums), and *Aconitum* (aconites). Plants are extremely toxic—a common trait of many members of the buttercup family. Hellebores are evergreen herbs with tough, leathery, peony-like leaves. The species range in height from less than 15 inches to nearly 3 feet tall at maturity. Flowers have five petals and come in a range of colors—white, pink, pale yellow, maroon, and lime green—thanks to modern hybrids. The dry fruits look like miniature peony pods and split open to release shiny, black seeds. The young green fruits are sometimes mistaken for small flowers. All parts of the plants are toxic if eaten. *H. foetidus,* as its name implies, has leaves that give off an unpleasant smell when crushed, making it difficult to imagine why anyone would consume them.

HOW TO GROW
Hellebores prefer well-drained, neutral to alkaline, organic soil. They require partial shade, and at the northern limit of their hardiness, they will perform best if protected from winter sun and wind. This can usually be accomplished by planting them in the shade of a building, fence, or hedge. Established hellebores sulk if moved. Useful in Zones 4 to 9, depending on the species.

HOW TO USE
These long-lived, clump-forming perennials make exceptionally fine ground covers when massed. When soil and siting conditions are favorable, plants will spontaneously self-seed to form ever larger drifts. Since hellebores bloom so early in the season and plants are attractive when flowering and fruiting, they have one of the longest seasons of peak interest of any ground cover. Plant them in drifts in shaded woodland gardens

to combine with summer perennials. Add groups to city patios and along cool, dark pathways, where they will bring elegance and beauty at a time when most perennials are still dormant.

H. foetidus

FEH-tid-us. Stinking Hellebore. The lime green flowers and boldly cut foliage make this species immediately recognizable from a distance. It is the tallest of the hellebores, growing to nearly 3 feet. A well-grown clump looks much like a small, glossy shrub mass.

H. niger   P. 86

NYE-jer. Christmas Rose. This species blooms from late winter to early spring in northern climates. Plant it in a humus-rich, moist, shady site. It will do best with some lime. Many named forms are available, although some selections are costly. All are appropriate for massing.

H. orientalis   P. 87

o-ree-en-TAHL-iss. Lenten Rose. This species blooms in very early spring and is one of the most reliable choices for northern gardens. It can be expected to reseed. Many named hybrids with some *H. orientalis* parentage are on the market.

❦ Hemerocallis

hem-er-o-KAL-iss. Daylily family, Hemerocallidaceae.

Hemerocallis species, commonly known as daylilies, are among the most ancient garden flowers—they are recognizable in Chinese artifacts from more than 2,500 years ago. The 15 to 20 wild species are native from northern India to China, Korea, Manchuria, the Russian Far East, and Japan. Daylilies were introduced into Europe by at least the sixteenth century and were brought to North America in the colonial era. They are so widely naturalized in much of North America that many people mistake them for native wildflowers. They are related to hostas and lilies, although these are technically divided into three separate but related families. Daylilies are tough, long-lived perennials with fleshy roots, spreading underground stems, and long, linear leaves that are partially folded to create a shallow v along much of their length. Leaves are often described as swordlike, but the v channel and gently arching outline create a leaf that is not flat or rigid, as in the case of an iris or sword. Foliage ranges from less than a foot long in dwarf cultivars to more than 3 feet in vigorous species and hybrids. The large flowers are funnel shaped or lily-like and last only a day—thus the common name. Immediately after bloom, flowers simultaneously shrivel and liquefy into a slimy mess—a process dignified by the word "deliquesce," for those readers who like botanical terms or good words for Scrabble™. They are usually held on slender stalks well above the foliage, and since several buds are present on each flowering stalk, peak bloom can last nearly a week. The name is Greek and means "beauty for a day."

HOW TO GROW

Easy to grow, untroubled by pests, and adapted to sun or partial shade, daylilies are well-deserved favorites of both gardeners and nurserymen. They are excellent examples of a plant that is generally clump forming but also spreads by rhizomes. Daylilies perform best in full sun to only very slight shade. They will persist and bloom acceptably with less than full sun, as happens when young trees mature over the decades and cast shade on what was once a sunny site, leading inexperienced gardeners to believe erroneously that daylilies prefer shade. Daylilies will grow in any type of fertile soil that is not waterlogged (although *H. fulva* has been known to survive even that) or so loose as to be unstable. They are excellent for binding slopes and banks. Useful in Zones 4 to 9.

HOW TO USE

Although daylilies are often thought of in the context of a perennial border, they serve equally well when massed, as they are tough, reliable ground covers that will enliven an area for decades. When considering daylilies as a ground cover, think about how you will view them and at what speed—from a distance in a moving car, as would be the case on a bank along the driveway, or up close and on foot, as when they are massed in dramatic drifts at the edge of a lawn or woodland. Consider, too, the height of both the foliage and the flower stalks if they are to be in a major sightline. For example, daylilies massed in a view from a terrace (such as a view to water) may be too high, in which case a dwarf form is preferable. By contrast, daylilies massed at a distance from the viewing location (such as along a property boundary) may need to be large. Remember that daylilies grown in partial shade or strong shadow (as from a building or solid fence) will turn toward the prevailing light, so if seeing the flowers is important to you, make certain you place them where the prevailing light is behind you. Some late-twentieth-century cultivars are distinctive for their rebloom—'Stella de Oro' is one well-known example. For effective use as a ground cover, your daylily selection needs to be vigorous at establishment, clump forming or spreading, useful in Zones 4 or 5 to 9, easy to find in nurseries or by mail order, and inexpensive enough to be purchased in large numbers. If money is no object, probably any contemporary daylily cultivar can be planted in large enough masses to create a ground cover. One species, *H. fulva*, is a reliable choice, but it is also considered an invasive pest in certain parts of the country. Several old cultivars, such as 'Hyperion', are reliable ground covers for large landscapes.

SPECIES

H. fulva   P. 87
FUL-vuh. Daylily, Orange Daylily, Tawny Daylily. This is the daylily found beside many ruined farmhouses and settlements. Native to East Asia, it remains one of the best and finest ground covering daylilies, with flowers complexly colored from coppery orange to burnt orangish red. Blooms are produced in abundance in early to midsummer, and plants tolerate salty sites. Totally reliable.

H. lilioasphodelus (H. flava)
LIL-ee-o-ass-fo-DEL-us. Lemon Lily. This Asian species is native from China and Siberia to Japan. Leaves are seldom more than 2 feet long. The very fragrant, clear yellow flowers are produced in late spring to early summer, making it one of the first daylilies to bloom. It spreads well.

CULTIVARS
Countless excellent cultivars exist. Among the most popular for mass planting are those listed here.

'Black-eyed Stella' grows 1 to 2 feet tall and has golden yellow flowers with a large, dark throat. Reblooms.

'Catherine Woodbury' grows to 2½ feet tall and has pinkish orchid color flowers with a greenish yellow throat.

'Eenie-Weenie' is only 10 inches tall. Its yellow flowers bloom over a long period.

'Frans Hals' grows to 2 feet tall and is a red and yellow bicolor.

'Green Flutter' grows to 20 inches tall and has bright yellow flowers with a green throat.

'Hall's Pink' reaches 20 inches tall and has light pink flowers.

'Happy Returns' grows to 18 inches tall and has yellow flowers. Reblooms.

'Hyperion' is up to 38 inches tall and has fragrant, clear yellow flowers.

'Kwanso Flore Pleno' ('Green Kwanso') is a very old selection that grows to 3 feet tall and has double, orange flowers.

'Stella de Oro' grows only 12 inches tall and has golden yellow flowers. Reblooms.

❧ Heuchera

HEW-ker-uh. Saxifrage family, Saxifragaceae.

The 35 to 50 species of *Heuchera* are native to North America, from the mountains of Mexico north into Canada. Within the saxifrage family, *Heuchera* is closely related to *Bergenia* and *Saxifraga,* and more distantly to *Astilbe.* Heucheras are deciduous or semievergreen perennials with tufted basal leaves and flowering stalks rising 1 to nearly 2 feet above the foliage. Leaves are simple and rounded or heart shaped. Many new cultivars have been developed with distinctive leaf coloration or mottling, especially in tones of purple or bronze. Flowers of garden forms are pale white, pink, coral, or red. Although they are individually small, they are presented in cloudlike sprays that are attractive to hummingbirds. The species tend to have less showy flowers and leaves than the numerous hybrids and cultivars. The name commemorates Johann Heucher (1677–1747), a professor of medicine in Wittenberg, Germany, at a time when many physicians were also trained botanists.

HOW TO GROW

Heucheras grow under remarkably variable garden conditions. Try them in moist, fertile, shaded sites with above-average organic content, as well as in drier, sunnier sites. For best performance, soils should be neutral rather than strongly acid or alkaline. The roots can heave in cold-winter areas. If planted too deeply, the crowns are prone to rot. Divide plants every 3 or 4 years for densest growth and discard the old woody centers. Useful in Zones 4 to 9.

HOW TO USE

Heucheras are hardy, deciduous or semievergreen clumpers that are often massed as ground covers in small areas. They can also be used in naturalistic settings or where they can be grouped so that other plants do not obscure their floral display. Many selections have been made for choice foliage colors, and plants are frequently used in perennial borders. They are equally effective as ground covers in transition zones from sun to shade, at the edges of woodlands, and in gardens where they can be admired at close range.

H. americana (H. glauca)   Pp. 89, 90

ah-mair-i-KAN-uh. Alumroot. This shade-loving species has purplish green, deciduous foliage and greenish white flowers in early summer. Designers can select among the many cultivars for foliage effects. Well-known selections include 'Chocolate Veil', with chocolate brown leaves, and 'Ruby Veil', in which red veins highlight the pale foliage. 'Cathedral Windows' has dark purple leaves with silver tones between the veins.

H. micrantha   Pp. 89, 90

mih-CRAN-thuh. This western North American native is useful in partial shade to full sun, depending on the climate. Var. *diversifolia* 'Palace Purple' is one of the most famous of all heucheras and was selected at Kew (England) for its excellent chocolate-colored foliage. Some material offered under this name may be seed (rather than clonal) propagated and thus not true to form.

H. sanguinea

san-GWIN-ee-uh. Coralbells. This western species is used in gardens with partial shade to full sun. It has green foliage only a few inches tall, and the tiny, coral or red, bell-like flowers are carried well above the leaves. 'June Bride' has white flowers. 'Splendens' has spikes of scarlet flowers. 'White Cloud' is a vigorous seed strain with creamy white flowers.

× *Heucherella*   P. 91

This is an intergeneric hybrid between *Heuchera* and *Tiarella* and can be grown and used as the parents. 'Bridget Bloom' is one of the best-known selections, with green foliage and tiny pink flowers.

Hosta

HOS-tuh. Hosta family, Hostaceae.

The 40 species of *Hosta* are native to Japan, Korea, and China. The genus is related to *Hemerocallis* (daylilies), even though they are technically in separate families. In Japan, homeland of most of the *Hosta* species, they are native to moist woodlands and open meadows in river valleys. Hostas are tough perennials with numerous broad, lance- or heart-shaped leaves rising from the well-defined root crowns. Leaves are green to blue-green, with an apparently infinite selection of leaf colors, ranging from variegated to multihued, with the major colors being white, gold, yellow, lime green, and blue-green. Numerous leaf textures also are available, from totally smooth to seersucker to quilted. Flowers are lily-like but small, often less than 2 inches long, although they can be more than 4 inches long in selections such as 'Honeybells'. Flowers are usually pendent, less often flaring, and grow on almost-leafless flower stalks. They are usually not very fragrant, with two noteworthy exceptions being *H. plantaginea* and 'Honeybells'. The name commemorates the Host brothers of Austria, botanists and physicians of the late 1700s and early 1800s. The common names plantain lilies and funkia apply to the genus as a whole, not individual species or selections.

HOW TO GROW

Hostas are versatile, elegant, and reliable perennials that will persist and slowly spread for generations if their basic needs are met. Grow them in moist but not wet soil and partial shade. Hostas perform best in slightly acid soil but will grow perfectly well in mildly alkaline soil if it has above-average organic content. Unless noted, they tolerate short-term dryness once established. Hardy from Zone 4 south, depending on the selection.

HOW TO USE

Hostas are often chosen only as accent plants for the garden, but many selections are useful as ground covers in perennial and woody plantings. There has never been a greater diversity of hostas available to the discerning gardener. They are ideal perennials for massing, provided the scale of the plant and the space are kept in mind. Large-leaved hostas require space for display as specimens, let alone for use in masses. Plant them in sweeps in shaded and woodland settings, where they make excellent cover for the dying leaves of early bulbs. Grow them in layers along pathways, mass them under spring-flowering trees, or allow them to stabilize the soil of banks or stream edges. As long as there is partial shade and adequate moisture, there is a hosta for any site and design. Hundreds of hosta selections are available, offering an immense spectrum of leaf color and form. Some gardeners will argue that every hosta can be used as a ground cover in the right situation, but to be listed here, the plant must meet many criteria. First, it must have a track record as a reliable performer in a range of shade conditions. Second, it must have a classic leaf form that is small to medium in size and recessive in coloration. Third, it must be eminently neglectable. And finally, it must be reasonably priced. These characteristics allow the plants to be massed beautifully in an overall composition without calling undue attention to themselves. These hostas are members of the "chorus"; it's up to you which plants, including other hostas, are the featured "stars."

S P E C I E S

H. lancifolia
P. 93

lan-suh-FOL-ee-uh. The glossy, relatively narrow leaves are dark green. Plants grow to more than 1 foot tall and spread quickly. The lavender-violet flowers appear in late summer.

H. plantaginea
P. 94

plan-tuh-JIH-nee-uh. Glossy, light green, heart-shaped leaves form the backdrop to large, spectacular, fragrant white flowers in late summer to early fall. Plants are medium size and full. This is one of the classic garden plants to mass in sites with light shade and adequate moisture, as it forms dense, fragrant, minimal-care masses.

H. sieboldiana var. elegans ('Elegans')

see-bol-dee-AH-nuh var. EL-uh-ganz. This is one of the best medium-size hostas, forming exquisite masses with its blue-gray and slightly quilted leaves. The white flowers bloom in summer.

H. ventricosa

veh-trih-KO-suh. A large, green-leaved hosta with heart-shaped leaves that have a slight ripple along the edge, this species forms substantial clumps and masses. The dark purple flowers appear in mid- to late summer.

C U L T I V A R S

'Allan P. McConnell' is one of the best hostas for ground cover and edging. It has small, oval, dark green leaves embellished with a white edge. The purple flowers are held on 15-inch scapes in midseason.

'Blue Cadet' is a very good glaucous form with blue-green, heart-shaped leaves to 6 inches tall. Plants clump well and spread. The lavender flowers appear in late summer.

'Francee' is one of the all-time classic hostas. It is medium size, with elongated, heart-shaped, green leaves edged in white. The lavender-purple flowers bloom in midsummer.

'Ginko Craig' is a vigorous grower that has narrow, white-edged leaves that reach 12 inches tall. The purple-lavender flowers appear in mid- to late summer.

'Golden Tiara' forms vigorous, compact clumps to 10 inches tall. The small green leaves are heart-shaped and have a golden edge all season. The deep lavender flowers appear in summer.

'Honeybells' is aptly named for the fragrant white or pale lilac flowers, which appear in late summer on stalks 3 feet or more tall. The large, pale green leaves are 18 inches or more long, and the plants grow rapidly.

'Pacific Blue Edger' is a vigorously growing and spreading, blue-leaved hosta that reaches 15 to 18 inches tall and is excellent for massing. The pale lavender blooms appear in midsummer.

❧ *Houttuynia*

hoo-TIN-ee-uh. Lizard's tail family, Saururaceae.

Ask someone to crush a leaf of *Houttuynia* and watch his or her reaction — the strong, bitter orange fragrance suggests that this is a plant with a potent personality. Native from Japan to the Himalayas of China and India, the single species of *Houttuynia*, which is in the same family as the California wetlands native *Anemonopsis*, is an aggressive perennial in marshy aquatic sites and moist soils and spreads rapidly by subterranean stems. The leafy stems typically grow to 18 inches or more tall. The alternate leaves are often heart shaped. The small, yellowish flowers are visible above the four showy, white bracts (modified leaves), which are often mistaken as petals. There are garden forms with double bracts, and several patterns of leaf coloration and variegation. Houttuynias are seriously invasive pests in moist soils and wetlands and should be considered for use only where they can be controlled, as by planting in sunken tubs and liners. When grown in drier garden soils, however, houttuynias are likely to die out within a few years. The name commemorates Dr. Martin Houttuyn, an eighteenth-century Dutch naturalist.

HOW TO GROW

Houttuynias do best in nearly full sun to partial shade and moist soils of average fertility. They benefit from more shade when soils are drier. To restrict their rampant growth, plant them in almost-dry conditions or containerize them. Hardy in Zones 6 to 9 and useful where they can be managed.

HOW TO USE

Named cultivars have special features that make them attractive garden plants, provided their growth can be restricted. Plant them in beds that are edged with metal or stone, or use them in front of large, vigorously growing shrubs. This ground cover will overwhelm most companion plantings.

H. cordata   P. 94

cor-DAH-tuh. The wild form of the species is rarely seen in gardens because of its weedy nature. 'Chameleon' ('Tricolor') has orange, red, green, and cream leaf markings and is highly ornamental. When planted in sites with moist soil and partial shade to morning sun, it will spread rampantly. 'Chameleon' is best reserved for large containers, where its brilliantly colored foliage can be enjoyed under optimum control. 'Flore Pleno' has green foliage and creamy white, double-bracted flowers, almost like those of a miniature gardenia. It is a less vigorous spreader.

🌿 Hydrangea

hi-DRAN-jee-uh. Hydrangea family, Hydrangeaceae.

Mention hydrangeas, and most gardeners envision shrubs with blue, white, pink, or red flowers in lacy or mop-headed displays. Of the 80 *Hydrangea* species, only a few are useful as ground covers. They are native to Europe, Asia, and the Americas, and are related to mock orange *(Philadelphus)* and deutzias. Hydrangeas are deciduous shrubs and climbing vines. The oval leaves are opposite and sometimes toothed. Flowers are individually small and arranged in large, flat or pyramidal displays. In many species, the outer clusters of flowers have showy, petal-like bracts up to ½ inch long, giving the flowering mass the appearance of a pancake garnished with flowers at the edge. The name is Greek and means "water vessels." The tiny, dry fruits do indeed look like the amphorae used in ancient times.

HOW TO GROW

H. anomala ssp. *petiolaris* naturally forms a ground cover. It will often grow very little for the first year or two after planting, but during this time, the plant establishes an impressive root system. After this establishment period, the plants will grow at a remarkable rate. When planting hydrangeas to climb or cover an object or wall, it is best to place them on the north or east side, where the soil tends to be cooler and moister. From this location, they will ramble to the sunnier and drier side. Useful in Zones 5 to 9.

HOW TO USE

Use *H. anomala* ssp. *petiolaris* in partial shade where it can spread and climb up tall, pruned trees, especially if there has been storm damage and you would like to cover an unsightly pruning cut. Think of turning a tall, skinny tree trunk into a column of creamy white flowers and rich brown stems. Or guide the hydrangea up a sturdy chimney, allow it to weave through a chainlink fence, or let it lie along the top of a wall. A story is told of an old hydrangea that had climbed high into a tall sugar maple. A storm took down the maple, but the owners rescued most of the hydrangea and laid it on top of an adjacent stone wall. The plant, now in full sun rather than shade, never missed a beat.

H. anomala ssp. *petiolaris* P. 95

ah NOM-ah-luh ssp. pet-ee-o-LAIR-iss. Climbing Hydrangea. Though usually thought of only as a vine, this hydrangea makes an effective carpet, rooting as it goes. It will clamber with agility over tree stumps, rocks, and walls. It prefers partial shade or woodland conditions. The creamy white flower heads develop with maturity. This is a plant for delayed gratification, and there is no substitute for time.

❦ *Hypericum*

hy-PER-i-cum. St. Johnswort family, Clusiaceae.

The 200 to 300 species of *Hypericum* are native to Europe, Asia, and the Americas, with a great number of them found from southern Europe to western Asia. Hypericums are perennials and shrubs, typically with opposite leaves. Leaves are dotted with oil cells, giving them the fanciful appearance of being pierced or wounded—literally, punctate (as in punctured). The flowers are bright to golden yellow and measure from 1 to more than 3 inches across. Only a few of the species are spreading, low shrubs useful as ground covers. The common and scientific names may have related meanings. *Hypericum* can be translated in various ways, one of which is "above the icon." It has been suggested that this may reflect early Christians' use of sprigs with religious images, where the punctate leaves were used to represent triumph over the Devil. The plant is believed to have been associated with the ancient midsummer feast of Walpurgisnacht, which became Christianized as the feast of St. John on June 24. In Europe and the Mediterranean, plants of this genus are known as the rose of Sharon.

HOW TO GROW

Plant hypericums in almost any well-drained, fertile soil. They will grow in full sun to partial shade, but bloom is better with more sun. In the southern part of their range, they need more water in sunnier sites. Hardiness depends on the species.

HOW TO USE

Use hypericums to carpet a steep slope, border a parking lot, or face down any number of trees and shrubs. They are lovely in flower (coveted by floral designers for their longevity) and adaptable to many garden situations. In the magnificent landscape of the Bloedel Reserve (Washington State), hypericums are used to make a memorable golden carpet anchoring a spectacular view.

H. calycinum   P. 95

kal-i-SY-num. St. Johnswort. This is an excellent ground cover for both sun and shade. It will grow in most soils and will tolerate some drought once established. Plants reach 1 foot tall, spread by rhizomes, and have semievergreen foliage. They are useful in controlling erosion on banks, but the strong root system may be invasive. Shear in spring to keep compact. Useful in Zones 6 to 9.

H. olympicum

oh-LIM-pick-um. This small European shrub grows to only 15 inches tall and makes an attractive, ground-hugging mass. The bright yellow flowers are displayed in clusters. Useful in Zones 6 to 9.

H. reptans

REP-tanz. This carpet-forming Chinese shrub with rooting branches spreads to more than 3 feet across. The small, light green leaves form a backdrop for the large, yellow flowers. Useful in Zones 7 to 10.

❦ *Iberis*

EYE-ber-iss. Mustard family, Brassicaceae.

The 30 to 40 species of *Iberis* are native to Europe and Asia, with many of the species native to the Mediterranean region. *Iberis* is related to *Alyssum* and all the mustards of culinary use. *Iberis* species may be annuals, perennials, or low shrubs. The small, evergreen leaves are linear or spatula shaped. The numerous flowers are only about ½ inch across but are massed in striking displays. Fruits are insignificant. The name honors Iberia, the European peninsula formed by Portugal and Spain, where many species are native.

HOW TO GROW

Grow *Iberis* in full sun. Soil should be well drained, alkaline, and sandy or gravelly. Plants perform best if you deadhead them after flowering. They will fuse into a dense mat within several years. Protect *Iberis* from drying winter winds. Useful as a ground cover in Zones 6 to 9, although they are root hardy in colder zones.

HOW TO USE

Like putting on a clean white shirt, adding *Iberis* to the garden makes everything appear neater and crisper. The contrast between the bleached white of the flowers and the lively green of the foliage suggests that *Iberis* be planted to define areas. Use it as a massed ground cover with clipped box domes, plant it along pathways as a base for more relaxed flowering shrubs such as *Viburnum burkwoodii* or *V. sargentii*, or use it to highlight a plant with beautiful bark. In general, *Iberis* seems most successful when combined with plants that have distinctive foliage, bark, or flowers. Note that *Iberis* may not do well if it is shaded.

I. sempervirens (I. commutata)　　　　P. 96

sem-per-VY-rens. Evergreen Candytuft. This pretty, matlike, perennial ground cover sparkles with some of spring's brightest white blossoms. It grows 6 to 12 inches tall, although the stems bend to the ground and root as they touch. Root hardy to Zone 4. 'Alexander's White' has a compact habit and early bloom, making it popular as a ground cover for sunny sites. 'Schneeflocke' ('Snowflake') has larger flowers than the species and dark green leaves.

ᴠᴪ *Ilex*

EYE-lex. Holly family, Aquifoliaceae.

Hollies are deciduous or evergreen shrubs and trees native to most of the world, with the majority of the 400 species originating in Asia, Europe, and the Americas. *Ilex* is in a family with no other important ornamentals. In a genus this large, it is no surprise that there is a great deal of variation in leaves. They can be deciduous or evergreen, less than ½ inch to more than 6 inches long, and spiny or not. Flowers are insignificant from an ornamental perspective, but plants are either male or female. The highly ornamental fruits, which can be red, orange, white, or black, grow only on female plants. Consequently, both genders should be planted to ensure good fruit production, although the planting can be heavily skewed toward females. The name is Latin and is thought to have been originally applied to an evergreen oak.

HOW TO GROW

There are relatively few ground-covering hollies. They need acid to slightly acid soil and full sun to partial shade, as is true of most hollies. Protect evergreen species from drying winter winds. Hardy from Zone 3 south, depending on the species.

HOW TO USE

In formal gardens, hollies and box are preferred for massing. Many ancient gardens in Europe, especially in Italy and France, include large plantings of hollies. Formal American gardens also use hollies, and in some areas, selections of *I. crenata* (Japanese holly) are used as box substitutes. For massing purposes, allow low-growing hollies to form gently swelling masses or, for a more dramatic effect, shear them into abstract drifts and forms. Dwarf selections of the deciduous species can be massed for dramatic fruit displays.

I. crenata   P. 96

kren-AH-tuh. Japanese Holly, Box-leaved Japanese Holly. The species is in general too tall for a ground cover, but smaller selections are available. Useful in Zones 6 to 9. 'Helleri' forms tight, spreading and mounding evergreen mats that grow to more than 3 feet across. This female selection always looks neat.

I. glabra   P. 97

GLAB-ruh. Inkberry. Although inkberry is typically a loose, open shrub, horticultural selections have been made to emphasize tighter and lower growth that is well suited to massing. Useful in Zones 4 to 9. 'Compacta' is a dwarf form with smaller leaves and tighter branches. It is a female selection.

I. verticillata   P. 97

ver-tiss-i-LAH-tuh. Swamp Holly. This deciduous North American native is normally thought of as a large shrub for moist sites in naturalistic landscapes in Zones 3 to 9. 'Nana' (possibly identical to 'Red Sprite') is much smaller and is useful for massing as a ground cover, as it matures to about 3 feet tall and spreads wider. The bright red fruits mature in fall as the leaves drop. To ensure the fruiting display, you must have a few males in the planting. 'Dwarf Male' is equally compact.

❦ Indigofera

in-dig-OFF-er-uh. Pea family, Fabaceae.

Indigofera is an enormous genus of nearly 800 species of perennials and shrubs native to warm zones throughout the world. It is in the pea family with *Trifolium* (clover) and *Lupinus* (lupines). The deciduous leaves are compound and have numerous leaflets, including one at the tip. Flowers are less than an inch long, pealike, and rose or pink. The small flowers appear in spikelike clusters that are produced all along the stem. One nonornamental species, *I. tinctoria,* is a traditional source of the blue dye indigo. The name is Latin and means "bearing indigo."

HOW TO GROW

Grow indigoferas in full sun. They are very deep rooted and demand a well-drained but fertile loam that is neutral to slightly alkaline. They may die back to the ground in cold winters but can be cut back and will return to flower on new wood. Indigoferas develop a strong crown at ground level, which must be mulched or covered to prevent damage in severe winters near the northern limit of their range. Like many members of the pea family, plants may sulk if moved after becoming established. Useful in Zones 5 to 9.

HOW TO USE

The charming blooms of indigoferas are the aboveground reward of these bank-stabilizing plants. Their suckering growth habit means a steady spread of the clean, pealike foliage. Their ability to fix nitrogen is a bonus that allows the extensive, spreading root system to improve the site for companion plants. Use with shrubs such as buddlejas and teucriums to create a charming, sun-tolerant combination.

I. incarnata

in-KAR-na-tuh. This low shrub produces fountains of branches that bear light pink flowers in late spring. Plants mature to less than 2 feet tall but are many times wider. Useful in Zones 7 to 10.

I. kirilowii P. 98

kir-uh-LOW-ee-eye. Smaller and hardier than *I. incarnata*, this slowly spreading shrub has pink cotton candy flowers. Useful in Zones 6 (with proper siting) to 10.

☙ *Iris*

EYE-riss. Iris family, Iridaceae.

More than 200 species of *Iris* are found throughout the Northern Hemisphere. *Iris* is an exceptionally variable and useful plant, with species for almost every imaginable type of garden or style, from true aquatics to dwarf species well suited to rock garden culture. Within the iris family, *Iris* is related to *Moraea, Gladiolus,* and *Freesia.* Leaves are flat, sword shaped, and typically arranged like a fan attached to the growing tip of the creeping rhizome. Flowers come in every imaginable color and are highly specialized for pollination by bees. Each flower has only three true petals, the other "petals" being modified floral parts that help attract and then orient the bees so that they can perform their pollinating service. The genus is named for Iris, the Greek goddess of the rainbow, reflecting the wide range of colors.

HOW TO GROW

The wild species of *Iris* grow in almost every imaginable habitat that is neither tropical nor arctic. Consequently, their cultural requirements and hardiness are equally diverse. In general, irises require full to partial sun (the woodland *I. cristata* is a notable exception). Soil should be rich and well drained, except for those species native to wet sites (such as river-banks and shallow water) or those native to drier sites in Mediterranean climates.

HOW TO USE

Beyond the beauty of individual flowers lies the architectural quality of iris foliage. *I. cristata* (the dwarf crested iris) forms low fans of pale green, sword-shaped leaves that curve effortlessly like waves breaking on a beach. Grown in partial shade to partial sun, they are effective summer-dormant ground covers in woodland gardens. *I. tectorum* (Japanese roof iris) has spiky foliage that grows to less than 12 inches tall but spreads to form stalagmite-like spikes. In a moist waterside planting, the magnificent stems of *I. versicolor* (blue flag) and *I. pseudacorus* (yellow flag) mass to hold banks, blur transitions from water to shore, and create brilliant bands of early-summer color. In warmer, drier climates, think of using *I. pallida* massed as a foliage accent on hillsides or creating broad swales of silvery gray swords.

I. cristata   P. 98

cris-TAH-tuh. Dwarf Crested Iris. This eastern North American native forms delightful woodland carpets. Flowers are two-tone lilac-blue and white. Leaves are only several inches tall and go dormant in summer in much of its range. Useful in Zones 3 to 8; hot, dry weather prompts summer dormancy. 'Alba' is a white-flowered selection.

I. pseudacorus   P. 99

sue-DAK-or-us. Yellow Flag. This European native thrives at the water's edge and will tolerate occasional brackish water inundations. The bold foliage provides a striking contrast to other waterside plants and grows to nearly 5 feet tall. Flowers are yellow. Use in extensive masses in landscape settings. Useful in Zones 5 to 9.

I. pumila   P. 99

PEW-mil-uh. Dwarf Bearded Iris. This low European and Asian iris grows to only 5 inches tall and spreads to form masses. Several color selections exist in purple, blue, yellow, and cream. Useful in Zones 4 to 8.

I. tectorum   P. 100

tek-TOR-um. Japanese Roof Iris. The name says it all. This species has leaves that grow to 10 inches tall and spreads moderately quickly in moist, acid soils—as would be found on old thatched roofs. Flowers are lilac-purple and white. Useful in Zones 6 to 9. 'Alba' is a white-flowered selection with a yellow crest.

I. versicolor
ver-si-CUH-lor. Blue Flag. This North American native is becoming recognized for its beauty and usefulness when massed. It requires moist to wet soil and full sun. Flowers are purple or blue. Useful in Zones 3 to 8.

❦ Juniperus
joo-NIP-er-us. Cypress family, Cupressaceae.

Junipers grow throughout the Northern Hemisphere, with the 60 species well distributed in Asia, Europe, and North America. *Juniperus* is in the same family as *Thuja* (arborvitae) and *Microbiota*. Junipers are woody, evergreen plants ranging from prostrate shrubs to trees more than 45 feet tall. All parts of the plants are highly aromatic. All species have juvenile needlelike foliage that is green to bluish green, the blue tones being caused by a natural waxy coating. This juvenile foliage may be retained for the entire life of the plant regardless of its ultimate size or age. Adult foliage is scalelike and not at all prickly. Juniper seeds are produced in fleshy cones commonly called berries. The cones are green when immature and develop distinctive bluish, blackish, or red tones when they mature. Birds prize the cones and eat them, thus dispersing the seeds. The "berries" from *J. communis* are a critical flavoring for gin.

HOW TO GROW
Grow junipers in full sun and well-drained soil. Junipers are not particular as to soil pH, but many species naturally thrive in stony or sandy, alkaline soils derived from limestone, dolomite, and similar rocks. Junipers cannot be rejuvenated from old trunks, so larger plants cannot be severely pruned. Most junipers are susceptible to a variety of diseases, including cedar-apple rust. Disease severity varies both by species and by region, so consult your local Extension Service and nurseries for specific advice. Hardiness depends on the species.

HOW TO USE
Few plants are as effective as ground-covering junipers in providing low-maintenance, evergreen cover for slopes, banks, and other difficult sites.

Prostrate junipers thrive in many seashore locations and are among the most tolerant of needled evergreens for alkaline soils. Those listed here serve well as ground covers on steep, sunny slopes or around buildings and rocks where little else will survive. When selecting junipers for use near paths and walks, remember that people usually find the prickly foliage of most junipers unpleasant. Junipers that are subjected to regular salt spray from surf or splash from salted roads will look much better if the salt is hosed off with fresh water. Hundreds of cultivars exist and vary by plant height, foliage color, and hardiness.

J. chinensis

chih-NEN-siss. Chinese Juniper. This species is native to northern Asia, and the cultivars are useful in Zones 4 to 9. 'San Jose' is a creeper that reaches 12 to 18 inches tall and more than 6 feet wide, with irregular branching. Needles are a muted sage green. 'Sea Spray' grows to 15 inches tall and more than 5 feet across and has blue-green foliage. Var. *sargentii*, Sargent juniper, is a ground-covering juniper native to coastal northern Japan. It will grow in almost pure sand. Plants are 1½ to 2 feet tall and spread to 9 feet. Needles are blue-green.

J. communis

kom-EW-niss. Common Juniper. This species is native to cold and temperate regions of Asia, Europe, and North America, with outlying populations high in the mountains far south of its typical range. Hardy in Zones 2 to 6, it does not perform well where summers are hot and muggy. 'Effusa' is a low grower that spreads to 4 feet across. It has green foliage with silver stripes on the underside.

J. conferta

con-FUR-tuh. Shore Juniper. Although the species grows wild only on the islands of Japan and Sakhalin (a Russian island north of Japan), its cultivars are useful in Zones 6 to 8 and grow well in sandy soils. 'Blue Pacific' is a low-growing and relatively heat-tolerant form that grows to 12 inches tall and 6 feet across. Its needles are blue-green. 'Emerald Sea' is dense, low, and relatively salt tolerant. Its emerald green needles have a gray band.

J. horizontalis   P. 100

hor-i-zon-TAL-iss. Creeping Juniper. This North American native grows wild from the Atlantic to the Pacific in northern regions, and some wild populations grow even in Zone 2. All forms are low growing and spread 5 to 10 feet over time. They are useful in Zones 4 to 9. 'Andorra Compacta' ('Plumosa Compacta') grows to 18 inches tall and has dense, gray-green foliage that bronzes in winter. 'Bar Harbor' was originally collected near its namesake town in coastal Maine. Its creeping stems have short side branches that grow up to 10 inches tall. Foliage is blue-gray. 'Blue Chip' ('Blue Moon') is a low spreader with blue foliage on short, upright tips that become purplish in winter. 'Wiltonii' ('Blue Rug') is a classic selection from coastal New England. It is very flat — rarely more than 6 inches tall — and dense. Needles are silvery green with a tinge of purple in winter. Perhaps the intense environment of its native shoreline habitat explains why this cultivar performs relatively well in the Deep South.

J. procumbens
pro-KUM-benz. This Japanese species is useful in Zones 4 to 9. 'Nana' has dense, irregular branches less than 12 inches tall that slowly spread to more than 10 feet. Needles are bluish green.

J. sabina   P. 101
suh-BEE-nuh. Sabin Juniper, Savin Juniper. This species is native to the mountains from central and southern Europe east through the Caucasus and into Siberia. It is useful in Zones 4 to 7 and will not tolerate hot climates. 'Tamariscifolia' is a popular landscape plant that grows to 18 inches tall and 10 to 15 feet across. Needles are light bluish green.

J. squamata   P. 101
skwa-MAH-tuh. Single-seed Juniper. This species grows wild in the mountains of Afghanistan east to China, including Taiwan. Useful in Zones 4 to 8. 'Blue Star' is dwarf (to 12 inches tall) and grows only 4 to 5 feet across. It has prickly, silvery blue foliage. 'Prostrata' is a creeping ground cover with needles that are bluish on top and all green underneath. Both cultivars are slow growing.

❦ Lamium
LAM-ee-um. Mint family, Lamiaceae.

Europe, the Mediterranean, and West Asia are home to the 40 to 50 species of *Lamium*, which are related to *Mentha* (mints), *Thymus* (thymes), and *Salvia* (sages). Dead nettle is the foreboding common name of some lamiums, and it maligns this useful group of garden plants. Wild *Lamium* species are annual or perennial, but all the useful garden forms are perennial herbs with mat-forming, stoloniferous stems. Leaves are opposite, with small, dull teeth. The primary leaf color is green, but the cultivars display a range of variegation and mottling. Flowers are mintlike with two lips, less than an inch long, and white, pink, or purplish mauve. The name is based on a Greek word meaning "throat" and refers either to the constriction in the flower's throat or their overall throatlike profile.

HOW TO GROW

Lamiums grow in deep to light shade and almost any garden soil, provided it is never soggy. Once established, they will persist in almost-dry conditions. If the soil is constantly wet, they will rot. Lamiums will form dense, spreading colonies when conditions are to their liking. Useful in Zones 3 (with careful siting) to 8 or 9.

HOW TO USE

The green or mottled foliage of lamiums, combined with their attractive flowers, makes them choice perennial ground covers for shade. Place them where their lighter tones can set off glossy *Abelia*, face down plantings of *Viburnum* 'Pragense' in light shade, or connect plantings of rhododendrons and cherry laurels with larger garden spaces. Some of the species are noted for their ability to "run for cover," as they quickly form colonies in shadier areas.

L. galeobdolon (Lamiastrum galeobdolon)   P. 102

gah-lee-OB-doe-lon. Yellow Archangel. The attractive, silvery, variegated foliage and bright yellow flowers in spring make this an excellent ground cover for dry shade. It has the ability to carpet large, open spaces and banks as a soil binder, and it serves as a "living light bulb" in dark areas. Expect it to cover a large area. 'Hermann's Pride' is a popular clumping form that adds taller decorative accents to the garden but does not serve as a ground cover unless planted *en masse*. 'Variegatum' ('Florentinum') develops purple-red markings on the foliage in fall. It has a trailing habit and spreads quickly.

L. maculatum   P. 102

mak-yoo-LAH-tum. European Spotted Dead Nettle. This clump-forming, herbaceous ground cover spreads modestly. A number of selections can be massed. All prefer rich loam and do poorly in droughty conditions. 'Aureum' ('Gold Leaf') has yellow foliage with white blotches along the midrib and prefers shade. 'Beacon Silver' has silver foliage edged with green and contrasting pink flowers. 'Chequers' is a popular selection with pink flowers. 'White Nancy' resembles a white-flowered form of 'Beacon Silver'. Both 'Beacon Silver' and 'White Nancy' do best in sites with partial sun and cool summers.

❦ *Lantana*

lan-TAN-uh. Vervain family, Verbenaceae.

The West Indies, tropical America, and South Africa are home to the 150 species of *Lantana,* but only two species are commonly grown in North America. *Lantana* is related to *Verbena* and *Petrea,* both ornamental plants for tropical climates. Lantanas are evergreen or deciduous perennials, shrubs, and vines. They are often treated as annuals in climates too cold for them to overwinter, but where they are hardy, several selections make excellent ground covers. Leaves are opposite, and veins appear to be deeply sunken. Some people find the scent of crushed leaves unpleasantly pungent. Flowers are individually small (about ¼ inch across) but are presented in colorful heads. Flower color is quite diverse, ranging from white to pink, red, yellow, orange, and various other sunset colors. Color often changes as the flowers mature. Fruits are small, black, berrylike, and attractive to birds. The name is an old Latin one for *Viburnum,* although this genus is quite unrelated to *Viburnum.*

HOW TO GROW

Grow lantanas as perennial ground covers in Zones 8 to 10. They are not particular as to soil, although it must not be waterlogged. Lantanas need full sun with good air circulation, as the leaves are susceptible to mildew if grown in partial shade. They have the potential to become weedy and invasive in warm climates, especially given the attractiveness of the fruits to birds. Check with your Extension Service to see if any of the lantanas are invasive in your area.

HOW TO USE

Lantanas are excellent at holding banks and eroding slopes. Where conditions are too muggy for South African succulents in genera such as *Carpobrotus, Lampranthus,* and *Mesembryanthemum* to survive, use one of the lantanas for a low, vibrant ground cover. Be sure to grow them in full sun to avoid unsightly mildew and fungal diseases. Plant them as ground covers along steps and banks, around pools, or anywhere you need a brilliantly colored flowering plant with a long blooming period. New selections are being tried and show promise for continuous bloom during the hot summer months.

L. camara

ka-MAR-uh. Lantana. Known to cold-climate gardeners as annuals for vibrant summer color, this native of South America grows well in dry and semidesert areas, where it is a familiar ornamental. In many tropical and subtropical regions, especially Hawaii, it escapes and is a noxiously invasive plant. *L. camara,* which has flowers with hot colors, has been hybridized with *L. montevidensis* to produce a number of named selections.

L. montevidensis (L. sellowiana)

mon-tay-vid-EN-siss. Trailing Lantana. This attractive species grows 12 to 15 inches tall and spreads 5 to 10 feet. Flowers are purplish pink. It is useful on slopes and dry hillsides, where it can be interplanted with other ground covers.

L. hybrids   P. 103

A wide and expanding range of warm colors—from cream and pale yellow to orange, red, and purple—are available. Among the lower-growing cultivars are the following. 'Cream Carpet' has pale cream flowers with yellow throats. 'Dwarf Orange' has bright orange flowers. 'Dwarf Pink' has pale pink flowers. 'Dwarf Yellow' has yellow flowers. 'Spreading Sunset' has orange flowers. 'Spreading Sunshine' has bright yellow flowers.

❦ Leiophyllum

ly-OH-fil-um. Heath family, Ericaceae.

The single species of *Leiophyllum* is native to the Carolinas, Georgia, and Tennessee, where it is a denizen of the sand hills on the coastal plain, as well as rocky slopes in the Appalachians. *Leiophyllum* is related to *Rhododendron* and *Ledum.* The small, glossy, evergreen leaves can be alternate or opposite. The small, starlike, white flowers are less than an inch across but are gathered into attractive clusters. Fruits are not ornamental. The name is from the Greek for "smooth leaf."

HOW TO GROW

Grow *Leiophyllum* in full sun to bright filtered shade and porous, loamy, moist but not wet, acid soil. Plants must have good drainage, or they will perform poorly, if at all. They can be difficult to establish, so be patient. Useful in Zones 6 to 8.

HOW TO USE

Use the prostrate form (rather than the species) as a distinctive low ground cover. Plant it where it can be appreciated at a pedestrian's viewing range rather than from a car. It is well suited to mass planting at the edge of a sandy wood, reminiscent of the low-country forests where it is native.

L. buxifolium P. 103

bux-ih-FO-lee-um. Box Sand Myrtle. The small, evergreen leaves are attractive year-round, and only in spring are they upstaged by the white flowers. *L. buxifolium* var. *prostratum* is a prostrate, naturally spreading form that is better suited as a ground cover than the species.

☙ *Leucothoe*

lew-KO-tho-ee or lew-KOTH-o-ee. Heath family, Ericaceae.

Most of the 45 species of *Leucothoe* are American natives, except for the handful that come from East Asia. The genus is related to *Vaccinium* (blueberries), *Oxydendrum* (sourwood), and *Pieris* (lily-of-the-valley shrub) and shares their cultural requirements. Leucothoes are shrubs that grow from 2 to 6 feet or more tall. Leaves of most of the species seen in cultivation are evergreen, but deciduous species do exist. Foliage is neat, glossy, and attractive. Leaves are elliptical, with smooth or slightly toothed edges, and often have a prolonged tip. Leaves of the evergreen species have a glossy upper surface that is as reflective as *Rhododendron* leaves. Flowers are white, urn shaped, and displayed in clusters either at the tips of the branches or from short branches along the stems. Fruits are not ornamental. The name recalls one of the brutal myths of ancient Greece, where Leucothea, daughter of a Babylonian king, offends her father and is buried alive for her intransigence. Apollo, horrified by this punishment (and most likely with a significant role in her demise), transforms her into a shrub. Since this particular shrub was unknown to the ancient Greeks, the name was probably used originally for a different genus.

HOW TO GROW

Leucothoes thrive in open woodland sites with rich, organic, acid soils that are well drained but never dry. Such soils are found on forested banks above streams and ponds and in rich, open forested valleys. In gardens, leucothoes thrive in the same kind of conditions preferred by rhododendrons and azaleas. Protection from strong winter sun and drying winds is required. Some species spread by suckers and also may root at the tips. This natural spread results in thickets of short stature—it is possible to see over the masses but not walk through them. From this come the common names fetterbush and dog hobble, as the plants thwart dogs on the hunt.

HOW TO USE

L. axillaris is an elegant, evergreen, ground covering shrub that can be used in formal and woodland sites. Plant it as the understory for large, deciduous trees along a driveway or in an entry courtyard. Mass it in drifts along woodland paths as a companion beneath dogwoods, silverbells, and maples. Use the glossiness of its foliage as a foil to more delicate perennials, such as epimediums, dicentras, trilliums, and Solomon's seal. Put its ground-stabilizing characteristics to work to maintain banks and slopes.

L. axillaris (L. fontanesiana) P. 104

ax-il-LAIR-iss. Fetterbush, Dog Hobble. This shrub is native to the southeastern United States. In humus-rich, acid, well-drained, woodland soils, the fountainlike arching branches and glossy foliage create an elegant form for massing in shady gardens. Over time, it will form a thicket compatible with many other natives. The small, white flowers appear in late spring. Foliage is reported to be unattractive to deer. Useful in Zones 6 to 9. 'Nana' is smaller and slower growing. 'Rainbow' has leaves brushed with cream, pink, and red.

❧ *Liriope*

le-RY-o-pee. Lily-of-the-valley family, Convallariaceae.

Liriope is a popular staple of warm-climate gardens, where its grassy, evergreen foliage provides a neat ground cover under trees and in shaded areas. The name lily turf is applied to any of the five or six species of *Liriope*, which are all native to China, Japan, and Vietnam. *Liriope* is related to *Convallaria* (lily-of-the-valley) and *Ophiopogon* (mondo grass). Indeed, *Liriope* and *Ophiopogon* are often confused. From a gardener's perspective, *Liriope* is hardier and has longer leaves, and the flowers are carried above the foliage. Leaves of *Liriope* range from only a few inches to nearly 18 inches long and from less than ¼ inch to more than 1 inch wide. Foliage is evergreen, except at its northern limit, where it becomes semievergreen in winter. Leaves form loose tussocks on the underground rootstock, and several of the species spread by runners. Flowers, which are a bonus rather than the main attraction, resemble grape hyacinths *(Muscari)*. They are followed by small, glossy, black berries. The name is from Greek mythology and commemorates the woodland nymph who was the mother of Narcissus.

HOW TO GROW

Liriopes thrive in loose, rich, moist, acid soils, but they are amazingly tolerant of a broad range of soil textures. Their extensive root systems develop nutrient- and water-storing nodules, so the plants are capable of withstanding drought, although they do better with periodic watering. Mow or shear in early spring to maintain a neat appearance. At their northern limit, they do best in partial shade to prevent winter sunscald. Once established, *Liriope* is a low-maintenance ground cover that can last for years. Useful with winter protection from Zone 5 *(L. spicata)* or warm Zone 6 *(L. muscari)* to Zone 9.

HOW TO USE

Liriope is not a substitute for a lawn if the intention is to walk on it with any regularity. Visually, however, it can be used to create a lawn-like carpet when viewed at a distance. The clumping species and cultivars of *L. muscari* make excellent ground covers for small areas, as they spread slowly. The vigorous spreading forms of *L. spicata* will form extensive masses given a situation to their liking. Use *L. spicata* on shaded slopes and in broad sweeps under woody plants. Do not plant it with weak companions, as its vigorous stolons will form an impenetrable, overwhelming mass. The larger forms of *L. muscari* and *L. exiliflora,* including variegated forms, are used as facing plants for shrubs and to create sweeping masses of color. 'Majestic' *(L. exiliflora)* is a taller selection with wider, solid green foliage. Useful in Zones 7 to 10. 'Arika-Janshige' ('Silvery Sunproof') has leaves with yellow and white stripes. It tolerates more sun than most others. Useful in Zones 7 to 10.

L. muscari P. 104

mus-CAR-ee. Lily Turf. This species has clumping, evergreen, grasslike foliage. Planted in masses, it can be used as a ground cover. Individual plants spread relatively slowly. A vast number of cultivars have been selected; some of the notable ones are listed here. They vary in foliage characteristics and hardiness. 'Gold-banded' ('Gold Band') has wide green leaves with a gold edge. Useful in Zones 7 to 10 and one of the best for massing. 'Monroe White' ('Alba') is similar to the species, but the plants are not as hardy and the flowers (not leaves) are white. Useful in Zones 8 to 10.

L. spicata P. 105

spy-KAH-tuh. Creeping Lily Turf. Since this species spreads rapidly, use it on banks and where a vigorous, dark green, weed-free ground cover is desired. Useful in Zones 5 (with careful siting, but deciduous) to 10. 'Franklin Mint' has narrow leaves and has a finer texture when massed. Useful in Zones 6 to 10. 'Gin-ryu' (usually offered as 'Silver Dragon') has dark green foliage with silvery white stripes. Useful in Zones 7 to 10.

❦ *Lonicera*

lon-ISS-er-uh. Honeysuckle family, Caprifoliaceae.

The 150 to 200 species of *Lonicera* are native to North America, Europe, North Africa, and Asia, including the Philippines and Malaysia. The genus is related to *Abelia* and *Viburnum*. Most species are shrubs from one to several feet tall; only a relatively few are twining vines. All species have opposite, usually deciduous (less commonly evergreen) leaves. Flowers are tubular and often flare open above a throat that holds very sweet nectar—thus the common name honeysuckle. Flowers open white, yellow, pink, or red and often change color as they age. The species with white flowers are fragrant and likely pollinated by moths attracted by the scent and nectar. In North American gardens, hummingbirds are attracted to some of the species. Fruits are succulent, unpalatably astringent berries beloved by birds. A distinctive feature of the flowers and fruits is that they are paired. Fruits often appear as the Siamese twins of the berry world. Several of the nonnative, shrubby and vining species are invasive pests in North America. *L. japonica* is the only ground-covering species in this category, but it should be planted only where it is not an ecological problem. The name commemorates Adam Lonicer, a German botanist (1528–1586) who wrote a respected herbal that was reprinted for more than a century after his death.

HOW TO GROW

Grow honeysuckles in any reasonably fertile garden soil that is not regularly flooded. Most species prefer light shade to full sun. Hardiness depends on the species.

HOW TO USE

Most species are shrubs (not presented here). Most of the vining species do not form effective ground-covering masses but are best displayed as specimens in garden settings. Use *L. japonica* as a tough, vining ground cover to hold eroding slopes and cover fences.

L. japonica P. 105

juh-PON-i-kuh. Japanese Honeysuckle. This vining species has been grown throughout North America for well over a century and is an established plant in many regions—so much so that most people mistake it for a native. Even so, it is still enjoyed for its sweetly fragrant flowers. The species is widely available, as are several named selections. Useful in Zones 4 to 9. 'Aureoreticulata' ('Variegata') has yellow-veined leaves and grows more slowly. It does best in Zones 5 to 9. 'Halliana' is evergreen in mild climates and semievergreen otherwise. It spreads by stems that root as they touch the ground and is very fast growing and often invasive. It has been widely used as a bank cover throughout most of the warmer regions of North America. 'Purpurea' has purple-tinged leaves and is useful in Zones 4 to 9.

❦ *Luzula*

LOOZ-yoo-luh. Rush family, Juncaceae.

The 80 species of *Luzula* are found throughout the Northern Hemisphere, especially in Europe and Asia. These wood rushes are related to the true rushes *(Juncus)*, which are denizens of moist or wet meadows and waterways. All luzulas are deciduous perennials with straplike leaves. Flowers are much-reduced, wind-pollinated affairs that are grouped into small, angular masses reminiscent of cleaning brushes or abstract art. The fruiting structures have a subtle appeal all their own. The scientific name is based on an Italian common name.

HOW TO GROW

Wood rushes are sturdy, trouble-free plants that are gaining in popularity as excellent ground covers for difficult sites. They add a unique textural effect to shady gardens, and some species are tolerant of the thin, rocky soils found in some forested regions. They require full to partial shade, as would be found in the forest, where sunlight is filtered to the forest floor for only minutes at a time. Well-drained, organic-rich soil is best for the woodland species. Specialty nurseries may offer species from rockier, more exposed sites. Useful in Zones 3 to 8, depending on the species.

HOW TO USE

Consider luzulas when you are faced with a shaded site with either dry or moist soil. They add an unexpected texture to more typical combinations of leaf shapes and flowers. Here is a plant that can spread in a controlled manner and add a linear, grassy element to shadowy areas. Since they are adapted to dry or moist soil conditions, luzulas are suited to most tasks in rooty, dark shade. Although they have grasslike leaves, they cannot be walked on.

L. luzuloides

looz-yoo-LOY-deez. This wood rush makes a dense, sprawling matlike ground cover in shady sites with moist or dry soils. Useful in Zones 3 to 8.

L. nivea   P. 106

nih-VEE-uh. Snowy Wood Rush. The hairy leaves are up to 1 foot long, and the flowers have a whitish cast. Seed heads are cottony. Useful in Zones 4 to 8.

L. sylvatica

sil-VAH-tuh-cuh. Greater Wood Rush. This species has broad, glossy, green leaves about 1 foot long. It masses well in semishade and most soils. Flowers have a tan cast. Useful in Zones 5 to 8. There are several selections for leaf color. 'Aurea' has yellow-chartreuse leaves reminiscent of the color of almost-ripe lemons. It is a bright addition to woodland gardens, where it will form a pool of light in shaded situations. 'Variegata' has evergreen foliage with narrow, creamy bands on the edges. It spreads slowly.

❦ Lysimachia

lis-e-MAK-ee-uh. Primrose family, Primulaceae.

The 165 to 200 species of *Lysimachia* are native throughout the Northern Hemisphere, with the vast majority coming from East Asia or eastern

North America. *Lysimachia* is in the same family as *Cyclamen* and *Primula* (primroses). Lysimachias are annuals, perennials, or small shrubs, but most of the garden species are creeping or erect perennials. Leaves are simple and deciduous, and they range from less than ½ inch to more than 2 inches in length. They may be alternate, opposite, or whorled. Flowers are white, yellow, or occasionally pink, with five to seven petals barely fused at the base. Several species can be quite invasive and become garden pests. The name either commemorates King Lysimachus of Thrace (c. 360–281 B.C.) or is based on a Greek term meaning "ending strife."

HOW TO GROW

All lysimachias prefer wet or moist soil, although they also perform well in merely damp garden sites. They are not particular as to soil pH, and they perform well in partial shade, especially if water is limited. Use the spreading, herbaceous perennials as ground covers in difficult, moist, shady sites, provided you can exclude them from nearby garden areas. Useful in Zones 4 to 8.

HOW TO USE

The lysimachias, especially *L. clethroides,* have deservedly bad reputations as invasive thugs in perennial borders. But planted in appropriate situations, as in sites with high woodland shade and moist, acid soil, their spreading rhizomes produce large drifts of attractive foliage and a floral display in summer. Indeed, some species, such as *L. clethroides,* also have good fall color. Plant smaller species, such as *L. nummularia,* to form glowing carpets of golden flowers (or, as in 'Aurea', golden flowers and leaves) under dark conifers or high-pruned shrubs or trees. The contrast can be stunning.

L. clethroides   P. 106

cleth-ROY-deez. Gooseneck. This handsome and aggressive perennial spreads rapidly and stoloniferously in moist soil. On banks prone to erosion or in large naturalistic settings it can offer vast sheets of clean foliage, arching white flowers in early summer, and attractive fall foliage and stems.

L. nummularia   P. 107

num-yoo-LAH-ree-uh. Creeping Jenny. This is a low (2 inches tall) spreader for quick cover. The yellow flowers are striking against the green leaves.

'Aurea' creates quite an impression with its large pools of yellow foliage. It needs sun to maintain its yellow color. Both forms need moisture and make extensive mats.

❦ *Mahonia*

ma-HO-nee-uh. Barberry family, Berberidaceae.

The 70 to 100 species of *Mahonia* are native to East Asia, North America, and the mountains of Central America. *Mahonia* is related to *Berberis* (barberries) and *Nandina* (heavenly bamboo). Mahonias are evergreen shrubs ranging from mat-forming creepers to bold specimens more than 6 feet tall. Leaves are evergreen and range in color from yellowish green to dark glossy green. They are dissected and have 3 to more than 40 leaflets, depending on the species. The bright yellow, fragrant flowers are individually small but massed into dramatic spikes and clusters in spring. Fruits are ornamental, blue or black (occasionally red) berries that are much loved by birds. The genus is named for Bernard M'Mahon, an early American horticulturist who published *The American Gardener's Calendar*.

HOW TO GROW
Grow mahonias in acid, well-drained but moisture-retentive garden soil. They prefer partial shade and need to be protected from winter sunscald in northern gardens. Useful as ground covers in Zones 6 to 9.

HOW TO USE
Mahonias add textural dimension to tapestries of evergreen ground covers in partial shade and, depending on location, sun. Use the ground covering species and cultivars for their glossy foliage, but plant them far enough back from walkways and paths that the spines on the leaves will not be a nuisance. The spring flowers and magnificent blue berries make this a delightful choice for gardens. The foliage on *M. repens* can turn brilliant red or burgundy, in striking contrast to the blue fruits. Combine with needled evergreens, such as *Microbiota*, and the grassy foliage of *Liriope spicata* for a year-round picture.

M. aquifolium
ah-kwi-FO-lee-um. Oregon Grape. This species is native to the Pacific Northwest and grows to more than 8 feet tall. 'Compactum' is an evergreen,

ground-covering shrub less than half as tall as the species. It is useful for banks and partially shaded areas.

M. repens

P. 107

REP-enz. Creeping Grape Holly. This North American native grows only 12 inches tall and slowly spreads by underground stems. It has blue-green, hollylike foliage and bright yellow flowers in spring. These are followed by grapelike clusters of blue fruits and purple-red foliage. Although full sun produces the best coloration, this *Mahonia* will thrive in high shade where it is not subject to drying winds or early-morning sun in winter.

❦ *Maianthemum*

may-AN-the-mum. Lily-of-the-valley family, Convallariaceae.

Maianthemum (false lily-of-the-valley) is a small genus found in cold and cool regions of North America, Asia, and Europe. It is closely related to *Convallaria* (true lily-of-the-valley), but it is far more cold tolerant and much smaller in stature. *Maianthemum* forms extensive colonies in suitable conditions, as the slender stems spread just under the soil surface. Leaves are deciduous, often only one or two per stem, and usually less than 3 inches long. Flowers are very small, and unlike the true lily-of-the-valley, where flowers are pendent from the arching flower stalks, they are clustered into attractive bottlebrush formations at the tips of the stems. They are mildly fragrant, and when large colonies are in bloom, the forest floor looks as if it has low drifts of flowers strewn across it. Fruits are small berries and rarely seen. The name honors both Maia, the mother of the god Mercury, and her namesake month, May.

HOW TO GROW

Maianthemum thrives in cool woodland conditions. The eastern American species *(M. canadense)* is native from near-arctic regions to cool woodlands in the southern Appalachian Mountains, while the western species *(M. kamtschaticum)* is native from Alaska south to California. For best growth, provide plants with a rich, moist (but not wet), woodland or naturalistic site. As with *Cornus canadensis,* establishing "sods" purchased from reputable nurseries produces quicker results than planting small starts. Protect plants from dry exposures and foot traffic, as they are unforgiving of being walked on. Hardiness depends on the species, but none do well where summers are hot and muggy.

HOW TO USE

In cool woodland and shade gardens, you can combine this petite lily-of-the-valley relative with other native plants such as bunchberry *(Cornus canadensis)*, Christmas fern *(Polystichum)*, columbines *(Aquilegia)*, and Virginia bluebells *(Mertensia)*. It can also be used by itself in small-scale drifts.

M. canadense

can-ah-DEN-see. False Lily-of-the-valley. This species has charmed viewers for centuries. Pierre Redoute, the famous French botanical artist of Napoleon's wife, Josephine, gave this equal treatment in his work on lilies. Only 6 inches tall but spreading quietly by rhizomes, the lovely, heart-shaped leaves clasp the stems of this woodland native. Spikes of little white flowers, followed by red fruits, enliven the area. The species thrives in cool, damp, shaded, acid, woodland soils in Zones 3 to 7.

M. kamtschaticum (M. dilitatum)   P. 108

campt-CHA-tuh-cum. Deerberry. Similar to *M. canadense* but larger, deerberry this one inhabits moist coastal woodlands from Alaska south to northern California. In the garden, it forms extensive colonies from creeping rhizomes when its woodland conditions are met. Hardy in maritime climates in Zones 4 to 8.

❧ *Matteuccia*

ma-TOO-see-uh. Wood fern family, Dryopteridaceae.

There are only two or three species of *Matteuccia,* and yet they are ubiquitous in most of the Northern Hemisphere. *Matteuccia* (ostrich ferns) is related to *Dryopteris* (wood ferns), *Onoclea* (sensitive ferns), and *Athyrium* (lady ferns). Ostrich ferns have dramatic, bold fronds that grow up to 5 feet tall in favorable conditions but are usually somewhat shorter. Fronds are deciduous and rise in clusters or crowns from the rootstocks. Rootstocks produce vigorous stolons that in turn produce new crowns, gradually making great swaths of plants. Spores are produced on separate brown fronds that never turn green. The name commemorates Carlo Matteuci, who did pioneering work on animal electricity.

HOW TO GROW

Ostrich ferns revel in cool, damp to wet, highly organic, acid soils, such as those found on streambanks, alongside ponds, and in wet woodlands of the far north. In garden situations, they must have ample water and should be protected from strong winds. Use as a ground cover in naturalistic settings or as a dramatic foil to a major water feature. When conditions are ideal, this fern will form extensive colonies. Hardy in Zones 3 to 8, but most prolific in Zones 3 to 7.

HOW TO USE

Before the urge to add skirts of shrubby foundation plantings gripped America, ferns were high on the list of desirable plants to use at the bases of houses. Still found at old homesteads in the northern states, ferns such as the *Matteuccia* species thrive on the runoff from gutters and in the deep shade of overhanging roofs. Their winter dormancy allows them to be planted where snow buildup or plowing would damage woody plants. Plant masses of ostrich ferns in moist soil where tall, luxuriant bands of green will add a cooling note to the landscape. They look elegant both near buildings and in naturalized settings of streams and woods.

M. struthiopteris   P. 108

stru-thee-OP-ter-iss. Ostrich Fern. This architectural fern makes a magnificent, deciduous, ground-covering mass that spreads by rhizomes. It thrives in shaded, moist, loamy soil that does not dry out. Protect from wind, or the fronds will break. Typically grows 3 to 5 feet tall and spreads indefinitely.

❦ *Mazus*

MAY-zus. Figwort family, Scrophulariaceae.

The 20 to 30 species of *Mazus* are native from East Asia to Australia and New Zealand. *Mazus* is related to *Mimulus* (monkey flowers), *Antirrhinum* (snapdragons), and *Linaria* (toadflax). All species are mat-forming perennials in moist habitats. The small, deciduous leaves are opposite or sometimes even alternate, dark to light green, and usually have soft teeth or serrations on the edges. Flowers are two lipped and usually bicolored white and blue, although pink and solid white flower forms exist. The name notes the two small bumps on the lower lip of the flower — from the Latin meaning "breasts" or "teats."

HOW TO GROW

Grow *Mazus* in moist, acid to neutral, organic soil. Full sun is acceptable if there is constant moisture. If the plants dry out, they will turn bronze and die. *Mazus* can withstand very light foot traffic where the soil is very moist. Hardiness depends on the species.

HOW TO USE

Plant *Mazus* between steppingstones or along paths, where the tiny flowers add spring color and the bright green foliage can be enjoyed. Or use it as a ground cover in small areas such as damp depressions along paths or pond edges. Plant it only where you will enjoy its determined if petite spread, although a single plant can quickly be divided to cover a considerable area.

M. pumilio

PEW-mil-ee-oh. Dwarf Mazus. This species is native to Australia and New Zealand. It is used in Zone 7 and warmer gardens as a mat-forming carpet. It prefers partial sun or shade and moist, well-drained soil. The pretty white and blue snapdragon-like flowers appear in early summer.

M. reptans P. 109

REP-tanz. Mazus. This blue-flowered, herbaceous creeper is only 1 to 2 inches tall until it blooms. It spreads vigorously where soil is moist, and it is frequently planted as a ground cover between steppingstones or at the edges of paths. Once established, it can magically throw a veil of green over large steppingstones and move on. Useful in Zones 5 to 8. 'Albus' has white flowers.

❦ *Microbiota*

mi-cro-BY-o-tuh. Cypress family, Cupressaceae.

Microbiota is a low-growing, needled, coniferous shrub that is often less than 2 feet tall and spreads beautifully to several feet wide. The sole species, *M. decussata,* is native to mountain ranges near Russia's Pacific coast, an area mistakenly called Siberia in most American references. This gives rise to the common names Siberian cypress and Siberian carpet juniper. *Microbiota* is related to *Juniperus* (junipers) and *Thuja* (arborvitae). We have seen it in the wild north of Vladivostok, growing in full sun on partially stabilized, rocky talus slopes, as well as in the partial shade of the adjacent birch and maple forests. Foliage is juniper-like and ranges from bronzy green to olive green. Seeds are borne singly, each in its own fragile wooden cone that soon breaks apart. The name means "small life" in Greek, possibly in humorous reference to the small stature of the shrub in relation to its arboreal relatives.

HOW TO GROW
Grow *Microbiota* in partial shade to full sun where a juniper-like texture is desired. It will grow well in more shade than junipers can tolerate, however. Foliage typically turns bronze or purple in winter—especially when planted in the sun—then greens back up the following spring. Use as a ground cover near walkways (it is not as prickly as junipers) and on slopes. Useful in Zones 4 to 7.

HOW TO USE
The soft texture and gently arching form of *Microbiota* can be used to develop repeating, low mounds on banks. One of the best evergreen shrubs for uniting a planting in both sun and shade, *Microbiota* combines well with broad-leaved ground covers such as *Mahonia repens* and *Ilex crenata*, as well as with many deciduous and evergreen carpeters, such as *Liriope spicata*, *Epimedium*, *Ajuga*, *Bergenia* (with which it grows natively) and *Vinca*.

M. decussata   P. 109
deh-koo-SAY-tuh. Siberian Carpet Juniper. This hardy, evergreen, ground-covering shrub is less than 3 feet tall but spreads widely. In the landscape, it looks like a juniper growing in partial shade and makes a wide, lacy mass. Given where it grows in nature, it is likely to be hardy to maritime Zone 3, provided there is a reliable snow cover.

❦ *Mitchella*
mit-CHEL-uh. Madder family, Rubiaceae.

The two species of *Mitchella* are native only to eastern North America and eastern Asia. Only the native American species, *M. repens*, is used (or is readily available) as a ground cover. *Mitchella* is related to *Galium* (bedstraw), *Gardenia* (gardenias), and *Coffea* (coffee). It is a prostrate, evergreen herb with small, glossy, green leaves that are only ½ inch or less long, opposite, and held close to the ground. Flowers are petite, white trumpets with four petal lobes, and they are almost always twinned. Fruits are attractive, red berries that typically fuse together to form a single larger, somewhat elliptical fruit. As implied by the common name, partridgeberry, these fruits are important food for birds and small animals in northern forests. The name commemorates John Mitchell (1711–1768), a doctor and botanist in colonial Virginia, who maintained a correspondence with Linnaeus.

HOW TO GROW

Mitchella requires partial shade and moist, well-drained, organic, acid soil. Plants form dense mats under trees and over shaded rocks where conditions are to their liking. In garden culture, they often do well in climates where *Cornus canadensis* or *Epigaea repens* can be grown as ground covers (see those entries). To maintain a full planting, remove fallen leaves that might smother this matting ground cover. Useful in Zones 3 to 7.

HOW TO USE

Partridgeberry can be one of the key plants for giving a sense of place to a developing woodland or an existing shaded site. Combine it with other northern natives such as bunchberry or mayflower as well as trilliums and ferns, or use it as a ground cover to enhance native dogwoods, rhododendrons, blueberries, and hemlocks.

M. repens   P. 110

REE-penz. Partridgeberry. An excellent ground cover for cool, acid, shady sites, this North American native grows close to the ground. The pink or white flowers bloom in spring and are followed by equally attractive red fruits. Since the carpeting mass expands slowly, it is best used in small areas.

❦ *Myoporum*

my-O-por-um. Myoporum family, Myoporaceae.

The 30-plus species of *Myoporum* are native from warm regions of East Asia, across the tropical islands of the Pacific, to Australia and New Zealand. None of the other genera in this family are grown in North American gardens. Related families include the figwort family, with snapdragons *(Antirrhinum),* and the bignonia family, with catalpa trees *(Catalpa)* and trumpet creeper vines *(Campsis).* Myoporums are evergreen shrubs or small trees. Leaves are alternate and range from less than ½ inch to more than 3 inches long. They have very small, clear or colored spots that can be seen when held up to the light. The small flowers are usually white and have five petal lobes. They are followed by dark, berry-like fruits that are dispersed by birds. The name is Greek for "closed pores," in reference to the tiny spots on the leaves.

HOW TO GROW
Myoporums require full sun and good drainage. They are very tolerant of seaside conditions but will do best if provided with supplemental water during dry periods. Ground-covering myoporums are very low and without thorns. They will not tolerate foot traffic. Useful in maritime and arid areas of Zones 9 and 10.

HOW TO USE
Gardeners in hot, dry regions can use evergreen, creeping *M. parvifolium*, as an antidote to the "windswept" look. With good drainage and minimal supplemental water, this species will spread quickly and maintain a well-groomed appearance throughout the year. Use low and prostrate selections as ground covers on banks and in areas where an evergreen cover is desired. Since flowers and fruits are seasonal, the foliage is the attraction and can be used to set off flowering ground covers and perennials.

M. parvifolium   P. 110
par-vuh-FO-lee-um. This prostrate shrub hails from the interior of Australia. It grows only 6 to 8 inches tall but can spread to more than 12 feet. It is popular as a heat-tolerant ground cover from southern California to Arizona, both in desert regions and along the coast, where it looks good with occasional watering. 'Putah Creek' has larger foliage than the species and is taller, reaching nearly 2 feet. It has white flowers in summer, followed by purple berries. 'Tucson' has small, bright green leaves and makes a dense ground cover.

❀ *Nandina*
nan-DEE-nuh. Barberry family, Berberidaceae.

East Asia is the homeland of the only species in this genus, *Nandina domestica*. The common name, heavenly bamboo, falsely implies a relationship with bamboos and grasses. Instead, *Nandina* is closely related to such non-look-alikes as *Berberis* (barberries), *Epimedium* (barrenworts), and *Podophyllum* (May apples). Nandinas are multiple-stemmed shrubs ranging from less than a foot tall in dwarf forms to more than 15 feet tall. The large, dissected leaves are evergreen and have a span of more than 2 feet. Many people mistake them for masses of small leaves on strange, stalklike stems. On close inspection, these leaves are remarkably similar to those of *Epimedium*—only evergreen and much, much larger in scale. The small flowers are white and clustered into huge panicles of blooms, although they may be much less dramatic on dwarf selections. Fruits are brilliant red berries about ¼ to ½ inch in diameter and are readily devoured by birds. In recent years, a number of dwarf selections with colored leaves have come into the trade and are useful for mass planting as ground covers. The normal forms are invasive in parts of the Southeast.

HOW TO GROW
Nandinas grow best in moist soil and light shade, although they can be amazingly tolerant of short droughty periods once established. They are not overly fussy about soil pH. Nandinas spread slowly, so they should be massed from the beginning. They require minimal maintenance. Reliably hardy in Zone 7 and warmer.

HOW TO USE
For a lacy, tropical appearance without the rampant character of bamboo, dwarf nandinas are unsurpassed. Their graceful appearance belies their persistence, so they should be featured where they can be appreciated for their glossy foliage, bright fruits, and dramatic fall and winter color. They make an excellent choice for massing at driveway entrances, along banks, and even on islands in parking lots.

N. domestica   P. 111

doh-MES-ti-kuh. Heavenly Bamboo. The typical form grows to a large, broadly spreading shrub. Dwarf selections are used as ground covers. 'Harbor Dwarf' grows to 18 inches tall and has red-bronze foliage in fall. 'Firepower' is a recent introduction from New Zealand that grows to 2 feet tall. When grown in the light shade of deciduous trees, the flaming red foliage lights up the winter landscape. 'Pygmaea' ('Nana') grows 2 to 3 feet tall and forms a dense mound. This is one of the older selections—be aware that several similar but not identical plants are offered under this name.

🐾 *Nepeta*

NEP-e-tuh. Mint family, Lamiaceae.

This large genus includes catnip and has between 150 and 250 species native to Europe, Asia, and Africa (especially northern Africa). *Nepeta* is related to *Salvia* (sages) and *Mentha* (mints). Plants are strongly branched herbs or subshrubs, usually reaching only 1 to 2 feet tall. Leaves are opposite, green or gray-green, and typically pungently aromatic. Flowers are individually small but are presented in spikelike blue, lavender, or white clusters at the ends of the stems or rising from the leaf nodes. The name is Latin for "aromatic plant," and some authors suggest that it refers to Nepete, an ancient city in Etruria.

HOW TO GROW

Grow nepetas in full sun to very light shade and well-drained garden soil. They thrive in alkaline to circumneutral soil but will tolerate more acid conditions. Nepetas do not live long when their roots are soggy, even seasonally. Hardiness depends on the species, but none of them thrive in muggy weather.

HOW TO USE

The classic combinations of nepetas and roses is but one of the many ways in which this handsome, aromatic herb can be used. Plant it in masses along walkways, allow it to spread under and around old-fashioned shrub roses, arrange drifts along sunny banks, or mix it with the arching stems of *Lespedeza* or *Buddleja*. Use it as a ground cover where the aromatic foliage and attractive flowers can be enjoyed, but not so close to passersby that the presence of bees (which also enjoy the flowers) is an issue. Be aware that cats do like *Nepeta* and will be attracted to the foliage.

N. × *faassenii (N. mussinii)*   P. 111

x fahs-SEN-ee-eye. Persian Catmint. This species makes an herbaceous, gray-foliaged, mounding ground cover. It looks best planted in masses, especially the lower-growing selections. It requires well-drained soil but needs occasional water in summer. Shear back after flowering to encourage new growth and a neater appearance. Useful in Zones 4 to 9. 'Blue Wonder' is lower growing than the species. It has larger leaves and abundant flowers.

N. phyllochlamys

file-O-clam-eez. This species forms a low carpet of silvery gray, aromatic leaves and blue flowers. Useful in Zones 4 to 8.

N. racemosa

ray-see-MO-suh. The low-growing cultivars can be massed as ground covers. Useful in Zones 4 to 8. 'Blue Ice' is a petite plant with frosty blue flowers. 'Walker's Low', reaching only 18 inches tall, is one of the best ground covers. Use it as an especially attractive base for summer-flowering bulbs.

❦ Oenothera

e-NO-the-ruh. Evening primrose family, Onagraceae.

The 80 species of Oenothera are native only to the Americas and the islands of the Caribbean. Most species are endemic to North America. Over the years, these attractive plants have become common garden ornamentals in Europe and Japan. Oenothera is related to Fuchsia (fuchsias) and Epilobium (fireweeds), and like those genera, the flowers are usually large, attractive, and brightly colored. Oenotheras are annuals, biennials, or long-lived perennials, but the species useful as ground covers are all perennials. Leaves are alternate, although they may be clustered into a basal rosette, from which the flowering stalks arise. The large flowers have four petals that together form a broad cup, or flaring bell, atop a very narrow and sometimes long floral tube that is filled with nectar. Flower color, time of bloom (day or night), and pollinators are all interlinked. White-flowered species are usually late-evening or night bloomers, whose pale colors and wafting fragrances attract hawkmoths and luna moths. The yellow, orange, and pink species bloom in the daytime or evening and are often less fragrant, as the butterflies that visit them are aided by the bright colors. In all cases, each flower lasts at most one day. The daytime-blooming species are often known as sundrops. The name Oenothera refers to a plant used in flavoring wines, a popular practice in ancient Greece, but since this genus is truly American, the name referred to some other plant in ancient times.

HOW TO GROW

Grow oenotheras in well-drained, barely moist garden soil and at least one-half to two-thirds full sun. They are not particular as to soil pH. They do need a good deal of summer heat to bloom profusely, so they may not perform well in cool maritime climates or near the northern limit of their range. The perennial species spread by runners that can be controlled by digging out. Useful in Zones 4 to 9.

HOW TO USE
Enjoy oenotheras where both the flowers and their pollinating butterflies and moths can be seen. Evening-blooming species star in naturalistic landscapes, where their spreading tendencies are a benefit. Feature them in large drifts at the edges of meadows and prairies to connect the garden with the wilder areas. Allow them to make striking bands of color along the grasses—perhaps set off by stands of little bluestem or *Panicum*—a thug to catch a thug. Refrain from trying to incorporate them as small-scale ground covers in more domesticated landscapes, as they tend to romp.

O. fruticosa (O. tetragona)   P. 112
fru-tih-CO-suh. Sundrops. This assertive ground cover grows to nearly 2 feet tall and is topped by bright yellow flowers up to 2 inches across in early to midsummer. Sundrops spread well into partly shaded sites, provided the soil is well drained and the sun bright. At the southern edge of its range, the basal leaves are evergreen. Useful in Zones 4 to 9. 'Fyrverkeri' ('Fireworks') has red stems and bold yellow flowers in late spring to early summer. 'Sonnenwende' ('Summer Solstice') has lemon yellow flowers that bloom throughout the summer. 'Youngii' is lower than the species and spreads more slowly. It has yellow flowers in early summer and low mats of red stems in winter.

O. speciosa (O. berlandieri)   P. 112
spee-see-O-suh. Mexican Evening Primrose, Prairie Evening Primrose. This species spreads by underground rhizomes to form mats several feet across. The fragrant flowers are pink or white. Useful in Zones 5 to 9. 'Siskiyou' has large, pink crepe paper–like, flowers during much of the summer. 'Woodside White' has white flowers with a green eye and the same spreading tendency as the species.

❦ *Omphalodes*
om-fa-LO-deez. Borage family, Boraginaceae.

The 25 to 30 *Omphalodes* species are native primarily from the Mediterranean to West Asia. All are annuals or small perennials with forget-me-not–like flowers. *Omphalodes* is very closely related to *Myosotis* (forget-me-nots) and *Pulmonaria* (lungworts) and does well in similar garden situations. Leaves are alternate, deciduous, elliptical, and slightly hairy. Plants rarely grow more than 12 to 15 inches tall, even in bloom. Flowers are individually small, only up to ½ inch across, and sky blue, pink, or white. They are carried above the foliage on highly visible stalks. When grown well, the flowering masses will form a cloudlike haze. Seeds are small and have a slight ridge around the edge—thus the common name navelwort (*wort* is old English for "plant" or "herb").

HOW TO GROW
Navelworts grow well in partial shade and soil that is more gravelly than organic, provided it never fully dries out during spring and early summer. *O. verna* is especially likely to spread unaided, both by seed and by expansion of the crown. Useful in Zones 5 (with proper siting) to 9.

HOW TO USE
Plant these heavenly blue flowers as delicately as a chef adds the final garnish to a culinary creation. Small drifts are perfect for capturing the unearthly quality of the early-spring skies. Set them off with the deep green of ferns or the lustrous tones of European ginger. Or perhaps use the blue to catch the eye and lead the viewer to a patch of *Epimedium*, or even *Sanguinaria*. It is a color to be treasured.

O. cappadocica   P. 113
cah-pah-DO-see-kuh. Navelwort, Blue-eyed Mary. This lovely species comes from Asia Minor. It has clear blue flowers in early summer. Plants spread quietly in cool soil and partial shade. 'Starry Eyes' is from Ireland and has unforgettable, deep blue flowers edged with white.

O. verna
VER-nuh. Navelwort. This ground-hugging species dances along the woodland floor and makes an effective companion for other naturalistic ground covers. 'Alba' is a white-flowering selection.

❦ Ophiopogon
oaf-ee-op-O-gon or oaf-ee-oh-PO-gon. Lily-of-the-valley family, Convallariaceae.

The 20 or so species of *Ophiopogon* are all native to East Asia. Only a few species are seen in North American gardens, where they share the common names lily turf and mondo grass with *Liriope*. The genus is very closely related to *Liriope*, with which it is often confused. From a gardener's perspective, *Ophiopogon* is less hardy, it has shorter and more grasslike leaves, and the flowers are often nearly buried in the foliage. As implied by the common names, the evergreen leaves, when used in masses, create a turflike or lawnlike impression. Unfortunately, this is only an impression, as *Ophiopogon* tolerates only occasional foot traffic. Flowers look like grape hyacinths *(Muscari)* and are carried partially within, rather than boldly above, the foliage. The small, berrylike fruits are easily overlooked from a distance. The scientific name is fanciful and means "snake's beard."

HOW TO GROW

Ophiopogon and *Liriope* have similar garden requirements. They grow best in partial to full shade (especially in shade created by tall, high-branched trees) and moist, well-drained, slightly acid soil. Mondo grass will spread slowly but determinedly by underground runners. Mass plantings may be mowed once a year early in the growing season. Useful from Zone 7 south.

HOW TO USE

Of all the color notes in a garden, black—the color of shadow—is the most unusual, and *O. planiscapus* 'Nigrescens' has it. A mass of this species can be an arresting contrast to expanses of golden or silver leaves, or it can serve as a dark shadow beside whites or pastels. Place it beneath golden hostas and watch the hostas be transformed. Don't ignore the green or variegated mondo grasses; they have an elegance and discreet charm that seems entirely Oriental and a certain neatness that is far removed from the more rambunctious liriopes.

O. japonicus
jap-PON-i-kus. Mondo Grass. This looks and behaves like a shorter, white-flowered *Liriope*. It spreads by underground runners. 'Compactus', 'Minor', 'Nana', and 'Nippon' are dwarf selections that may be used between flag-stones and in other small-scale applications. 'Silver Mist' has variegated green and white foliage that grows to 6 inches tall and spreads slowly.

O. planiscapus 'Nigrescens' ('Arabicus', 'Black Dragon')   P. 114
plan-i-SCAPE-us. Black Mondo Grass. This most unusual ground cover has the blackest foliage of just about any perennial. It spreads extremely slowly but is worth the wait for the unique impression it makes in the landscape when used boldly.

❦ *Osmunda*

os-MUN-duh. Royal fern family, Osmundaceae.

Of the 10 to 12 species of *Osmunda*, only three natives are used as ground covers in North American gardens—*O. cinnamomea* (cinnamon fern), *O. claytoniana* (interrupted fern), and *O. regalis* (royal fern). All of these species have wide geographic distributions, ranging from cool temperate zones to the tropics. They are large, long-lived ferns that prefer moist to wet, woodland soils. They have coarse leaves (technically fronds) that in exceptionally favorable conditions may reach nearly 6 feet in length. Most leaves arise from the stubby crown that is just above ground level, but in spreading forms, the runners give rise to small plants between the crowns. The green leaves never produce spores. Instead, spores are produced seasonally either on specialized, brown, spore-bearing leaves or on one brown section of the otherwise green fronds. In the latter case, the frond looks "interrupted" in the middle and is the source of the common name interrupted fern. The scientific name is from Scandinavia and refers to Thor, the powerful and crafty god of thunder.

HOW TO GROW

Osmundas require moist to swampy organic soil and partial shade. *O. regalis* needs the most moisture, as it grows in seasonally flooded forests. *O. cinnamomea* will tolerate the relatively drier conditions of moist garden soils, while *O. claytoniana* is surprisingly tolerant of typical garden soils once established. In no case should any of these ferns be planted in soils that are allowed to dry out fully, or they will go into a permanent decline. Shade should be at least one-third to two-thirds, except near the northern limit of the species, where they will tolerate more sun once established. Useful from Zone 3 south.

HOW TO USE

Few ferns can match *Osmunda* for their distinctive beauty and majestic character. Place them in recurring masses—perhaps separated by an equally assertive moisture-loving neighbor such as *Clethra* or *Darmera peltata*—and see how the richness of the fronds attracts attention. Osmundas add a certain primeval quality to a garden, and even when they are planted in small drifts, that sense of "raw nature on the loose" comes through.

O. cinnamomea   P. 114

sin-uh-MO-mee-uh. Cinnamon Fern. The cinnamon stick–colored fronds emerge from the center of the crowns and mature to pale green. Depending on conditions, they can reach 3 to 5 feet tall and spread quickly to form dense masses. This fern has an unmistakable architectural quality.

O. claytoniana

clay-TOE-nee-ay-nuh. Interrupted Fern. Similar in many respects to cinnamon fern, interrupted fern is usually shorter and is literally interrupted —individual fronds look gap-toothed. This gap in each large frond makes masses appear somewhat shaggier and wilder than masses of cinnamon fern. Once established, interrupted fern is more tolerant of dry conditions, stonier soils, and more sun than many ferns.

O. regalis

ree-GAL-is. Royal Fern. A magnificent plant for wet or flooded sites, royal fern establishes an elegant mood in settings that are otherwise "just a swamp." The divided fronds emerge bright green, gradually mature to a deep majestic hue, and arch up to several feet long. Spores are presented on specialized, brown fronds. Use these ferns for a dramatic effect in sites where water stands for at least part of the year. They need partial shade and can be accented with wetland-loving, forest-edge plants such as cardinal flower *(Lobelia cardinalis)*, monkey flower *(Mimulus)*, and swamp holly *(Ilex verticillata)*.

❦ *Osteospermum*

os-tee-o-SPERM-um. Aster family, Asteraceae.

South Africa is home to most of the 70-plus *Osteospermum* species. Wild species include annuals, perennials, and low shrubs, but only the perennial species are used in North America. Leaves are alternate, semievergreen or evergreen, and highly variable in shape, ranging from linear to elliptical to deeply dissected. Flowers are daisylike and range in color from dusty violet to rose, lilac, and almost white. The small seeds are very hard, a condition reflected in the scientific name, which means "bony seeds."

HOW TO GROW

Osteospermums require full sun and excellent drainage. Soil should be of medium fertility and only average organic content. Although established plants will tolerate a great deal of drought, they will perform better if given supplemental water during the dry season. Plants can be rejuvenated by cutting them back to firm growth. Useful as a perennial ground cover in Zones 9 and warmer; otherwise useful grown as an annual.

HOW TO USE

Freeway daisies they may be, but the beautiful *O. fruticosum* deserves a place in any garden. Mass them in drifts along walkways, driveways, and slopes in warm, dry climates. Fill planters with them in cooler climates. Whether they are the spoon-shaped cultivars or the more relaxed yellow or purple selections, they will have an impact.

O. fruticosum (Dimorphotheca fruticosa) P. 115

fru-tuh-CO-sum. Freeway Daisies. Frequently planted along highways in southern California, these daisies have thick, mat-forming stems that are less than 12 inches tall but spread to 4 feet or more. They are considered relatively fire retardant and salt tolerant. Foliage is evergreen, and stems root as they trail. Cultivars include white-flowering selections under names such as 'Hybrid White,' 'Snow White,' and 'White Cloud.' Purple-flowering selections are sold as 'African Queen,' 'Nairobi Purple,', and 'Tresco Purple.'

❦ Pachysandra

pak-e-SAN-druh. Box family, Buxaceae.

One of the ubiquitous ground covers in the eastern United States, *Pachysandra* species are excellent workhorse plants. Only two of the four or five species are seen in cultivation, and one, *P. terminalis*, is the most frequently grown. Pachysandras are native to East Asia, with one species, *P. procumbens*, native to the Appalachian Mountains. They are deciduous or evergreen perennials. Leaves are up to 3 inches long and elliptical or oval. Flowers are individually tiny, off-white, and presented on short flower stalks, looking ever so much like stubby, worn-out, white bottle-brushes. The scientific name describes the anthers (pollen-bearing parts) as "thick."

HOW TO GROW

Pachysandras require at least partial shade. They thrive in the filtered light of large, high-branched trees. Soil should be moisture retentive and slightly to strongly acid. Once established, pachysandras are extremely tolerant of neglect, and colonies will slowly spread to the limits of the suitable conditions. At their northern limit, they need to be sited out of strong winter sun. Useful in Zones 5 to 9.

HOW TO USE

If the common pachysandra were rare and difficult to grow, it would be a highly sought-after component of shaded gardens. But sometimes a plant gets a bad reputation just because it is too successful. *Pachysandra* is one of those plants. Plant it under tall, deciduous trees where its glossy foliage can lighten and brighten the shadows — *P. terminalis* 'Green Sheen' is an excellent choice for this situation. Add *Pachysandra* to formal landscapes to blend carpets of taller woody plants into a pleasing composition. Place it as the transition layer between *Carex* or *Luzula* and low-growing conifers. Include variegated forms where their shier growth habit and gray-green foliage can make a striking effect. *P. procumbens* (Allegheny Mountain spurge) is considered a choice and sophisticated plant. Use it massed in woodland gardens, perhaps with native azaleas or kalmias, where its early-spring blooms and low form can complement the other plants' exuberance.

P. procumbens   P. 115
pro-CUM-benz. Allegheny Mountain Spurge. This pachysandra grows 8 to 12 inches tall and slowly spreads (think glacier) as much as 2 to 4 feet. Leaves are a matte green with earth tones and become evergreen at the southern limit of the species. The spikes of pale creamy white or greenish white flowers appear before the new leaves. This is an attractive, slow-growing woodlander appropriate as a small-scale ground cover.

P. terminalis   P. 116
ter-min-AH-liss. Pachysandra. This well-known plant forms a dense, spreading, evergreen ground cover. Leaves are dark green. The tiny, white flower spikes appear in spring. The small, berrylike fruits may be found occasionally on long-established plants. This plant thrives in acid soil, shade, and woodland conditions in northern North America. 'Green Sheen' has glossy, almost varnished, foliage. 'Kingwood' has medium-green leaves and deeply cut teeth at the leaf tips. 'Silver Edge' has gray-green foliage edged with creamy white. It is slow to establish and spread.

🌿 *Parthenocissus*

par-then-o-SIS-us. Grape family, Vitaceae.

Boston ivy, Virginia creeper, and woodbine are the most common names for the ornamental species grown in our gardens. East Asia and eastern North America are the homelands of the 15 species found in the wild. These are deciduous vines that are equally useful as carpeting ground covers, as they are adept at ascending trees, walls, and cliffs. Plants climb both by weaving young stems among supporting objects such as fences and also by affixing tendrils that encircle small branches or other objects of support. Once they are climbing, some species also may root from the stems and nodes and require no further means of support. *Parthenocissus* leaves are lobed (as in Boston ivy, *P. tricuspidata*) or compound, with five to seven leaflets per leaf (as in Virginia creeper, *P. quinquefolia*). All the species, especially Virginia creeper, are noted for exceptionally fine autumn colors. Flowers are tiny and of interest to botanists. Fruits are dark purple-black or black and relished by birds. The common name Virginia creeper accurately reflects the origin of one species in eastern North America, including the colony of Virginia, named for the Virgin Queen, Elizabeth I. The scientific name means "virgin birth vine" and may refer to the fact that the flowers and fruits are not obvious. It also may be a playful allusion by Linnaeus (a Swede) to Virginia and its queen.

HOW TO GROW

Grow these plants as ground covers where a slightly shaggy carpet that reflects the contours of the ground is desired, as in seminaturalistic settings. Plants are not particular as to soil, but it should be of at least average fertility and not subjected to periodic flooding. To maintain the plant's vigor as a ground cover, cut off stems that begin to grow up trees, walls, or other structures so that all the plant's energy is directed to maintaining the living carpet. Useful in Zones 4 or 5 and warmer.

HOW TO USE

Use Boston ivy and Virginia creeper as ground covers where an informal but extensive expanse of uniform foliage in partial shade is desired. Examples include open or disturbed woodlands, small groves or woodlots, along driveways, or partially shaded sites for statuary or art. The clean but low foliage will complement the trees, objects, or major shrub masses that are part of the composition. *Parthenocissus* will overwhelm weaker-growing plants, so if a mixed planting is desired, the other herbaceous selections should be in defined areas within the larger expanse of *Parthenocissus*. It does not tolerate being walked on, so pathways through this ground cover should be defined by steppingstones, logs, constructed edges, or paved surfaces. For best fall color, grow *Parthenocissus* with at least a half day of sun. Plants climbing on walls, structures, and tree trunks will have the best color where they get the most sun.

P. quinquefolia   P. 116
kwink-eh-FO-lee-uh. Virginia Creeper. This vine makes a dense, deciduous ground cover. The mature height is 6 to 8 inches, with indefinite spread. It is effective on banks and for erosion control. It will climb unless controlled by pruning.

P. tricuspidata   P. 117
try-cus-puh-DAY-tuh. Boston Ivy. This Asian species is best used as a climber rather than a ground-covering mass. It is the "ivy" of the Ivy League colleges, where it traditionally covers numerous campus buildings.

❦ *Paxistima*
pak-IS-te-muh. Spindle tree family, Celastraceae.

This uncommon genus of attractive, low-spreading, evergreen shrubs is slowly becoming better known in gardening circles. All five species are native to the mountains of North America, with one species *(P. canbyi)* found only in the Appalachians and the others in the West. It is related to buckthorn, but of an entirely different scale, and it behaves very differently in the garden. The narrow, evergreen leaves are small, often less than 1 inch long, and their edges may be toothed or not. The tough leaves range from alternate to opposite, even on the same stem. Flowers and fruits are ornamentally insignificant. This is a plant chosen for its foliage and growth form.

HOW TO GROW
Grow paxistimas in well-drained soils with at least average organic content. Widely reported as requiring acid soils, at least *P. canbyi* grows well and retains its foliage color on alkaline soils with other lime-loving plants such as lilacs, clematis, and pinks. Plants do best in partial shade and need some protection from winter sun. Hardiness depends on the species.

HOW TO USE

Paxistima can be used in landscapes where the effect of a small-leaved boxwood would be attractive but the gardener prefers a looser, more informal effect. Plant *Paxistima* as a low, evergreen mass under deciduous trees or to face down needled evergreens. Or try it as a loose, informal sweep where a garden merges into partial shade. It makes an attractive mass with other broad-leaved evergreens (such as kalmias and rhododendrons) with mahonias, or with deciduous or evergreen hollies.

P. canbyi   P. 117

KAN-bee-eye. This neat, mounding shrublet with small, holly-like, dull green foliage slowly spreads to several feet across. Branches root as they touch the soil. Useful in Zones 5 to 7.

P. myrtifolia (P. myrsinites)

mer-te-FOL-ee-uh. Oregon Box Holly. Taller and less spreading than *P. canbyi*, but still useful for massing in naturalistic landscapes, this western native does well in cool coastal conditions. Useful in Zones 6 to 8.

❦ *Phalaris*

fa-LAR-iss or FAL-ar-iss. Grass family, Poaceae.

Phalaris, commonly known as ribbon grass, is an extremely useful ground cover that has been misused enough that it has received a bad rap. The 15 species of *Phalaris* are native to North America, Europe, Asia, and North Africa, but only one, *P. arundinacea,* is commonly used as a ground cover. Ribbon grass forms a thick mass of stems and leaves that can grow several feet tall in exceptional conditions. Several variegated forms have been selected over the centuries, and these are the ones most commonly seen in gardens. Plants are strongly stoloniferous and spread vigorously. In some parts of the country, ribbon grass is an invasive pest. Flowers and fruits are both insignificant.

HOW TO GROW

Ribbon grass grows well in a number of difficult sites. It is excellent for erosion control in moist to nearly dry soils and thrives if periodically flooded. It will grow in full sun, provided there is adequate moisture, and will tolerate partial shade. If plants are allowed to dry out, the leaves will turn brown, but a shearing may promote new growth rather quickly. Useful and persistent in Zone 3 and warmer.

HOW TO USE

Plan to grow ribbon grass as a mass you can control—for it will mass with little encouragement from you. Try planting it near the entrance to a driveway, especially if this is a moist or poorly drained area. The light green and white color of the variegated forms will catch car headlights at night, and the area can be mowed in midseason to encourage a flush of new growth. This is also an excellent choice for an area that needs to be seasonally cleared, perhaps for snow removal. At all times, ribbon grass roots should be controlled, either by a physical barrier (such as a path, roadway, or watercourse) or by buried obstacles.

P. arundinacea   P. 118

ar-un-din-AY-see-uh. Ribbon Grass. This species spreads by underground runners. It will move quickly through rich, well-drained soils but will slow down in heavy wet soils. Plant it with care; once established, it is difficult to eradicate. *P. arundinacea* var. *picta* has green and white foliage. 'Feesey' ('Feesey's Variety') is a vigorously spreading selection with narrow foliage that is pinkish as the new leaves emerge.

✿ *Phlox*

floks. Phlox family, Polemoniaceae.

Phlox needs no introduction to most gardeners, although many are familiar only with the brightly flowering species used in borders and as cut flowers. The 60 species of *Phlox* have great natural diversity and include several that are best used as ground covers. All do well in most parts of North America, since all except one, an Asian species, are native here. Phlox are annuals or perennials. They have deciduous, opposite leaves that are usually soft and several inches long, but some species, such as *P. subulata*, have needlelike foliage. Flowers are produced in late spring to early summer and are held above the foliage. Their five petals flare to produce a flat, trumpet-shaped blossom in shades of white, pink, red, lavender, or purple. The colors are bright signals to the butterflies that pollinate the flowers. Fruits are not ornamental. The scientific name is Greek for "burning" or "flame," in reference to the bright colors.

HOW TO GROW

Phlox require full sun to partial shade, depending on the species. Woodland species, such as *P. divaricata*, require partial shade and moist, rich soil with above-average organic content. These species should never be allowed to dry out completely, or they will go dormant and not regrow well that season. The species native to rocky slopes and exposed areas, such as *P. subulata*, require full sun to minimal shade. Blooming vigor decreases rapidly with increasing shade. These species like garden situations that mimic their natural haunts—well-drained, gritty soils with some moisture retention—but constant moisture will cause the plants to rot. Phlox are not particularly fussy about soil pH, provided their moisture and drainage needs are met. Hardiness varies by species.

HOW TO USE

Many species of carpeting phlox are among the most charming and hardworking spring flowers. Use *P. divaricata* to create a woodland scene where its blue, purple, or white blossoms will float above the low mat of green foliage and complement spring-blooming azaleas and mountain laurels. Consider a carpet of *P. divaricata* under *Halesia*, to be followed by ferns or hostas. *P. stolonifera* is one of the hardiest spring-blooming perennials, adding its own low drifts of color in eastern and northern woodlands and shaded gardens. Since these species may be summer dormant, be sure to mask the empty spaces with late-appearing ferns, other perennials, or summer annuals. For a sunny wall, choose *P. subulata* to add a cloak of color. You also can use it in other sunny areas with excellent drainage, such as rocky slopes and gravelly banks. Remember that you can shear *P. subulata* back after flowering to increase its spread and discourage ranginess.

P. divaricata (P. canadensis) P. 118

dih-var-i-KAH-tuh. Wild Sweet William. This wild blue phlox is native to the western United States. Hardy to Zone 3, it makes a low, spreading, matlike ground cover that grows 8 to 12 inches tall and spreads several feet. It does best in moist, humus-rich soil with adequate water and high shade. It is summer dormant in dry climates. 'Clouds of Perfume' has fragrant, ice blue flowers. 'Fuller's White' is a time-tested selection with white flowers. 'May Breeze' is a new cultivar with pale blue flowers. *P. divaricata* ssp. *laphamii* 'Chattahoochee' has mauve-blue flowers.

P. × procumbens

x pro-CUM-benz. Many cultivars bred from *P. subulata*, including those with the name 'Millstream', are often listed under this species.

P. stolonifera

sto-lo-NIFF-er-uh. Creeping Phlox. This species prefers light to full shade and usually goes summer dormant. 'Blue Ridge' has lavender-blue flowers. 'Bruce's White' has pure white flowers and semievergreen, matlike foliage. 'Sherwood Purple' has mauve flowers and is a vigorous grower.

P. subulata   P. 119

sub-yoo-LAH-tuh. Moss Pink. This low-growing, carpetlike spreader has a mossy appearance but a prickly texture. It blooms exuberantly for 2 to 4 weeks in spring, and although it requires full sun, it is quite drought tolerant. 'Emerald Cushion Blue' has blue-lavender flowers on dense, evergreen foliage. 'Emerald Cushion Pink' has pink flowers. 'Red Wings' has rose-red blooms with dark centers. 'White Delight' has white flowers.

Pleioblastus

ply-o-BLAST-us. Grass family, Poaceae.

The number of species in *Pleioblastus* depends on which botanist wrote the text. When *Pleioblastus* is broadly defined (as it is here), it is a diverse genus of bamboos with well over 150 species from warm climates throughout the world (although all the species included here are Asian). When the narrow definition is used, many of the species listed here move over to *Arundinaria*. *Pleioblastus* species are woody-stemmed grasses ranging from less than 2 feet to more than 15 feet tall. Leaves are linear, usually less than 1 inch wide and 6 inches long. Flowers are insignificant and, as with most bamboos, usually signal the end of the plant's life. These bamboos are vigorous spreaders by means of underground stems and have the potential to be both weedy and persistent. The name means "more buds," as there is usually more than one bud where the side branches sprout from the canes.

HOW TO GROW

These bamboos do best in light shade and are completely intolerant of repeated drying. Consequently, soil texture and content are not as important as consistent moisture, without being soggy or desiccated. Plants will spread vigorously if their requirements are met, and thus they must be sited carefully to control their spread. Barriers such as major foundations, extensive impenetrable surfaces, and control edges (try buried conveyor belts) will limit spread. Hardiness depends on the species. *Pleio-*

blastus species are often root hardy to one zone colder than where the aboveground part is winter hardy.

HOW TO USE

Plant *Pleioblastus* only where its aggressive tendencies can be controlled. If you have ever seen photographs of hillsides in Asia completely covered by bamboo, you will understand the importance of this warning. At the Royal Botanic Gardens at Kew, England, the staff has installed old industrial conveyor belts to control the plants' spread. When restricted by natural or installed barriers, they become magnificent, low-maintenance ground covers. To establish bamboos, plant them in spring in moist soil and light shade. Consider bamboos for erosion control and low-maintenance plantings in shaded city lots, where nearby sidewalks and roadbeds can act as barriers.

P. auricomus (Arundinaria viridistriata) P. 119
aur-IK-o-mus. Yellow-stripe Bamboo. Growing to 2 feet tall and with fluorescent yellow foliage, this species is less invasive than *P. pygmaeus* and is distinctive for its brilliant color. It requires sun and good drainage. Useful in Zone 7 (Zone 6 with careful siting) and warmer.

P. pygmaeus (Arundinaria pygmaea)
pig-MEE-us. Dwarf Running Bamboo. With grassy foliage to only 1 foot tall but of unlimited spread, dwarf running bamboo is useful for difficult sites, such as a steep bank between walls, where it will make a quick and effective ground cover. This bamboo must be physically controlled, or it will invade adjacent areas until the limits of suitable conditions are met. Useful in Zone 8 and warmer.

🌿 *Plumbago*
plum-BAY-go. Sea lavender family, Plumbaginaceae.

Plumbago includes 12 species of perennials, shrubs, and shrubby vines native to several warm regions around the world. They are commonly known as leadworts. Like the related sea lavenders *(Limonium)* and thrifts *(Armeria)*, leadworts are native to and tolerant of salty, calcareous, rocky, and otherwise difficult, dry sites. They have simple, alternate leaves that are usually elliptical in outline, although they may be lobed at the base. Leaves are deciduous or semievergreen. Flowers are generally showy and clustered into headlike arrangements reminiscent of garden phlox. They range in color from white through a spectrum of blues. Flower color of a particular plant is fixed for life, but plants do vary in hue, so if precise color matching is critical, it is important to select individual plants when in bloom. The only commonly grown species in North America is *P. auriculata*, a vigorous, semievergreen shrub or vine that reaches 6 to 8 feet tall and spreads 10 to 12 feet. In most parts of North America, when gardeners refer to "plumbago," they mean the plant included in this encyclopedia as *Ceratostigma plumbaginoides*.

HOW TO GROW
P. auriculata requires perfect drainage and, once established, is quite drought tolerant. It is not particular as to soil, provided it is in full to only partial sun. Useful in Zone 9 and warmer.

HOW TO USE
Gardeners in the Pacific states can use *P. auriculata* as a ground-covering shrub or vine for dry banks and slopes where its height and spread can make a visual barrier, as at the back or top of a slope. It is also useful as a hedge or barrier plant where ocean salt may be a problem.

P. auriculata (P. capensis)   P. 120
aur-IK-yoo-lay-tuh. Cape Plumbago. This South African native is adapted to mild, moist winters and hot, dry summers. It makes an effective, sprawling ground cover in southern and interior California in well-drained soil. Occasional supplemental watering will keep the plants full. Flowers are blue and may be bleached out in hot desert areas. *P. auriculata* var. *alba* has white flowers.

P. larpentiae See *Ceratostigma plumbaginoides*

❦ *Potentilla*
po-ten-TIL-uh. Rose family, Rosaceae.

The 500 species of *Potentilla* are native throughout the world, with most growing in the Northern Hemisphere. *Potentilla* is closely related to *Rosa* (roses) and in general will do well in a similar range of garden conditions. Leaves are deeply lobed or dissected into numerous leaflets. They are arranged as a tight basal rosette or are alternate along the stems. Flowers are five petaled, usually white or yellow, and very similar in size and shape to those of wild blackberries and raspberries. The dry fruits are insignificant. The Latin name means "powerful," as the plants were used in traditional medicines.

HOW TO GROW

Grow the species listed here in a wide range of good garden soils, provided they are well drained but not excessively dry and of only average fertility. Plants do best in full to nearly full sun. Hardiness depends on the species.

HOW TO USE

These evergreen and deciduous shrubs and perennials make attractive mats and masses. Some of the perennials are evergreen except in extreme temperatures. Many woody species will tolerate high temperatures and can be massed effectively in hot, dry conditions. Be prepared to prune and shape woody specimens to create billowy mounds.

P. cinerea (P. tommasiniana)

sin-eh-REE-uh. This ground-covering species makes a low carpet to 4 inches tall with gray or silver leaflets. It grows in full sun to very light shade. Useful in Zones 5 to 9 and may be evergreen in warm coastal areas.

P. neumanniana (P. tabernaemontana, P. verna)

new-man-ee-AH-nuh. Spring Cinquefoil. This versatile ground cover is sometimes planted as a "viewing lawn"—eyes only, no feet. It is a tufted creeper that grows to 6 inches tall and has soft yellow flowers. This fast-spreading ground cover is often used as a carpet below and after spring bulbs. There are several named cultivars in the trade. Useful in Zones 5 to 9.

P. tridentata (Sibbaldiopis tridentata) P. 120

try-den-TAY-tuh. Wine-leaf Cinquefoil, Trident Cinquefoil. This is a fast-growing ground cover for banks or rocky situations in Zones 3 to 7. It does best in full sun and sandy, well-drained soil, but it needs some moisture to become established.

❦ Pratia

PRAY-tee-uh. Bellflower family, Campanulaceae.

Most gardeners seeing *Pratia* in bloom would correctly think they were looking at something related to *Lobelia* or *Scaevola,* and indeed the genus is very close to *Lobelia.* Like lobelias, pratias are perennials that like moist to wet, acid soil, but unlike lobelias, they are native only from Australia and New Zealand to South America, with 1 species (of the 30) native to southern Africa. Pratias are creeping plants that root along the stems. The small, alternate, rounded leaves are almost succulent. Flowers are five petaled; lilac-blue, rose, or white; and reminiscent of lobelia flowers. The succulent, berrylike fruits are purplish red. The name commemorates a French naval officer who set off on a fabled natural history expedition in the early 1800s but who died only days after the vessel departed France.

HOW TO GROW

These plants are rather unfamiliar to most North American gardeners, since they are only partially frost tolerant and quite demanding in their moisture requirements. Where these conditions can be met on the Pacific, Gulf, and Atlantic Coasts, the plants make dramatic, small-scale ground covers. Pratias need moist, soggy, or boggy soil that is also organic and acid. They also require cool soil, as is provided by running water coming from springs or coastal mountains. They prefer full sun to partial shade. They are useful as perennials from Zone 8 south.

HOW TO USE

If you live in a warm climate or in a colder climate but have a solarium attached to your home, use this charming creeper between steppingstones or at the edges of paths in wet areas. The tiny, round leaves look like "baby tears," and the flowers come in rich shades of blue, rose, and white. Plants will tolerate an occasional footstep, although they should not be walked on.

P. angulata (Lobelia angulata)   P. 121

an-gule-AY-tuh. This low, mat-forming ground cover with dark, zigzag stems has blue and white flowers in spring and early summer. It prefers light shade and abundant moisture in warm climates.

❦ *Prunella*

proo-NEL-uh. Mint family, Lamiaceae.

Prunella species include worthy garden perennials and one well-known lawn weed *(P. vulgaris)*. The 7 to 12 species are native to meadows and woodlands from Europe to western and central Asia. Growing conditions to their liking can be found in gardens in much of North America. Prunellas, commonly called self-heals, spread by creeping rootstocks. The deciduous leaves are opposite, are usually only 1 to 2 inches long, and may be entire or deeply lobed. Flowers are individually small, bright to dark purple, and clustered into tight but showy heads. Each flower is two lipped, with the lower lip forming a landing platform for bees that probe the flower's throat for nectar. The common and scientific names refer to this throat, and the traditional medicinal use of these plants was for the treatment of quinsy, soreness and inflammation of the throat. In German, this condition was called *braume*, which became Latinized as *brunella* and later misspelled as "prunella."

HOW TO GROW

Prunellas thrive in garden conditions similar to those in their native woodland glades and meadows. Soil should be partially moist and never allowed to dry out during the summer. Plants will grow well in nearly full sun if the soil is constantly moist, as is the case in damp meadow seeps. They are not particular as to type of soil, provided it is fertile, friable, and neither too soggy nor too dry. Useful in Zones 4 to 8.

HOW TO USE

Prunellas are versatile and undemanding ground covers for woodland and naturalistic sites. Use them to face down shrub masses or to informally tie together larger areas with a consistent foliage. Other woodland or shade ground covers may be mixed in for a mosaic or to play a bolder foliage, such as that of hostas, against this finer one.

P. grandiflora (P. × webbiana)   P. 121
gran-dih-FLOR-uh. Showy Self-heal. This European native is a low-maintenance ground cover for sites with full sun to partial shade and average soil. The small flowers are purple. 'Pagoda' is a seed strain with a broad range of flower colors. 'White Loveliness' has white flowers.

❦ *Pulmonaria*

pul-mon-AIR-ee-uh. Borage family, Boraginaceae.

The mottled leaves of *Pulmonaria*, commonly known as lungworts, are attractive to contemporary gardeners, but to medieval European herbalists, these leaves were a sign that the plants were useful in treating lung diseases. The 10 to 12 species are native to Europe and adjacent regions of Asia. These perennial herbs with slowly creeping rhizomes are relatively easy to grow in most parts of North America. The coarse, hairy leaves are alternate but usually clustered into tight basal rosettes. Leaves are usually deciduous but may be evergreen near the southern limits of the species. Flowers are carried above the foliage on hairy, curiously curved flower stalks. Individual flowers are five-angled funnels or bells about ½ inch long and usually pink or blue. The common and scientific names come from the medicinal use implied by the shape of the leaves.

HOW TO GROW
Lungworts make low, clump-forming, slowly spreading ground covers in rich, well-drained soil. They need light shade and adequate moisture during the growing season. They perform well in woodland settings or under trees, provided they are not allowed to dry out, in which case they will go prematurely dormant. All are quite tolerant of soil pH, and several (such as *P. rubra*) do well in alkaline soils. Useful in Zones 4 to 8 (unless otherwise noted) where summers are not hot and dry.

HOW TO USE
Pulmonarias are classic ground covers for woodland and shade gardens, especially as they are reputed to be unpalatable to slugs and deer. The choice foliage makes them an excellent hosta substitute where hostas cannot be grown. With adequate moisture, they maintain an attractive appearance from early spring through summer. The large range of attractive silver, white, and green variegation makes them unique among shade-tolerant plants, which rarely have silver foliage. Plant *P.* 'Excalibur' for a brilliant splash of silver in a dark spot, or work in the long leaves of *P. longifolia* or *P. longifolia* ssp. *cevennensis* for a dramatic spreading mound in contrast to the rich foliage and flowers of oakleaf hydrangeas. Many new cultivars are being developed and introduced.

P. angustifolia   P. 122
an-gus-ti-FO-lee-uh. This early-blooming lungwort has dark green leaves and deep blue flowers.

P. 'Excalibur' P. 122

'Excalibur' has dramatic, silver foliage and red flowers that fade to pink.

P. longifolia

lon-ji-FO-lee-uh. This species is distinctive for its long, narrow leaves, which grow to 12 inches long. The hairy, green leaves are splashed with silver. Flowers are blue. 'Bertram Anderson' has rich blue flowers and narrow, dark green leaves that are heavily spotted with silver. *P. longifolia* ssp. *cevennensis* is one of the most effective ground-covering lungworts because it forms wavy mounds. Leaves are exceptionally long, often more than 15 inches, and well textured. Flowers are blue.

P. rubra (P. angustifolia 'Rubra')

ROO-bruh. This lungwort has hairy, light green foliage and pinkish flowers. 'Redstart' has salmon or peach flowers.

P. saccharata 'Mrs. Moon' P. 123

sak-ah-RAH-tuh. This is one of the time-tested classics. The hairy, light green leaves have strong silver spots. Pink buds open to sapphire blue flowers.

✿ Pyracantha

py-ra-KAN-thuh. Rose family, Rosaceae.

Pyracantha species, commonly known as firethorns, were very popular garden shrubs in the post–World War II housing boom and development of metropolitan suburbs, but the intervening decades have allowed a clearer assessment of how best to use these 6 to 10 species of European and Asian origin. The basic problem is that like their relatives — cotoneasters *(Cotoneaster)*, quinces *(Chaenomeles)*, and hawthorns *(Crataegus)* — firethorns can be very susceptible to fire blight, which is debilitating in their case. Most firethorns are large shrubs to almost small trees with tough, spiny branches. In all cases, leaves are small, rounded or oval, and semievergreen, with tiny serrations or indentations on the edges. The small, white flowers are presented in clusters. The fruits are the main ornamental feature. They are bright orange or orange-red and splayed across the shrubs with an exuberance that can be breathtaking.

HOW TO GROW

Low-growing firethorns are popular and tough ground covers for western gardens. Give them acid to neutral, well-drained soil and occasional deep watering, and they will thrive in full sun to partial shade. In the humid East, they are subject to destructive fire blight, scale, and aphids. Hybrids with *P. coccinea* are considered among the hardiest in the genus, but they are not necessarily the best suited for ground-cover use. Do not overwater. The cultivars listed here are useful in Zones 8 to 10.

HOW TO USE

Plant pyracanthas in full sun on banks and to drape over walls. Their small, white flowers and masses of red berries are displayed beautifully cascading down a stone wall or spreading widely along a slope. They can be easily trained against walls, either pruned as espaliers or pinned to make a flat, lustrous, hanging rug. They also make attractive carpets under taller shrubs in warmer southwestern gardens.

P. koidzumii   P. 123

koyd-ZOOM-ee-eye. 'Santa Cruz' is a prostrate, spreading form that grows to 3 feet tall and 6 feet wide and is often planted on slopes.

P. 'Tiny Tim'

This selection has dwarf leaves and a tight growth form that finally reaches 3 feet tall.

❦ *Rhaphiolepis*

raf-ee-o-LEP-iss. Rose family, Rosaceae.

Although there are 10 species of *Rhaphiolepis* in Southeast Asia, only a few are found in North American gardens, and only one, *R. indica* (Indian hawthorn), is useful as a ground cover. Used extensively in the South, especially in the Gulf states, and in California, in coastal, inland, and some protected desert regions, this versatile shrub can be kept low, massed to form a large-scale ground cover, or clipped into an informal hedge up to 5 feet tall. The alternate leaves are glossy, dark green, elliptical, and without serrations or teeth. The foliage creates a very dense backdrop that is difficult to see through. The white or pink flowers are produced in early spring and are followed by dark blue-black fruits later in the season.

HOW TO GROW

Indian hawthorn thrives in a wide range of garden soils. Full sun is required for best growth and best bloom. Plants also require regular moisture throughout the growing season. Once established, Indian hawthorn can withstand fairly dry, but not desiccated, conditions for short periods. Useful in Zone 8 and warmer.

HOW TO USE

Indian hawthorn is an excellent choice as a sun-tolerant, spring-flowering shrub mass for the South. Flowers are elegantly displayed, foliage is a rich green, and plants are well adapted for formal gardens. Beyond its normal uses, it can be massed to form thick drifts along walkways, on banks, or facing down larger shrub masses.

R. indica   P. 124

IN-di-kuh. Indian Hawthorn. Native to southern China and parts of Indonesia, where it grows in coastal conditions and low woodlands, this evergreen shrub requires moisture and warm subtropical winters. The species is too tall for most ground-covering purposes. 'Ballerina' is a compact, low-growing shrub (2 to 3 feet tall and wide) with pink flowers and is often used for massing. 'Clara' grows slightly taller (3 to 5 feet) and has white flowers. 'Dancer' is a compact selection growing only to 2 to 4 feet.

❦ *Rhododendron*

ro-doe-DEN-dron. Heath family, Ericaceae.

Only a few rhododendrons spread well enough to be truly effective ground covers, but many are used as large-scale shrub masses, because of their heavy foliage and attractive spring flowers. There are more than 500 *Rhododendron* species native throughout the north temperate zones, as well as countless hybrids, but native-plant enthusiasts will have to look elsewhere for ground covers, since none of the selections listed here is native to the Americas. Rhododendrons and azaleas (a distinction made by gardeners but not accepted by botanists in charge of the scientific names) are shrubs with alternate, deciduous or evergreen leaves. Leaves range from less than 1 inch to more than 6 inches long, depending on the species. In many cases, the undersides of leaves are sparsely to totally covered with white or brown hairs, which give the entire plant a luxurious visual texture. Flowers range in color across the spectrum, except for blue and black, and are usually funnel shaped or flaring trumpet shaped. They are often clustered into dramatic, headlike displays that can be seen from considerable distances. The name means "tree rose," in reference to this bright floral display.

HOW TO GROW

Rhododendrons require loose, acid, humus-rich soil with a constant source of moisture and humidity. Even established shrubs do not like to dry out. Partial shade is required, as leaves will scorch in full sun. In northern gardens, it is best to protect rhododendrons from winter sun, although azaleas will accept full sun or morning sun and may even require it to flower adequately. Rhododendrons should be mulched at least annually with an organic material, such as rotted wood chips, leaves, or old compost. Useful from Zone 5 south (non-ground-covering species are hardy farther north), depending on the species.

HOW TO USE

Use the selections listed here massed as ground covers rather than as specimens or foundation plantings. In shade and woodland gardens, these rhododendrons are most effective when grouped as "choruses" rather than planted as "soloists." Companion plants for textural compositions include *Hosta, Ilex, Leucothoe,* and *Pieris.*

R. hybrids   P. 124

Thousands of selections exist, and it can be argued that all look good when massed. The best way to find one that will meet your needs and be reliable in your climate is to visit local gardens specializing in these plants. Exceptional collections can be seen at Callaway Gardens (Georgia), Middleton Place (South Carolina), Rhododendron Species Foundation (Washington State), U.S. National Arboretum (Washington, D.C.), and Winterthur (Delaware). Only a few well-known selections are listed here.

'Alexander' is a creeping azalea that forms irregular mounds to 3 feet across. It has flaming red-orange flowers. Useful in Zones 6 to 9.

'Delaware Valley White' is perhaps the most frequently planted evergreen, white-flowering azalea in the Mid-Atlantic region and Northeast. It grows to 4 feet tall. Useful in Zones 6 to 8.

'Joseph Hill' is a dwarf creeping azalea with vivid red flowers. Useful in Zones 7 to 9.

'Pink Cascade' forms an evergreen, ground-covering mat less than a foot tall. Flowers are coral-pink. Useful in Zones 7 to 9.

'Pink Pancake' is a prostrate shrub that reaches barely 6 inches tall and grows several feet wide. It has pink flowers in summer. Useful in Zones 7 to 9.

✿ *Rhus*

rhoos. Cashew family, Anacardiaceae.

More than 250 *Rhus* species are found throughout the world, but the finest ground covers for North American climates are all native species and ornamental selections made from them. These species, commonly known as sumacs, are clonal shrubs that spread by underground stems to make dense thickets over time. Since the leaves are deciduous, the stark winter profile of the plants should be considered when locating them. Leaves may be compound with 3 leaflets (such as *R. aromatica*) or more than 15 leaflets (such as *R. typhina*). Flowers are individually small and clustered into small groups (as in *R. aromatica*) or into large structures that become even more evident as the brightly colored fruits mature and display a range of red to tawny shades.

HOW TO GROW

Sumacs require full sun for best growth and best fall foliage color. They are tolerant of a wide range of soil textures and types, provided soils are well drained and never soggy. These species spread by underground runners, with new plants appearing with almost volcanic suddenness, sometimes at quite some distance from the mother plant. Typically, the masses form gently rounded shapes, with height depending on the species. *R. aromatica* is the lowest-growing species and the most useful as a ground cover in garden situations. The other native species are larger and develop into thickets better suited to large-scale situations. Hardiness depends on the species.

HOW TO USE

Sumacs' wide-spreading colonies stabilize banks, provide cover for wildlife, and offer some of fall's most brilliant foliage. Although sumacs are considered weedy by some gardeners, few will deny the impact of a mass of flaming autumn foliage on a roadside or mountain bank. Because they tolerate poor dry soil, drought, and cold and heat (though not soggy or boggy conditions), their landscape potential is enormous. Be sure to plant them where the fall foliage can be enjoyed.

R. aromatica   P. 125

air-o-MAT-i-kuh. Fragrant Sumac. This is an excellent ground cover for big areas, growing 2 to 5 feet tall and spreading into large colonies. The shiny, green foliage turns brilliant scarlet in fall. 'Gro-Low' is a selection that matures to 2 feet tall and spreads 6 to 8 feet. Useful in Zones 6 to 9.

❧ *Rosa*

RO-suh. Rose family, Rosaceae.

Roses include a spectacular range of plant sizes, and modern ground-cover roses are becoming popular in the nursery trade and with home gardeners. Even among the species (of which there are at least 250 in temperate regions), there are several that are useful as ground covers when allowed to grow freely. Ground-cover roses are woody shrubs with either naturally prostrate branches or arching canes that cascade well across the ground. These roses are deciduous (unless noted otherwise), with typical rose foliage and flowers. A wide range of floral colors is available, but most of the familiar garden roses (such as hybrid teas, floribundas, and miniatures) are not useful here. The name refers to both the flower and the color.

HOW TO GROW

Roses prefer full sun and deep, rich soil with adequate moisture throughout the growing season. Deviations from these conditions will result in less impressive floral displays or weaker vegetative growth. Hardiness depends on the species and selection.

HOW TO USE

Grow roses in beds, on slopes, over walls, as foundation plantings, or even as hedges. For a contemporary look, mass them with perennials such as nepetas, artemisias, or low asters. Roses do not tolerate being walked on, but many are remarkably adapted to urban pollution, salt, and poor soils, although all will grow better in rich soils with good feeding and adequate moisture and sun. Ground-cover roses require less maintenance than roses in display beds, and gardeners should learn to enjoy these shrubs for their natural growth and seasonal changes, rather than try to groom them as if they were display plants.

SPECIES

R. banksiae   P. 125

BANKS-ee-ay. Lady Banks Rose. This Chinese species has almost thornless
cascading stems that, when supported, climb 15 to 20 feet. It has white or
pale yellow, lightly fragrant flowers. It can be used as a cascading ground
cover to spill down banks and over walls, in which case the stems will rise
only a few feet above the ground as they travel. Plants are evergreen in
mild winters. Useful in Zones 8 to 10. 'Alba Plena' has double, white flowers. 'Lutea' has double, yellow flowers. 'Lutescens' has single, yellow flowers.

R. nitida

NIT-id-uh. Shining Rose. This native of northeastern North America grows
to 2 feet tall and makes a thicket. The small, shiny leaves provide excellent
fall color. Flowers are pink and are followed by attractive hips. Useful in
Zones 4 to 7.

R. rugosa   P. 127

roo-GO-suh. Rugosa roses are native to the north Pacific coast of Asia and
are virtually indestructible shrubs. They grow to well over 4 feet tall, but
with severe pruning to within 4 inches of the ground in late winter, they
will sucker vigorously to make spectacular flowering ground covers. They
are very salt tolerant. Useful in Zones 3 to 8. The many cultivars in the
trade should be reliable, provided they are on their own roots. The necessary severe pruning will cause the rootstocks to sucker.

R. wichurana

wi-shur-AY-nuh. Memorial Rose. This Asian native is a procumbent shrub
usually less than 18 inches tall but spreading to 15 feet. Stems root as they
travel, thus making it an excellent choice for banks and erosion control.
The semievergreen leaves form the backdrop for the single, fragrant,
white flowers. Useful in Zones 5 to 9.

CULTIVARS

'Baby Blanket' grows to 3 feet tall and 5 feet wide and is a repeat
bloomer. The pink flowers are delicately fragrant. Useful in Zones 5 to 10.

'Garden Blanket' stays under 4 feet tall and spreads to 8 feet, with repeat bloom. The lavender-pink flowers are white in the center and have a
mild, fruity fragrance. Useful in Zones 5 to 9.

'Hiawatha' is often listed as a cultivar of *R. wichurana* and has a similar spreading, prostrate form, reaching 6 to 12 feet across. It has bright red flowers. Useful in Zones 5 to 9.

'Magic Blanket' grows to 3 feet tall and 6 feet across, with repeat bloom. The fragrant flowers open pale apricot and mature to white. Useful in Zones 5 to 10.

'Magic Carpet' grows only 18 inches tall but spreads to nearly 4 feet, with repeat bloom. The lavender-mauve flowers have a deliciously spicy fragrance. Useful in Zones 5 to 10.

Meidiland roses were bred in France as landscape (read "groundcover") roses and are gaining in popularity in North America in Zones 4 to 10. They tolerate a wide range of growing conditions, provided they have sun and good drainage. Some of the better-known selections are listed here. There are also some excellent cultivars that are not as winter hardy. Most of these rebloom, several have very ornamental hips, and the taller ones all mass well. 'Alba Meidiland' is less than 3 feet tall and spreads to 5 feet. Flowers are very double and white. This selection is considered very hardy. 'Bonica' grows 3 to 4 feet tall and 5 feet wide. Flowers are double and soft pink. 'Carefree Delight' is less than 3 feet tall and grows to 5 feet wide. Flowers are soft pink and presented in clusters of 3 to 15 blooms. 'Fuchsia Meidiland' is less than 2 feet tall and spreads to 4 feet. Flowers are a strong pink. 'Magic Meidiland' is 2 feet tall and 6 feet across. The deep magenta flowers have a spicy fragrance. 'Pearly Meidiland' is just over 2 feet tall and spreads to 6 feet. Flowers open pale pink and mature to a pearly white. 'Scarlet Meidiland' grows to 3 feet tall and 6 feet wide. It has scarlet flowers, tolerates more shade than most, and is very winter hardy. 'White Meidiland' is 2 feet tall and 6 feet wide and has white flowers.

'Nearly Wild' is a reblooming floribunda that has stood the test of time as a ground cover in cooler parts of North America. The shrubs grow 3 to 4 feet tall and 4 feet wide and have fragrant, rose-pink flowers that look much like those of wild roses. Useful in Zones 4 (Zone 3 by some reports) to 9, but they grow larger in climates with mild winters.

'Paulii' is one of the few older roses to scramble down slopes and form an excellent, almost impenetrable, thorny ground cover. It grows to more than 4 feet tall and 12 to 15 feet wide. Flowers are white and mildly fragrant. Useful in Zones 4 to 8.

'Red Ribbons' is less than 3 feet tall but more than 6 feet wide and has a long to continuous blooming season. Flowers are brilliant red and lightly fragrant. Useful in Zones 5 to 10.

'Rushing Stream' is a David Austin introduction growing to less than 3 feet but spreading to 5 feet with repeat bloom. Flowers open blush pink and promptly turn white. Useful in Zones 6 to 10.

'Sun Runner' is less than 2 feet tall and up to 5 feet wide, with repeat bloom. The yellow flowers have golden centers and a light citrus fragrance. Useful in Zones 6 to 10.

Rosmarinus

rose-mar-EYE-nus. Mint family, Lamiaceae.

The rich fragrance of rosemary has garnished many chicken and lamb dishes. In its prostrate form, it makes an equally attractive living garnish for the garden. *Rosmarinus* species are evergreen shrubs native to the Mediterranean region, but only one of the three species is commonly grown for garden use. If left unclipped, the shrubs will grow to more than 3 feet tall and spread to 5 feet or more. Or they can be shorn annually and kept shorter for dramatic mass plantings. Leaves are evergreen, about an inch long, and narrow. The fragrance comes from oils that are released when a leaf is brushed or bruised. Flowers are individually small, lavender-blue or white, and strongly two lipped, as is typical of the mint family. The name comes from the Latin for "sea dew," evidently an allusion to these species' appearance on cliffs within range of the sea's spray.

HOW TO GROW

Rosemary can be used outside the herb garden, but the same cultural conditions are needed to ensure vigorous plants. Full sun, good drainage, and fertile but not rich soil are the keys to its success. Overly rich soil or heavy fertilization will lead to lank growth and lack of hardening off for winter. Rosemary is useful for massing from Zone 8 (warm Zone 7 with summer heat) south.

HOW TO USE

Use where you can appreciate the fragrance by lightly brushing by the plants. Rosemary makes an attractive, low ground cover in front of flowering shrubs with similar cultural requirements. Plant 'Prostratus' or 'Lockwood Variety' to drape over walls or cascade down banks. Plant 'Benenden Blue' ('Collingwood Ingram') where it can be clipped in tighter masses; it looks especially attractive when kept as flat, aromatic squares in a formal garden or clipped into a hedge.

R. officinalis

P. 128

o-fiss-in-AL-iss. Rosemary. Many selections appropriate for ground covers are available. The cultivars vary by flower color and foliage grayness, as well as overall matting ability. 'Benenden Blue' ('Collingwood Ingram') grows 1½ to 2 feet tall and spreads to 4 to 6 feet. It has deep purple-blue flowers and upturned stems. 'Huntington Blue' ('Huntington Carpet') makes a dense ground cover several feet across and little more than 1 foot tall. Flowers are bright blue. 'Prostratus' grows 12 to 15 inches tall and has pale blue flowers and a spreading, cascading habit. 'Lockwood Variety' ('Lockwood de Forest') is similar to 'Prostratus' but has deeper blue flowers.

❦ Rubus

ROO-bus. Rose family, Rosaceae.

Many *Rubus* species are all too eager to become ground covers. A few are welcome as intentional additions to the landscape, where their foliage and flowers are foils to other plants. *Rubus* includes all blackberries and raspberries—more than 250 species worldwide in a wide range of habitats. Many species have the characteristic trait of branches growing from the root crown the first year but flowering and fruiting only in the second year. Individual branches will grow for a number of years, then decline. The plant, however, tends to send up new stems from the root crown each year. Stems, especially the tips of branches, typically root when they come in contact with the ground, thus forming masses. Leaves are alternate and deciduous in the species listed here. They range from large, shallowly lobed leaves (such as *R. odoratus*) to dissected leaves with five or more leaflets per leaf. Leaf stalks (petioles) and veins, as well as branches, may be densely thorny to almost thornless. Flowers are five petaled, about an inch across, and white or rose-pink. Fruits are the well-known raspberries and blackberries, although some species have poor, almost mealy, fruits. The name comes from the Latin word *ruber*, or "red," in reference to the fruit color.

HOW TO GROW

Plant *Rubus* species, commonly called brambles, in full sun for best growth. They can take partial shade, but they will not be as dense. (*R. odoratus* is an exception that prefers partial shade.) They are not particular about soil, provided it is not waterlogged. When used as a ground cover, the plants will benefit from a severe cutting back to near the ground every several years to renew the stems and give you an opportunity to remove other plants. Useful in Zones 3 to 9, depending on the species.

HOW TO USE

Brambles are useful and adaptable ground covers for large areas where the main need is for a dark summer-foliage mass. Flowers and fruits are additional benefits. Note that the species listed here vary greatly in height. *R. pentalobus* is a welcome addition to the list of plants that make semievergreen, weed-suppressing carpets in sunny sites in Zones 7 to 9. The crinkled foliage contrasts well with other sun lovers, such as sedums, geraniums, or low roses. The plants have the added advantage of being adapted to partial shade, although they may thin out as shade increases. *R. odoratus* is an excellent plant for massing in a naturalistic garden. It grows well in partial sun to shade and quickly spreads to form a foliage mass up to 3 feet tall. Enlivened with pretty, pink, roselike flowers, it can create a midsize swath in the garden. It also will tolerate salt-laden winds and has been known to thrive as far north as Mount Desert Island, Maine.

R. odoratus

o-dor-RAH-tus. Flowering Raspberry. This eastern North American species spreads to form extensive colonies that reach 3 feet tall in partially wooded sites. The rose-purple flowers are borne in loose sprays and look like small wild roses, but the fruits are insignificant. Useful in Zones 4 to 8 except where summers are dry.

R. pentalobus (R. calycinoides)   P. 128

pen-tah-LOW-bus. Creeping Raspberry. This species forms a dense, spreading mat of crinkly, round-lobed leaves that measure 1 to 2 inches across and turn burgundy in winter. Leaves may be semievergreen or evergreen in warm maritime climates. Useful in Zones 7 to 9. 'Emerald Carpet' makes a handsome, low ground cover that grows only 4 inches tall. Its small, bright green leaves turn burgundy in fall.

🌿 Sagina

sa-JY-nuh. Pink family, Caryophyllaceae.

Irish moss and pearlwort are descriptive names for the one species, *Sagina subulata,* that is used as a ground cover. There are 20 to 30 annual and perennial species of *Sagina* native to the Northern Hemisphere. *Sagina* is related to *Dianthus* (carnations) and *Gypsophila* (baby's breath). It is a prostrate, mat-forming perennial with tiny, semievergreen, needlelike, bright green leaves only a fraction of an inch long. In late spring, the mats are covered with tiny white flowers, each with four or five petals. The main attraction is the foliage mat, which is truly mosslike in color, scale, and texture. The name means "fodder" and stands as a reminder that sheep were fattened on a related species subsequently exiled by botanists to an obscure genus.

HOW TO GROW
Saginas grow best in damp, well-drained soil and partial shade. They tolerate a wide range of soil pH but not waterlogged soils. Even though the plants form prostrate mats, they do not like being walked on, so they are most effectively used between steppingstones but not in lieu of a turf path. Useful in Zones 4 to 8.

HOW TO USE
The mossy texture and brightly colored leaves of *S. subulata* show to advantage among stones and in sandy, loamy, damp, well-drained soil. Use among steppingstones or as a small-scale lawn substitute in cool locations where the "turf" will be viewed but not trod on. Note that saginas sometimes "hump up" as they grow. This can be remedied by cutting the mat of plants and flattening it out.

S. subulata   P. 129
sub-yoo-LAY-tuh. Irish Moss, Pearlwort. This perennial, evergreen herb grows in dense tufts of tiny foliage that rapidly creep to form carpets 3 to 4 inches tall. It has small, starlike, white flowers in summer. 'Aurea' has golden yellow foliage.

❦ *Salix*
SAY-liks. Willow family, Salicaceae.

Mention willows, and most gardeners are likely to think either of pussy willows or weeping willows. It may come as a surprise that among the nearly 500 *Salix* species native to the Northern Hemisphere, several are very low growing, long-lived shrubs that make exceptionally fine ground covers. Willow leaves are deciduous and alternate and usually taper to a point, although some species have leaves with blunter shapes. Flowers are totally inconspicuous (other than the forms known as pussy willows), with male and female flowers on separate plants. Seeds are tiny, very short-lived, and produced in prodigious numbers, with each carried aloft on a tuft of silky hairs.

HOW TO GROW

Willows in garden cultivation prefer moist, but not necessarily wet, soils. Soils may vary from clayey to loamy, provided they are not so well drained as to dessicate the plants. None of the willows will perform well if subjected to a long dry period or unrelenting hot, dry weather. Willows do best in full to nearly full sun, and plants grown in partial shade will be spindly and not nearly as vigorous. Useful in Zones 2 to 9, depending on the species.

HOW TO USE

The silvery foliage and ground-hugging qualities of the creeping willows make them especially attractive when used as masses to drape over rocks, near streams, to add texture to a pond-edge, or on a slope prone to runoff.

S. apoda

eh-PO-duh. This ground-hugging species has horizontal branches. Though relatively slow growing, it will evenutally cover a large area. Useful in Zones 4 to 7.

S. repens   P. 129

RE-penz. Creeping Willow. This low ground cover spreads by running stems, reaching 2 to 3 feet tall and more than 8 feet wide. It grows especially well along streams and in low, marshy areas. Useful in Zones 4 to 8.

S. retusa

re-TOO-suh. A native of European mountains, this is a low shrub rising only a few inches above ground level. Its crowded leaves partially cover the stems and ground. Useful in Zones 2 to 7.

S. uva-ursi

OO-vuh-UR-see. Bearberry Willow. This North American native ranges from New England to Greenland. It is a prostrate, mat-forming shrub with branches up to 1 foot long. It makes an excellent cover for rocky areas and cool, windswept slopes. Useful in Zones 2 to 4.

❦ Salvia

SAL-vee-uh. Mint family, Lamiaceae.

For hundreds of years, salvias, or sages, have been valued for their culinary, medicinal, and aromatic qualities. Found throughout temperate and tropical zones from sea level to more than 11,000 feet, the more than 700 *Salvia* species include shrubby and herbaceous plants. Many of the species are known to most North American gardeners as tender plants (if at all), but in mild regions of the Pacific states, several make exceptionally fine, eye-catching ground covers. Salvias have opposite leaves that are usually deciduous. Leaves are aromatic due to the oil cells in them. Flowers are tubular and often flare at the open end into an upper lip and a lower lip. The species that are pollinated by bees tend to have relatively small blue or lavender flowers, which are clustered into very attractive heads. The species that are pollinated by hummingbirds often have red flowers, which are usually less tightly clustered. *Salvia* is derived from the Latin word meaning "to heal," as is seen in related words such as "salve" and "salvation."

HOW TO GROW

Grow salvias in full sun to light shade, depending on the species. All species need fertile, well-drained soil. Nearly all will not tolerate deep shade and if grown there will succumb to rot. Salvias are not particular as to soil pH, and the genus includes many species from the dry and desert regions of the western United States and the mountains of Mexico, all of which do well in neutral to alkaline soils. Hardiness varies depending on the species, but in general the ground-covering species are useful in Zone 8 and warmer.

HOW TO USE

Unlike the culinary selections, ground-covering salvias come in a range of heights and from a broad range of growing conditions. In western gardens, especially in southern California and parts of Arizona, Nevada, and Texas, salvias make excellent ground covers in partial shade to full sun. Selected species grow in woodlands and at the edges of woods into old fields, or in garden situations with fertile soil and partial shade. None grows especially fast, but all can be coaxed into forming sizable perennial swaths of attractive foliage and flowers.

S. arizonica

air-i-ZON-uh-kuh. This creeping perennial, native from Arizona to Texas, makes large patches in partially shaded sites. In garden situations, plants prefer well-drained, fertile soil and supplemental watering. The small, blue flowers appear in summer. Useful in Zones 7 to 9.

S. blepharophylla   P. 130

blef-air-o-FIL-uh. Eyelash sage. This spreading perennial, native to Mexico, grows to 18 inches tall and forms small masses. It needs partial shade and well-drained, rich soil. Flowers are scarlet. Useful in Zones 9 and 10.

S. cacaliifolia

cah-cal-ee-FO-lee-uh. This Central American native has been a favorite in European gardens for many years. The creeping rootstocks form masses with flowering stems that reach more than 2 feet tall. The bright green, triangular leaves are a good foil to the brilliant blue flowers. Useful in Zones 9 and 10.

S. chamaedryoides (S. semiatrata)   P. 130

came-uh-DROY-deez. Germander Sage. This small shrub grows to 2 feet tall and spreads several feet. It needs well-drained soil and full sun. The small, gray leaves and light blue flowers are a welcome addition to a warm-climate hillside site. Useful in dry Zones 7 to 9.

S. mellifera 'Terra Seca'

mel-IF-er-uh. This selection of a California native grows to 2 feet tall and more than 6 feet wide. It has pale lavender flowers and is a good ground cover for sunny sites in warm, arid areas of Zones 9 and 10.

S. sonomensis

so-no-MEN-siss. Sonoma Sage. This California native is a woody perennial that forms low mats. It is excellent for dry gardens with heavy shade and good drainage. The pungent leaves are usually narrow and vary in gray- ness. Flowers are lavender or purple. Useful in Zones 8 to 10.

❦ Santolina

san-tol-EYE-nuh. Aster family, Asteraceae.

Whether known by the English name lavender cotton or the Latin *San- tolina* (perhaps from *sanctum linum,* or "holy linen"), these plants have long evoked a sense of their being important textile plants, which they most certainly are not. The 8 to 10 species of *Santolina* are all small, aromatic cushion-shaped shrubs native to the western Mediterranean. Leaves are alternate, gray-green, and fragrant when brushed. Flowers, as is typical of the aster family, are individually tiny but clustered into buttonlike flower heads that are carried well above the foliage. None of the flowers have obvious petals, so the heads look like tight, dusky golden pincushions.

HOW TO GROW
Santolinas require full sun and well-drained soil. Plants will tolerate a range of soil pH but prefer warm, gritty, alkaline soils. They will bulk up, but they will not spread, so plants must be massed together from the beginning. Plants can be shorn several times a season if a low mass is desired, but they will not flower as well. Useful in Zones 7 to 9.

HOW TO USE
When developing a Mediterranean-style landscape, you can use santolinas as an important visual component. Their tight foliage and aromatic qualities are welcome characteristics in cooler climates where true Mediterranean species may not grow. Santolinas mound and spread like slowly melting scoops of ice cream on a plate. Though not likely to "merge," plants will broaden out to achieve adequate cover. Mass santolinas on banks, along walkways and driveways, and in drifts outside their normal use in perennial plantings and gravel gardens.

S. chamaecyparissus (S. incana)   P. 131
kam-ee-sip-ar-ISS-us. Lavender Cotton. This low, spreading shrub has gray foliage and bright yellow, buttonlike flowers. It needs well-drained soil, full sun, and little supplemental water. Trim it back immediately after flowering to prevent the plants from becoming rank and falling apart. 'Compacta' is a low, mounding shrub that grows to 1 foot tall.

❦ *Sarcococca*
sar-ko-KOK-uh. Box family, Buxaceae.

Sweet box is the perfect name for this small Asian genus of low, evergreen shrubs, since the flowers are deliciously fragrant, and the genus is closely related to *Buxus* (box). Unlike box, the leaves of sweet box are 1 to 2 inches long and up to one-third to one-half as wide, giving the plant a pleasantly shaggy appearance (in contrast to the tight foliage of box, even when little clipped). The pale white flowers are individually tiny (about ¼ inch) and as inconspicuous as those of *Ilex* (holly). Their presence is unmistakable, however, as their fragrance wafts on the spring breeze. Fruits are dark, fleshy berries, and the scientific name comes from a Greek term meaning just that.

HOW TO GROW

Sweet box prefers moist, acid, organic soil and partial to full shade. Near its northern limit, it needs protection from winter sunscald, which can cause it to decline. Plants are slow to spread by underground stems, but in time they will form tight colonies up to several feet across (much more if conditions are perfect). Useful in Zone 7 (Zone 6 if well sited) to 9.

HOW TO USE

Plant *Sarcococca* in shaded areas, whether the shade is from buildings or larger plants. Use it in masses near entryways where people coming and going will enjoy its delicate fragrance. The shrub's small stature creates drifts that fit neatly in front of or under the taller branches of other evergreens, such as viburnums, hollies, photinias, or needled conifers. Just be sure that sweet box receives adequate moisture and food when planted in competition with larger companions.

S. hookeriana var. humilis   P. 131

hook-ur-ee-AY-nuh var. HEW-mil-us. Dwarf Sweet Box, Himalayan Sweet Box.
This is a low, spreading, evergreen, stoloniferous, woody shrub. It grows 1 to 2 feet tall and spreads to 6 feet. It does best in moist, acid, shady sites.

❦ Sasa

SAS-uh. Grass family, Poaceae.

Sasa is a genus of Asian bamboos, only a few of which are hardy in temperate North America. They have deciduous or evergreen leaves (in part depending on the species, in part depending on the climate) that are usually less than 12 to 15 inches long. The aerial stems are less winter hardy than the buried stems and roots, making the plants worth a try for adventuresome gardeners who live outside the apparent northern limit. The underground stems spread vigorously in suitable conditions, eventually growing many yards beyond the initial planting. As is typical of many bamboos, flowering is extremely uncommon. When it does occur, the grasslike flowers are abundantly produced. Flowering is somehow synchronized among widely separated plants—even worldwide—and often results in the plants' death or severe decline. Fortunately, flowering plants usually produce abundant seeds. The scientific name is Japanese, transliterated into Latin.

HOW TO GROW
Sasas will tolerate very difficult sites, provided there is both adequate moisture and good drainage. Examples include dry, exposed banks of ponds and streams or the high shade of rarely but temporarily flooded sites. As with most bamboos, regardless of their size, sasas will provide intense root competition for any other plants in the area and choke out plants shorter than themselves. Once they are planted, stand back! Hardiness depends on the species.

HOW TO USE
Despite their bad reputation, sasas can be used effectively under large trees, where you can make the most of their aggressive nature. Use them near lawns, if the roots are contained, or along watercourses, where the roots cannot survive drowning. Or try massing them as foundation plantings near a stone driveway and let the cars cope with their invasive shoots. They are useful in dark, shaded corners, especially *S. veitchii,* since its fading leaf edge will give the plants a variegated look in winter. Smaller members of the clan, such as *S. pygmaea,* should be planted only where there is, for example, severe erosion on a bank and the roots can be contained at the edges. When correctly used, it produces an elegant, low, green carpet.

S. pygmaea
pig-MEE-uh. This extremely vigorous, spreading dwarf bamboo provides fast cover and will continue spreading indefinitely. Plant only when barriers are used. Useful in Zones 7 to 9.

S. veitchii (Arundinaria veitchii)   P. 132
VEET-chee-eye. One of the feared running bamboos, *S. veitchii* moves more slowly than many, forming an attractive ground cover to 2 feet tall in shade and heavy soil. In winter, the edges of the leaf blades senesce, giving them an interesting striped appearance through the cold weather. Useful in Zones 6 to 9. Plant with care, since the invasive roots must be controlled.

❦ Saxifraga

sax-a-FRA-ga or sax-IF-ra-ga. Saxifrage family, Saxifragaceae.

There are more than 350 species of *Saxifraga* native from the arctic south to the temperate regions, with a few species found far removed from the rest at high elevations in the Andes. Many are beloved by rock garden enthusiasts, and a few are useful as ground covers. Saxifrages are perennial herbs that usually form a definite rosette. The ground-covering species tend to have less well-defined rosettes. In addition, they spread by runners, thus fusing the rosettes into a living mat. Leaves are deciduous and usually toothed or lobed. Foliage is dark green in the species listed here and may be mottled with darker or lighter colors. Flowers are individually small and with a clear left and right mirror-image arrangement of the petals. They are usually white and carried well above the foliage on strong, multiflowered stalks. The name means "rock breaker" and refers to the predilection of many species to make their natural homes in rock faces and cracks.

HOW TO GROW

The ground-covering species are a bit atypical of the genus in that they prefer moist, partly shaded sites. Soil should be moist, above average in organic content, and weakly acid to nearly neutral. Plants will not tolerate more than half sun without additional moisture, and even then the foliage may acquire a reddish or bronze tint. These species are useful from Zone 6 south, depending on the species (non-ground-covering species may be much hardier).

HOW TO USE

In the high shade of oaks or maples, *S. stolonifera* or *S. umbrosa* spreads quickly to make an eye-catching ground cover. The tiny runners seem to pad across the bed, quickly forming a broad patch of marbled foliage with pink or white flowers. Plant these species in shade where their attractive foliage can be seen. Use as masses in woodland gardens to catch the light or in shaded urban gardens where sunlight cannot penetrate. They also look good beside streams, pools, and fountains.

S. stolonifera (S. sarmentosa)   P. 132

sto-lo-NIF-er-uh. Strawberry Begonia. Not a begonia at all, this denizen of shady cliffs in China makes a low, stoloniferous, herbaceous ground cover that grows to 8 inches tall. The pretty foliage has silvery markings that set off the small, white, airy flowers. Useful in Zones 6 to 9. 'Eco Butterfly' has chartreuse leaves marked with a "butterfly" in the center.

S. umbrosa P. 133

um-BRO-suh. London Pride. This well-known saxifrage makes rosettes of green foliage with heuchera-like clusters of pink flowers on long, wiry stalks. Useful in Zones 6 to 9. 'Variegata' ('Aureopunctata') has leaves splashed with yellow.

S. veitchiana

veet-chee-AH-nuh. This charming, deciduous creeper has rounded leaves held only a few inches above the ground. It forms weed-choking mats in moist sites with light shade, such as in front of camellias or photinias. Flowers are white. Useful in Zones 7 to 9 and may be evergreen at its southern limit.

❧ Scaevola

SKEE-vo-luh. Goodenia family, Goodeniaceae.

These Australian natives have flashed onto the North American market over the past several years and fortunately have so many ornamental merits that they have been adopted into widespread use. The nearly 100 species of Scaevola are perennials, shrubs, and trees in tropical and warm climates. There are no close relatives used in ornamental horticulture in North America. The perennial species in cultivation are also grown as annuals well beyond their hardiness zones. Leaves are alternate, often slightly toothed, and, where the plants are hardy, evergreen. Plants are typically less than a foot tall but have branches up to several feet long. The showy flowers are asymmetrical and usually blue with white markings. The overall effect is of a sprawling, shrubby lobelia, and indeed lobelias are in a closely related family. The scientific name refers to the one-handedness of the flowers.

HOW TO GROW

Scaevolas require full sun to partial shade and soil that is well drained but rarely completely dry. Useful as a perennial ground cover in Zones 9 and 10, they are also effective as annual ground covers throughout much of North America where summers are hot, as long as they are kept watered.

HOW TO USE

Plant scaevolas as perennial ground covers in warm-climate gardens, in broad masses along banks, and as connectors between grasses and roses. In temperate and cooler zones, plant them as annual masses to edge paths and to create cool, blue bands of color.

S. aemula   P. 133

EH-mew-luh. Fan Flower. This low-spreading, fleshy perennial has green foliage and lobelia-like flowers. There are many cultivars in the trade. 'Alba' has white flowers. 'Blue Wonder' has particularly dense foliage and prolific blue flowers.

S. 'Mauve Clusters'

This cultivar makes a dense carpet and has lavender-mauve flowers.

❦ Sedum

SEE-dum. Stonecrop family, Crassulaceae.

The more than 500 species of *Sedum* include perennials and subshrubs native to northern temperate zones, as well as the mountains of Mexico and central Africa. Many are well adapted to harsh, dry situations, not only because of their succulent leaves but also because they have special physiological adaptations. The succulent leaves are usually pale green or bluish green, with the blue tints caused by wax on the leaves' surface. They are quite variable in size, ranging from less than ½ inch to more than 2 inches long. Flowers are individually small, five petaled, and white, pink, or yellow, depending on the species. They are carried on complex stalks held well above the foliage, where they are typically pollinated by bees. In ancient times, the name *Sedum* was used for a variety of succulents.

HOW TO GROW

Sedums need full sun for vigorous growth as ground covers. Soil should be of average fertility and well drained. Rich soils or the use of fertilizers will result in leggy but flaccid growth, and a subsequent lack of hardening off before winter. If soils are not well drained, the roots and crowns will rot, a usually fatal condition. Sedums are not overly particular as to soil pH, but they will perform best in neutral to mildly alkaline soils. Hardiness depends on the species.

HOW TO USE

Plant low-growing sedums as carpets in sunny, exposed sites, such as along driveways or on slopes. They also make excellent rugs in tapestry plantings. In naturalistic gardens, taller sedums—such as the selections 'Herbstfreude', 'Indian Chief', and 'Mohrchen'—are often planted to form dramatic bands of color in association with ornamental plants (such as *Pennisetum* or *Helictotrichon*) or *Rudbeckia*. Be sure to leave the attractive seed heads on during the winter, whether or not the plants will be covered by snow.

There are many additional species and cultivars for planting in warm, dry climates. The selections here are useful in a wide range of growing conditions.

S. acre P. 134

AY-ker. Mossy Stonecrop. This ground cover grows rampantly and may become weedy. The succulent leaves are less than 1 inch long but rise on stems to form an irregular carpet 1 to 2 inches tall. Mossy stonecrop has bright yellow flowers in spring. Useful in Zones 3 to 8. *S. acre* 'Aureum' has foliage with golden tips in spring.

S. anglicum

ANG-lik-um. This mat-forming sedum from England grows to 2 inches tall and spreads widely. It has white flowers in late spring. Useful in Zones 3 to 8.

S. brevifolium

brev-if-O-lee-um. This Mediterranean species has gray-green foliage, grows to 3 inches tall, and spreads to form a neat mat. Flowers are white but scarce. Useful in Zones 6 to 9.

S cauticola

caw-TIK-o-luh. This Japanese species is only 3 inches tall but creeps relatively quickly. It is more tolerant of soil moisture and humid air than most sedums. Useful in Zones 4 to 8.

S. kamtschaticum (S. floriferum) P. 134

kamt-SHAH-ti-cum. This succulent ground cover comes from northern China and the Pacific coast of Russia. It spreads relatively slowly but has dark, semievergreen leaves. Flowers are bright orange-yellow. Useful in Zones 3 to 8. 'Variegatum' has leaves with creamy white margins.

S. spectabile

spec-TAB-uh-lee. Showy Stonecrop. Looking like green broccoli in spring, *S. spectabile* does one of the best ground-cover transformation acts. In late summer, these galactic pincushions, which grow to 2 feet tall, display flower heads in tones from rosy pink to deep red, depending on the selection. These heads gradually mature to a chocolate hue that remains throughout the winter. Named cultivars are used for massing purposes. 'Brilliant' has lavender-pink flowers. 'Indian Chief' has carmine red flowers.

S. 'Herbstfreude' P. 135

Also called 'Autumn Joy', this cultivar is similar in most respects to *S. spectabile* and has rose-pink flowers.

S. spurium P. 135

SPUR-ee-um. Two-row Stonecrop. This moderately fast creeper grows to 6 inches tall. The small leaves are often bronze. Useful in Zones 4 to 8. There are many horticultural selections. 'Fuldaglut' ('Fuldaglow') has bronze foliage all summer and rosy flowers. 'Schorbuser Blut' ('Dragon's Blood') has bright red flowers and bronze foliage that turns red.

❦ Senecio

see-NEE-see-o. Aster family, Asteraceae.

Senecio aureus, or golden groundsel, is the one native North American ground-covering species worth considering out of this huge genus, believed by many to be the largest genus of flowering plants, with 2,000 to 3,000 species. Almost every plant form, from annuals to shrubs, is found in the genus, as well as virtually every leaf shape and condition. The leaves of golden groundsel are clustered into strong rosettes at the top of the root crown. Leaves are deciduous, variable in outline but predominantly elliptical, and gently toothed. Flowers are golden or orange-yellow and clustered into tight but showy heads typical of the aster family. These flower heads are held well above the foliage in late spring. Seeds are carried on the wind like miniature dandelions. The name humorously refers to these fuzzy gray parachutes. It means "old," as in the scraggly beard of a senile (same root word) old man.

HOW TO GROW

Golden groundsel thrives and forms open masses in moist, fertile soils, such as those found in old floodplains, on the margins of moist meadows, and in similar transitional habitats in eastern North America. It does not perform well in dry or sandy soils. Useful in Zones 5 to 8.

HOW TO USE
Golden groundsel is a native perennial of moist, open habitats in eastern North America, such as along partly sunny woodland streambanks and meadows, where it is a spectacular element in the spring wildflower bloom. Plant it as a transition between grassy uplands and moist pools and streamsides, to enhance swampy woods, or to give low-lying, poorly drained pockets a dash of sunshine in spring. Useful for naturalizing in moist, open woods with companions such as Joe-Pye weed, bonesets, white wood asters, and touch-me-nots.

S. aureus (Packera aurea) P. 136
AW-re-us. Golden Groundsel. This species makes a good ground cover for moist woodland sites with partial sun to shade. It is used spectacularly well at the Mount Cuba Center for the Study of Piedmont Flora (Delaware), where it creates a tall haze of golden daisies on long, wiry stems in midspring.

Stachys
STAY-kees or STAK-eez. Mint family, Lamiaceae.

Lamb's ears is the common name for the most common species of *Stachys,* although there are more than 200 species native to the tropics and subtropics worldwide. The hardy species are stoloniferous perennials with opposite, often densely felted, leaves that may be better described as "ever-white" than evergreen. Flowers are pinkish or lavender-blue, individually small (less than ½ inch long), and clustered into short, dense spikes carried above the foliage on short, stout flower stalks. The name means "spike" in Greek and refers to the flowers and their stalks.

HOW TO GROW
Hardy *Stachys* species perform best in well-drained sites. Soil should be coarse, sandy, or gravelly loam from which water drains freely. Though reputed to like hot, dry sites, these species do best in sites with temperate summers and full sun. Avoid full exposure in arid climates. Wet or rich soils will cause the plants to rot over time, especially during the winter. Useful in Zones 5 to 8.

HOW TO USE

Grow with *Helianthemum, Rosa* (roses), small species of *Alchemilla,* or other low-growing perennials that could use a handful of silver. *Stachys* is a charmingly tactile plant, but one that looks tattered and ratty after a winter in an exposed site. Silver lamb's ears were planted by Gertrude Jekyll in masses at Hestercombe (England), where she used them like icing on a cake to set off the spiky textures of other perennials. For best massing, choose 'Silver Carpet', a nonflowering selection. In sites that are slightly moister, create broad drifts with 'Big Ears' (or 'Countess Helen von Stein').

S. byzantina (S. lanata, S. olympica)   Pp. 136, 137

bih-zan-TEE-nuh. Lamb's Ears. Few can resist stroking lamb's ears—the fuzzy leaves just call to be touched. The species has purple or mauve flower spikes in early summer and spreads moderately. Useful in Zones 4 to 8. 'Big Ears' is a robust form with leaves that are nearly 8 inches long. It is useful in some larger-scale plantings. 'Silver Carpet' is a nonflowering, dense ground cover.

S. macrantha (S. grandiflora, S. spicata)   P. 137

mah-CRAN-tha. Big Betony. This species has bright green foliage and pink flowers. It tolerates light shade. Useful in Zones 5 to 9.

❦ *Stephanandra*

stef-an-AN-druh. Rose family, Rosaceae.

The four species of *Stephanandra* are native to eastern Asia, but only one, *S. incisa,* is commonly encountered in North American gardens. *Stephanandra* includes small to medium-size shrubs and is related to *Physocarpus* (ninebark) and *Potentilla.* The 'Crispa' cultivar listed here has low, sprawling branches that are usually less than 2 feet tall but spread to several feet. *Stephanandra* leaves are alternate, deciduous, and shallowly or deeply lobed. Flowers are greenish white, five petaled, and well under ½ inch across. The subsequent fruits are woody capsules of no ornamental significance. The name literally means "a crown of men," a reference to the anthers (the male parts of the flowers), which persist in a ring around the tiny, dry fruits.

HOW TO GROW

Stephanandras grow best in full sun to partial shade. They are not particular as to soil, provided it is moist and without prolonged droughts or flooding. Useful in Zones 4 to 8.

HOW TO USE

Plant *Stephanandra* where its delicate foliage and mounding form can be seen to best advantage. On flatter sites, it will quickly form low, irregularly shaped masses. On banks and slopes in full sun to partial shade, it will cascade over rocks and ground irregularities, quickly adding a froth of bright green foliage. It is excellent in colder zones in a transitional planting between sun and shade and is equally at home in woodland and more formal gardens.

S. incisa 'Crispa' ('Prostrata')   P. 138

in-SY-zuh. Dwarf Cut-leaf Stephanandra. This species makes a charming, low, woody ground cover that grows to 18 inches tall and spreads to more than 5 feet. It billows effectively across banks and is demure in appearance, with tiny foliage and white flowers in early summer.

❦ *Symphoricarpos*

sim-for-ih-CAR-pos. Honeysuckle family, Caprifoliaceae.

Coralberry and snowberry are common names for two of the native North American species of *Symphoricarpos,* and all 17 species are native here, except for one found only in China. These are low, colonizing shrubs native to open woods and rocky places, primarily in the mountains. All are deciduous, with simple leaves that are seldom more than an inch long. Flowers are pendent, pinkish white urns that are much visited by bees but easily overlooked by casual visitors to the garden. The dramatic, pulpy or fleshy fruits are bright pink or white and usually in pairs or tight clusters. *Symphoricarpos* species were long promoted as large-scale ground covers for erosion control, cover for wildlife, and winter forage for birds. However, the fact that fruits are often persistent long into the winter indicates that they are not preferred foods if alternatives are available. The name means "fruits borne together," in reference to the dramatic clusters.

HOW TO GROW

Grow in partial shade and a wide range of soils, including somewhat dry woodland soils. These shrubs make a superb underplanting in open woods in northern climates. Plants will form superior masses if colonies are severely cut back every several years and forced to grow new stems. Hardiness depends on the species.

HOW TO USE

Symphoricarpos is almost equally successful in shade and sun. Plant *S.* × *chenaultii* in woodland gardens in moderate to deep shade where it can serve as a transition planting. Use it to highlight the trunks of large, magnificent trees and as a marker along a woodland trail. *S. orbiculatus* is a good choice for sunnier transition areas from woods to open gardens.

S. × *chenaultii*   P. 138

x shen-O-ee-eye. Chenault Coralberry. This low, spreading, woody ground cover grows to 3 feet tall and 6 feet across and is supposedly not preferred by deer. Berries turn pink where they face the sun. Useful in Zones 4 to 8. 'Hancock' is lower, just 2 feet tall, and spreads widely.

S. orbiculatus   P. 139

or-bik-yoo-LAY-tus. Coralberry. This suckering, woody shrub grows 2 to 4 feet tall and has small, red or purple berries in fall. Useful in Zones 3 to 7. 'Leucocarpus' has white fruits.

❧ *Taxus*

TAX-us. Yew family, Taxaceae.

Yews are an ancient group of evergreen shrubs and trees that are distantly related to pines and junipers. The 10 species of *Taxus* are native primarily to the Northern Hemisphere, with several species ranging into mountains bordering desert and subtropical regions. Although they are very common as garden shrubs and some selections are useful as ground covers, most gardeners are unaware that yews can live for centuries. Some wild plants are believed to be more than 500 years old. Yews are very unusual conifers in that they can be clipped and very severely cut back, then regenerate new growth on old wood. The leafy, broad, evergreen needles are alternate, but on side branches and twigs, needles are often oriented so that the top surfaces are all aligned, creating a pleasing frondlike appearance. Plants are male or female. Males sport very small pollen cones in early spring, and these produce yellowish dust clouds when the pollen is released. Females produce seeds that are partially enclosed in the succulent, bright red structures commonly called fruits (botanists have other terms). The name is the ancient Latin one and comes from the Greek word for "bow." The English yew, *T. baccata,* was used to make the finest bows of the legendary archers of medieval England. Yew leaves and especially the seeds (but not the red, fleshy parts) are extremely toxic to fatal if chewed and eaten. This toxicity has given rise to a number of myths about their magical powers. Homeowners should be careful to use the plants where infants and young children will not eat the seeds or their attractive fleshy coverings.

HOW TO GROW

Yews prefer fertile, well-drained, humus-rich, acid soil, but they will tolerate a wide range of conditions. They are very easily drowned in clayey soils or low-lying areas where high water tables or faulty irrigation systems flood the root zone. Plants grow well in full sun to shade. Hardiness depends on the species.

HOW TO USE

All yews are severely grazed by deer. For a rich, dense, evergreen ground cover, few plants can come close to equaling yews. *T. baccata* 'Repandens' and *T. cuspidata* 'Low Spreading' are especially useful as mounding forms in the landscape, massed in deep shade near buildings, or for areas where low light and poor soil would make most shrubs curl up and die. If treated well, these shrubs become elegant components of the landscape.

T. baccata 'Repandens'   P. 139

bah-KAH-tuh. Spreading English Yew. The typical wild form is arboreal, but 'Repandens' is a female selection that grows to 3 feet high and spreads widely and elegantly to more than 12 feet. Plants are slow growing and have a good green color. Useful in Zones 5 to 8.

T. canadensis

can-ah-DEN-sis. Canadian Yew. Imagine a shag rug scaled up to gargantuan proportions to conjure up an image of this species. Low growing (usually less than 3 feet tall) and spreading, this species naturally forms a shaggy forest ground cover. Plants root along the stems to form sizable colonies. Foliage is yellower than that of other yews, and it bronzes in strong winter sun. Wild stands are often severely grazed by deer. Mass in naturalistic landscapes where summers are cool. Useful in Zones 2 to 6 with sufficient snow cover.

T. cuspidata

kus-pi-DAH-tuh. Japanese Yew. Several low cultivars of this tree serve as ground covers and are useful in Zones 4 to 7. 'Cross Spreading' grows 3 to 4 feet tall and nearly 10 feet across and is resistant to winter burn. 'Low Spreading' is one of the lowest ground-covering cultivars of this species. Plants seldom reach 3 feet tall and spread vigorously. Foliage is dark green.

❦ Tellima

tel-LY-muh. Saxifrage family, Saxifragaceae.

The one species of *Tellima*, commonly called fringecups, is a wildflower native from California to Alaska that is useful in woodland and naturalistic gardens throughout the Northern Hemisphere. Its cultural conditions are similar to those of its close relatives, *Heuchera* and *Tiarella*. The leaves of fringecups are deciduous, up to several inches long, and shallowly lobed or toothed. They are produced on short, rhizomatous rootstocks, resulting in a low, leafy crown and, where conditions are right, a vigorously spreading mat. Flowers are small, greenish white, and not very showy, but they are fragrant.

HOW TO GROW
Fringecups thrive in moist, organic, acid, woodland soil and partial shade. Plants should not be allowed to dry out, or the leaves will burn and the plants will go dormant prematurely. Useful in Zones 4 to 7, they can be used in cool maritime areas farther south.

HOW TO USE
Fringecups naturally form clumps and can be massed to make an attractive ground cover in semishaded sites, to complement other woodlanders such as *Tiarella* and *Heuchera*, and for naturalizing. They are lovely with ferns and *Hosta* and provide a carpet beneath the vertical stems of such summer shade royalty as *Cimicifuga*. Plant in woodland areas where they can spread in cool, shaded soils. For design purposes, 'Forest Frost' brings

an unusual touch of copper into the green of the deep woods, although it requires more moisture than the species to survive.

T. grandiflora
P. 140

gran-di-FLO-ruh. Fringecups. This Pacific Northwest native grows in partial shade to shade and cool, moist, woodland soil. It quickly forms clumps that reach 12 inches tall and spreads much farther. Some gardeners confuse this with its eastern cousin, *Tiarella*, but the flowers of *T. grandiflora* are less showy. 'Forest Frost' is a charming copper-leaved selection growing to 2 feet tall. Flowers are greenish white in spring and then fade to pink.

❦ *Teucrium*

TOO-cree-um. Mint family, Lamiaceae.

The 300 species of *Teucrium* are native throughout the Northern Hemisphere, with a concentration of species around the Mediterranean. They are slightly aromatic perennials and subshrubs. Leaves are deciduous or evergreen, depending on the species and environment. They range from less than an inch to more than 2 inches in length, are often oval or elongated heart shapes, and are lightly felted with short hairs. Flowers are less than an inch long and two lipped. They come in tones of pink, yellow, purple, and lavender. Flowers are individually insignificant but are presented in slightly congested spikes. The name honors Teucer, king of ancient Troy, who used it as a medicine.

HOW TO GROW

In the wild, *Teucrium* species grow in open forests with humus-rich soils as well as on dry, rocky slopes in full sun and with perfect drainage. The prostrate species listed here prefers average to infertile, well-drained, slightly alkaline soil and full sun to light shade. Flowering decreases as the shade increases. Useful in Zones 4 to 9.

HOW TO USE

These tough plants are well suited to rocky, poor soils and full sun to very light shade. *T. chamaedrys* is well known as a neat hedge in herb gardens. The prostrate form can be massed to form spreading, bushy carpets on open banks, along driveways, and in other areas where its attractive flowers can be enjoyed.

T. chamaedrys 'Prostratum'
P. 140

cam-EE-driss. Ground Germander. This cultivar makes a better ground cover than the species. It has small, pink flowers and forms a mat about 4 inches tall and up to 2 feet wide by means of runners. It prefers sun and well-drained soil, but once established, it will tolerate some drought. The overall appearance can be neatened by light shearing after flowering.

❦ Thymus

time. Mint family, Lamiaceae.

Parsley, sage, rosemary, and thyme may be the lyrics of a traditional folk song, and although all these plants are essential residents of an herb garden, thyme alone stands out for its many uses in a flower garden. The 300 to 400 species are native to Europe and Asia, where they are perennials or mat-forming shrubs. The tiny, aromatic leaves are opposite, evergreen or deciduous, and, depending on the abundance of hairs, greenish to grayish. The small flowers are two lipped and clustered into tight, dramatically showy, white, pink, rose, lavender, or purple heads at the tips of the branches. The species and cultivars can be very difficult to distinguish, even for the experienced gardener or botanist. This is the name by which the ancient Greeks knew this plant.

HOW TO GROW

Grow thymes in infertile, dry, well-drained soil and full sun. They will rot if grown in too rich or too moist of a site. It is difficult to give thymes too much sun and heat, although they will not survive in desert or salt-laden conditions. Useful in Zones 5 to 9, depending on the species.

HOW TO USE

Think of the much-photographed carpet of massed thymes at Sissinghurst (England). Countless gardeners have tried to emulate this picture, many finding that in much of North America, the carpet develops "holes" because of the more humid conditions there. Many thymes available are suited to ground-covering functions, however. All do best in sunny, well-drained, lean, gritty or sandy soils. Be aware when planting that bees are just as fond of thymes as humans. For dramatic effects, mix several species to get an abstract mosaic of foliage and floral colors.

T. pseudolanuginosus (T. lanuginosus)   P. 141

SOO-do-lah-nue-jih-NO-sus. Woolly Thyme. The flat mats of gray foliage and tiny, pink flowers in midsummer show well along and among stepping-stones. Unlike many other thymes, this species tolerates a modest amount of foot traffic. Useful in Zones 5 to 8.

T. serpyllum   P. 141

ser-PIL-um. Mother-of-thyme, Creeping Thyme. This much-loved thyme has handsome green foliage and is striking when in bloom. Plants creep to form dense mats usually less than 2 inches tall but of irregular outline. Flowers in the species are pink, but many cultivars have been selected for flower color. Useful in Zones 4 to 9. Var. *coccineus* is blanketed with crimson flowers. 'Pink Chintz' has pink flowers and gray foliage. 'Victor Reiter' has pink flowers and deep green, semievergreen leaves. It is a recent introduction from the Mediterranean and, unlike the others, is useful in Zones 6 and warmer.

❦ *Tiarella*

tee-a-REL-uh. Saxifrage family, Saxifragaceae.

In full bloom, *Tiarella* makes frothing, foaming sweeps, whether it is carpeting the oak woods at Longwood Gardens (Pennsylvania) or in the Appalachian forests. The few species are native to eastern and western North America, East Asia, and the Himalayas. The deciduous, maplelike, fuzzy leaves grow directly from spreading rhizomes, creating dense foliage carpets 3 to 8 inches tall. Many foliage selections have been made for distinctive markings and colors. The small flowers are clustered into loose, bottlebrush stalks held well above the leaves in spring. Flowers are white or pink. The name means "small crown" and is closely linked to the idea of a jeweled tiara — take a close look at the individual flowers with an imaginative eye.

HOW TO GROW

Tiarella species, commonly known as foamflowers, thrive in moist, acid to neutral, woodland soils and partial shade. Such soils are frequently found where shrub and perennial beds have been mulched for several years with organic materials such as wood chips, ornamental bark, or compost. Plants will be most vigorous if divided every several years. Useful in Zones 4 to 8.

HOW TO USE

Foamflowers form colonies in their native woodlands. They are spectacular when exuberantly massed below trees, in front of shaded shrub borders, or carpeting the ground on the shaded north sides of structures. The diversity of foliage forms allows designers to use them with hostas, heucheras, and other shade-loving perennials. Recently, some introductions from tissue culture laboratories have included pronounced leaf markings and new flower colors (pink tones) that expand the design potential.

T. cordifolia   P. 142

cor-di-FO-lee-uh. Foamflower. This stoloniferous, eastern North American species grows 12 to 18 inches tall and has creamy white flowers in spring. The wild form spreads prolifically by runners to carpet moist, woodland sites. 'Slickrock' was found in the wild in North Carolina and has smaller leaves than the species. It grows 8 to 12 inches tall and performs well in shade.

T. wherryi (T. collina)   P. 142

WHERE-ee-eye. Foamflower. This Appalachian species does not spread by runners, but instead forms thick patches that mass supremely well in shade. Plants are 10 inches tall and have pale pinkish white blooms.

❦ *Tolmiea*

TOLE-mee-uh. Saxifrage family, Saxifragaceae.

Tolmiea is a genus with only one species, commonly called piggyback plant, which is a staple of the houseplant sections of many supermarkets. It also makes a charming and effective ground cover in warmer climates. *Tolmiea* is native to the Pacific Northwest and is very closely related to *Tiarella* (foamflower). Both have essentially identical horticultural uses, although *Tolmiea* needs moister growing conditions. Piggyback plant differs from foamflowers in the leaves, as the former frequently produces new plantlets ("baby plants") where the leaf blade joins the petiole. Flowers are creamy white and not significant. The name honors Dr. William Tolmie, a surgeon with the fabled Hudson's Bay Company.

HOW TO GROW

See *Tiarella*. Plants will not tolerate dry soil.

HOW TO USE

See *Tiarella*. In cool maritime climates such as the Pacific Northwest, piggyback plant can be used in moister sites than foamflowers and in ground-covering compositions, such as with foamflowers, heucheras, or epimediums.

T. menziesii   P. 143

men-ZEEZ-ee-eye. Piggyback Plant. Distinctive for the small plantlets that form at the base of the leaf and seem to be hopping off the mother plant's back, this species makes a low, spreading ground cover that expands indefinitely. It must have moist soil and shade and will even colonize saturated soil. Useful in Zones 7 to 10.

🌿 *Trachelospermum*

Tra-key-lo-SPER-mum. Dogbane family, Apocynaceae.

Confederate jasmine is one of the regional names for the 30 species of *Trachelospermum*, which include fragrant-flowered vines native from India to Japan, as well as in the southern United States. The genus is related to *Vinca* (periwinkle) and is useful both as a ground cover and a climbing vine but not nearly as cold hardy. *Trachelospermum* vines form spreading mats or climb by twining stems. The dark green leaves are evergreen, opposite, and rather tough without being coarse. They are entire and usually quite glossy, and variegated cultivars are commonly encountered. The fragrant flowers are five lobed, with the narrow lobes joined atop a long tube. In the wild, these flowers are undoubtedly pollinated by moths that use the fragrance and pale color to locate them in twilight hours. The name's meaning is precise and peculiar—it combines the technical terms for "throat" and "seed."

HOW TO GROW

Trachelospermums thrive in partial shade and fertile soil that is never fully dry. Given these conditions, they will form extensive, weed-choking carpets of dark green or variegated foliage. For best flowering, stems need to climb, such as over a trellis or trained on a wall. Control climbing by severely clipping back the plants, as once they begin climbing, they will continue to do so vigorously. Hardiness depends on the species.

HOW TO USE

Few fragrances are as hauntingly sweet as that of *T. jasminoides* (Confederate jasmine), which can be used as a richly scented, vining ground cover in light shade to full sun. It looks lovely under trees and shrubs, as an edging for a walkway, in raised beds, or an entry courtyard, perhaps surrounding camellias, provided it is controlled. *T. asiaticum* (star jasmine) is another attractive, stoloniferous ground cover. Be aware that it is frost sensitive and will quickly turn brown when frozen.

T. asiaticum (T. majus)

ai-see-AH-tik-um. Star Jasmine. This species is ubiquitous in southern landscapes. When the temperature falls to freezing, it dies back, but then returns from the roots. As a ground cover, it grows to 12 inches tall and 10 feet or more wide, rooting as it goes. Flowers are yellow. In light frosts, the foliage turns dark red. It is hardy and reliably attractive in Zones 8 to 10 in moist, well-drained soils that never fully dry out.

T. jasminoides   P. 143

jas-min-OY-deez. Confederate Jasmine. This well-known ground cover spreads 10 to 15 feet, and though technically a vine, it is not always a strong climber. The fragrant white flowers are produced in spring, mostly on branches that are climbing or draped over walls and structures. Plants do best in moist, rich, loamy soils. Useful in Zones 9 to 10. 'Variegatum' has leaves mottled with white.

❦ *Vaccinium*

vak-SIN-ee-um. Heath family, Ericaceae.

Blueberries, cranberries, and crowberries are the most familiar members of this diverse genus of nearly 400 species. *Vaccinium* species are native throughout the Northern Hemisphere and at high elevations of tropical mountain ranges as well. They are low to stout shrubs — sometimes almost small trees — with deciduous or evergreen leaves, depending on the species. Leaves are often smaller than a human fingernail, and the deciduous species often have spectacular and intense fall colors. Flowers are small, pendent urns that are narrow at the mouth (urceolate to botanists and Scrabble™ masters) and creamy white, sometimes tinged with pink. Fruits are edible (some more pleasant than others) and mature to blue, nearly black, or red, depending on the species. Fruits and leaves may have a gray cast caused by naturally secreted waxes. The name is the classical Latin one for the blueberry shrub.

HOW TO GROW

Vacciniums thrive in moist, acid soils enriched with humus. They are quite tolerant of full sun in northern climates if they are provided with enough water during the growing season. In garden culture, they perform well in partial shade, provided their soil requirements are met. *V. angustifolium* is often planted from sods in the Northeast. Selections of ornamental blueberries are in development for the South. Hardiness depends on the species.

HOW TO USE

Bringing back scenes of cool Maine summers or walks along East Coast pine bogs, vacciniums are ideal plants to use in a naturalistic, somewhat wild landscape. When planting *V. angustifolium* and *V. vitis-idaea*, look for propagated sods from farms that specialize in growing the plants. Then lay the sods in full sun to partial shade and keep the soil evenly moist until the plants are established. These vacciniums thrive in maritime conditions, similar to that of the Maine coast. *V. crassifolium* is native to pine bogs in the South but grows well in created landscapes with well-drained soil that can be kept moist. Plant them as understories to taller shrubs such as rhododendrons; to create transitions between open, sunny areas and woodland edges, such as with hostas; or around rocks and in crevices. Enjoy the brilliant fall color and the tiny edible berries.

V. angustifolium

an-gus-ti-FO-lee-um. Lowbush Blueberry. This is a Northeast native carpeter that grows 1 to 2 feet tall and spreads widely in acid, sandy, well-drained soil that is enriched with humus or top-dressed with a peat and manure mixture. White flowers in spring are followed by edible berries in summer; fall brings brilliant red leaf color. Plants are best from sods planted in spring and need moisture to become established. They thrive in partial shade to full sun. Useful in Zones 3 to 7.

V. crassifolium   P. 144

crass-i-FO-lee-um. Creeping Blueberry. This is a native of southeastern pine bogs, where it forms carpeting mats of small, evergreen leaves that often have bronze tones. Flowers are pinkish or red and are followed by small blueberries. It thrives in moist, well-drained soil and full sun to partial shade. Useful in Zones 7 to 9. 'Wells Delight' has glossy, evergreen foliage, with red tones in new growth.

V. vitis-idaea var. *minus*

VY-tus-eye-DEE-uh var. MINE-us. Dwarf Lingonberry. The species grows across far northern regions of Asia, Europe, and North America, where it is a low, creeping or prostrate shrub with evergreen leaves. *V. vitis-idaea* var. *minus* is slightly smaller in all respects, forming dense mats to 6 inches tall with dense foliage that has red tones in fall. The white flowers are followed by bright red and somewhat bitter berries. Plants do best in cool, boggy soils or cool soils that are moist, sandy, and acid. They will not thrive in high heat or summer humidity. Useful in Zones 2 to 6.

❦ *Vancouveria*

van-coo-VER-ee-uh. Barberry family, Berberidaceae.

It is rare that a city and a plant genus commemorate the same person, and even more remarkable when the city is near the natural range of the genus. Yet such is the case with Vancouver, British Columbia, and *Vancouveria*, a genus of three close relatives of *Epimedium* (barrenworts) native to the Pacific Northwest. Vancouverias are rhizomatous woodland herbs that are very similar in appearance and cultural requirements to epimediums. Leaves are twice compound, with each leaflet being both vaguely heart shaped and tending to have three lobes. The small but striking flowers are carried above the foliage on slender stalks, with several pendent flowers on each. Flowers are white or golden yellow. *Vancouveria* is named for Captain George Vancouver, an English explorer of this botanically rich part of North America.

HOW TO GROW

Closely related to epimediums and needing very similar conditions, these species are medium- to slow-spreading, herbaceous ground covers for shaded, humus-rich, woodland soils that maintain some moisture in summer. Hardiness depends on the species, and when they are grown in garden conditions, they may require winter protection near their northern limit.

HOW TO USE

Use *Vancouveria* with ferns and spring wildflowers in shade gardens and on woodland floors where its needs can be met. Let it slowly creep in shade gardens in more formal areas, where its neat appearance will add an elegant, small-scale mass and light green foliage color.

V. hexandra   P. 144

heks-AN-druh. Inside-out Flower. American Barrenwort. This species performs well as a deciduous ground cover in cool, moist, woodland and shade garden conditions. It grows 12 to 18 inches tall and spreads well in deep shade. The small, white flowers appear in spring. Protect these plants from drying winds. Useful in Zones 5 to 8.

V. planipetala

plan-i-PEH-tuh-luh. Inside-out Flower. This species is slightly shorter than *V. hexandra,* reaching only 8 to 12 inches tall. It has evergreen leaves and creamy white flowers and spreads slowly to form a fine woodland carpet in ever-moist soils. It is not as hardy as *V. hexandra* but tolerates more shade. Useful in Zones 6 to 8.

❀ *Verbena*

ver-BEAN-uh. Vervain family, Verbenaceae.

Verbenas are annual, biennial, and perennial herbs native throughout North, Central, and South America, with most of the 250 species inhabiting the American tropics. A few species are native to Europe. Verbenas have opposite, hairy leaves that are usually toothed or deeply dissected. Flowers are individually small, sometimes less than ¼ inch long, but are presented in spectacularly showy heads and spikes. The individual flowers are tubular, with five petal lobes at the top. The petal lobes often flare away from the floral tube to form a broad landing platform for bees and butterflies. Flowers are available in most colors except true blue, and in many cases the top of the floral tube has a different color from the lobes, creating an "eye" pattern on close inspection. The name is from Latin and refers either to a European species that was used for eye diseases (perhaps because of the "eye" in the flower) or to *verbenae,* a sacred bundle of olive, laurel, and myrtle used in ancient rituals.

HOW TO GROW

Ground-covering verbenas are perennials that thrive in hot, sunny sites with well-drained soil and good air circulation. Plants grown in moist, rich soils will usually rot, and plants in less than full sun or in sites with poor air circulation are prone to mildew. In North America, the species grown as ground covers are usually deciduous, or else treated as annuals, even though they are longer-lived in warmer regions. Plants need heat and sunlight to bloom well. Water them deeply, though rarely, to promote good root growth and prevent fungal diseases that come with cooler temperatures and poor watering techniques. Useful as reliable perennials in Zone 7 *(V. canadensis)* or Zone 8 *(V. peruviana)* to Zone 10.

HOW TO USE

Gardeners in warm climates, especially in the West, know ground-covering verbenas for their brilliant colors and rapid growth. In the muggier East, they are not as popular, although some tests in South Carolina suggest that some will tolerate high heat and humidity. Use verbenas to create brilliant mats of color on sunny banks, along driveways, in parking medians, and wherever there is full sun and well-drained soil. Cut them back in the fall to encourage a reflush of growth. Use them as vibrant accents on slopes to help control erosion.

V. canadensis   P. 145

can-ah-DEN-sis. Rose Verbena. This native of eastern North America has a loose, trailing growth form and is usually less than 12 inches tall. Flowers are rosy violet to purple. Hardy in Zones 5 to 9, it is reliable only as a perennial ground cover from Zone 7 south. 'Alba' is a new, white selection highly rated for its vigor.

V. peruviana (V. chamaedrifolia)

per-oo-vee-AH-nuh. With sufficient room to make luxuriant growth, this subtropical perennial will grow 8 inches tall and 3 feet or more wide. In tight quarters, however, it can look weedy and unkempt. Foliage is dark green and dense, setting off the red or crimson flowers. Plants root where stems touch the ground. Useful in Zones 8 to 10, but it is reported to be hardier in dry, well-drained, high-desert conditions. 'Red Devil' makes a very low, dark green mat with bright red flowers.

V. tenuisecta

ten-yoo-i-SEC-tuh. Moss Verbena. This spreading South American peren-nial grows to 12 inches tall and up to 4 feet across. The shiny, dissected leaves form a carpet on which are displayed violet flowers. It requires sun and good drainage, but even so may die out after several years. Useful in Zones 8 to 10.

V. hybrids   P. 145

Many noteworthy ground-covering hybrids are often listed in the trade under one of the parent species. Since the parent species vary in hardi-ness, so do these.

'Aphrodite' is a low-growing ground cover with green, dissected leaves. The purplish pink flowers are edged in white. Hardy in Zone 8.

'Dorothy Burton' is a vigorous plant that grows to 15 inches tall and more than 5 feet across. Flowers are large and purplish pink. Hardy in Zone 9.

'Homestead Purple' is a vigorous, spreading variety originally dis-covered by Allen Armitage and Mike Dirr in Georgia. Hot-purple flowers keep on coming throughout the summer. This heat-loving variety needs only a little water to get established. Probably hardy in Zone 7, but it grows so vigorously that it is effectively used as an annual bedding plant.

'Sissinghurst' is a robust ground cover that reaches 4 feet or more across and has large clusters of deep rose-pink flowers. Hardy in Zone 8.

'Taipen Blue' has dark green foliage and violet-blue flowers. 'Taipen Pink' is similar, with pink flowers. Both are hardy in Zone 9.

'Tex Tuff Red' has bright red flowers and is hardy in Zone 8.

❦ Veronica

ver-ON-a-cuh. Figwort family, Scrophulariaceae.

Speedwell is one common name for this genus of 250 to 300 species of annuals and perennials. They are in the same family with snapdragons *(Antirrhinum)* and monkey flowers *(Mimulus)*. Most veronicas are native to the Northern Hemisphere, where many of the infrequently encoun-tered species live at high elevations or in subalpine habitats and are thus prized by rock gardeners. The growth forms range from low, weedy an-nuals to mat-forming and colonizing perennials. Leaves are deciduous and usually opposite, but they can be whorled or alternate, especially on the flowering stems. Flowers are individually small, four lobed, and displayed individually or clustered into showy spikes. The meaning of the name is contested. Some authorities consider it to honor St. Veronica, who captured the image of Jesus (*hiera eicon* in Greek) in her shroud during his Passion. Others contend that it is a misspelling of another plant with similar foliage. The common name speedwell can be interpreted as an Old World blessing of departure.

HOW TO GROW
Several dozen species are garden worthy, and of these a few are effective ground covers. Grow them in full sun to partial shade and fertile, well-drained loamy soil. Hardiness depends on the species. Some, such as *V. incana*, are best suited to drier summers, although they are very tolerant of cold temperatures. Others, such as *V. peduncularis*, require a milder, moister climate to thrive.

HOW TO USE
Use veronicas in full sun to partial shade, depending on the zone, where they will form large patches of brilliantly colored flowers in spring to summer. Commonly used as edgers in borders, they also mass to form lovely pools of color alongside paths and in areas that merge back into shade. Some of the species can be massed to make effective, even rampant, ground covers. Give them regular water through the growing season.

V. chamaedrys
kam-EE-dris. Baby-blue-Eyes, Angel's Eyes. This mat-forming European native spreads by stolons to make small-scale mats with stems rising to more than a foot tall. The pale blue flowers appear in spring. Useful in Zones 5 to 8.

V. pectinata
pek-tin-AY-tuh. This creeping species is native to West Asia and grows in drier conditions than most garden veronicas. Foliage is covered with white hairs, and the small flowers are blue. It requires good drainage. Useful in Zones 5 to 9. 'Rubra' has pink flowers.

V. peduncularis 'Georgia Blue' ('Oxford Blue')   P. 146
pee-dunk-yoo-LAIR-riss. This striking selection was discovered by British plant explorer Roy Lancaster in the Republic of Georgia (formerly part of the Soviet Union). It makes a low cluster of dark green foliage and gradu-

ally spreads into tight mats. The small, blue flowers appear in spring, and the foliage acquires purple hues in winter. Useful in Zones 6 to 8.

V. prostrata (V. rupestris)

pros-TRAH-tuh. This European native forms mats that spread vigorously and send branches up to 10 inches tall. The bright green leaves are semievergreen and act as a foil to the dark blue flowers at the ends of the branches. Useful in Zones 5 to 9. 'Heavenly Blue' has dazzling blue flowers in midspring and emerald green foliage. 'Trehane' has yellow foliage and bright blue flowers.

V. repens

RE-penz. Creeping Speedwell. This species has tiny, semievergreen leaves and forms flat mats with pale blue flowers in spring. Native to Spain and the island of Corsica, it is useful in Zones 7 to 9.

V. hybrids

Several hybrids are excellent ground covers.

V. *spicata*, 'Goodness Grows', reaches 12 inches tall. Though not a spreader, it masses well, since it forms bushy clumps that bear blue flowers all season long. It survives hot, muggy summers better than most veronicas. Useful in Zones 7 to 9.

'Waterperry Blue' is named for the famous horticultural school in England. It has trailing stems that form a low mat to 6 inches tall, and it spills well over walls and rocks. It has lustrous, small leaves that are evergreen in warmer climates and spikes of light blue flowers in spring. Useful in Zones 6 to 8.

❦ Vinca

VIN-kuh. Dogbane family, Apocynaceae.

Periwinkle, creeping myrtle, and graveyard grass are some of the common names for these very commonly used, evergreen ground covers. There are fewer than a dozen species of *Vinca*, all of which are native to Europe, North Africa, and Asia. The most commonly grown species, V. *major* and V. *minor*, rarely climb, but instead the pliable young stems form dense, leafy mats along the ground. Leaves are opposite. Flowers are tubular, about an inch long, and with five petal lobes flexed to make a landing platform for visiting insects. They are blue, white, and, less commonly, pink. The name is the classic Latin one and derives from the Latin verb meaning "to bind." The meaning behind *Vinca* lingers in the familiar English word "invincible" — descriptive of a person who repeatedly is not defeated, not a captive, and thus not bound with rope or subject to another ruler.

HOW TO GROW

Among the most popular evergreen ground covers, vincas tolerate a broad range of garden soils and light levels. They thrive in moist, loose, organic-rich soil and light shade. They are not particular as to soil pH, provided the soil is acid to slightly alkaline. Both species listed here can be slow to establish and may need regular watering during the first year, when they may grow very little. This is only a pause before the rampant growth begins. *V. minor* is the hardier of the two and is replaced farther south by *V. major*. Both are widely naturalized and persistent (even invincible) after a site has been abandoned. Many a periwinkle patch in the woods marks the site of a long-vanished homestead. Vincas have the potential to be aggressive, exotic pests. Hardiness depends on the species.

HOW TO USE

V. major and *V. minor* both have a vigorous, almost rampant, trailing habit, and they root where the stems touch the soil in partial to full shade. Both are excellent for large-scale uses. *V. minor* is neater and tighter growing. Its crisp character and reliability make it an excellent choice for large-scale plantings in formal landscapes, flowing under shrubs and around trees and making a base for small bulbs. Try interplanting it with *Scilla sibirica*. *V. major* is less formal to weedy, but in sites where it can be controlled, the massive carpets will face down much larger evergreen tree and shrub masses.

V. major

MAY-jor. Bigleaf Periwinkle. This tough, evergreen ground cover has foliage and stems rising 10 to 18 inches above the soil surface. Flowers are pale blue-lilac and more than 1 inch across. It prefers partial shade and is useful in Zones 7 to 9. 'Variegata' ('Elegantissima') has leaves edged and mottled with creamy white.

V. minor Pp. 147, 148

MY-nor. Myrtle, Periwinkle, Graveyard Grass. This persistent, evergreen ground cover has foliage rising to 6 inches above the soil surface. The flowers are pale blue and well under 1 inch wide. In its northern range, it grows well in full sun with ample water. But in its southern range, it needs at least partial shade, or it will scorch. Useful in Zones 4 to 8. *V. minor* f. *alba* (commonly called 'Alba') has white flowers and leaves that are slightly smaller than those of the species. 'Alba Variegata' ('Alba Aureavariegata') has white flowers and yellow-edged leaves. 'Argenteovariegata' is vigorous with irregular white markings on pale green leaves. 'Atropurpurea' ('Purpurea', 'Rubra') has reddish purple flowers and green foliage. 'La Grave' ('Bowles' Variety', as it was chosen by the great plantsman E. A. Bowles) has larger, deeper blue flowers. 'Gertrude Jekyll' has smaller, white flowers and narrow foliage. Some consider it the best white-flowered form. 'Multiplex' ('Double Burgundy') has double, purple-red flowers. 'Sterling Silver' has rich blue flowers and foliage with bright white edges.

❦ Viola

vy-O-luh. Violet family, Violaceae.

Violas, or violets, are a gardener's dream and a taxonomist's nightmare. The more than 500 *Viola* species include wild ones that are often garden worthy, as well as domesticated forms, such as Johnny-jump-ups and pansies. Violas are annuals or perennials, with the perennial species having stout, creeping stems from which deciduous, heart- or lance-shaped leaves arise. Flowers are of two kinds — the obvious ones with five showy petals and then, later in the season, tiny flowers that rarely or never open yet set abundant seeds. It is these later flowers that cause botanists so much angst, since they set seeds without any pollinators. The resulting seedlings are almost perfect copies of the mother plant, so any strange or unusual forms (to botanists) may propagate themselves indefinitely. It is these seeds, of course, that help make violas such effective ground covers, for they are dispersed in abundance. *Viola* is the ancient Latin name for violets and is closely related to the Greek term *ion,* which also means violet.

HOW TO GROW

Grow violets in fertile, moist, well-drained, rich, organic soil and partial shade. The perennial species are deciduous and usually go dormant by late summer. Lack of summer water will hasten their demise. All perform best with periodic watering. Useful from Zone 4 or 5 south, depending on the species. Cultivars are often less hardy, sometimes significantly so.

HOW TO USE

Is there a patch of white violets in your lawn? Some Johnny-jump-ups seeding happily among the perennials? The cheery faces of pansies, violas, and violets are found in hundreds of thousands of gardens. The wild plants are often considered lawn weeds, but they are also useful as small-scale ground covers in formal areas and as larger ground covers for bigger naturalistic settings. Combine them with massed spring bulbs. The selections of *V. odorata* are often best treated as specialty ground covers and grown as pure stands.

V. hederacea (V. reniforme)

hed-er-AY-see-uh. Australian Violet, Ivy-leaved Violet. This species makes a tight, leafy ground cover that grows 2 to 4 inches tall and spreads widely. It has occasional scentless flowers throughout the year held above rounded leaves. A very attractive ground cover for moist soils in Zones 9 and 10.

V. labradorica   P. 148

lab-rih-DOR-ih-kuh. Labrador Violet. One of the best species for ground covers in temperate zones, Labrador violet has deep green leaves, often with a purplish cast, and grows to 6 inches tall. Flowers are dark violet and essentially scentless. It performs best in sites with partial shade and adequate moisture, where it will make a handsome ground cover, perhaps in front of rhododendrons. Useful in Zones 2 to 7.

V. odorata

od-or-AH-tuh. Sweet Violet. Beloved of poets and symbol of romance because of its sweetly fragrant flowers, this species grows 6 to 8 inches tall and spreads by runners and seeds. Plants will make sizable carpets over time. They will benefit from supplemental water and should be lightly mulched. Flowers are available in almost any color. Useful in Zones 6 to 9, but plants will fade out under hot conditions. 'Clive Groves' has reddish purple flowers and is a strong spreader. 'Lamb's White' has white flowers and self-seeds readily. 'Princesse de Galles' ('Princess of Wales') has large, strongly fragrant, lavender-blue flowers. It makes clumps rather than spreading assertively. 'White Czar' has large, white flowers.

✴ *Waldsteinia*

wald-STY-nee-uh. Rose family, Rosaceae.

Barren strawberry is one uninspiring name for this small genus, which is indeed related to *Fragaria* (strawberries). Waldsteinias are native to central Europe, northern Asia, and North America. They are perennials with slowly creeping, underground rhizomes. Leaves form as rosettes atop the rhizomes. They are evergreen in warm climates and deciduous near the species' northern limit. Leaves are remarkably similar to those of *Fragaria,* having three to five deep divisions, sometimes so deep that there are three to five leaflets. The yellow flowers have five petals and are presented just above the foliage. Fruits are insignificant, as implied by the common name. The Latin name commemorates Count Franz Waldstein, an Austrian botanist who coauthored a book on the plants of Hungary.

HOW TO GROW

Barren strawberries thrive in dry woodland settings with half sun to light shade. Unlike many other woodlanders, waldsteinias are quite tolerant of relatively dry, loamy soils. They perform well with supplemental water. These species are hardy (and fully deciduous) to Zone 3 but differ slightly in their useful ranges.

HOW TO USE

Imagine a carpet of green, strawberry-like foliage under tall river birches, or perhaps as a ground cover for spring-flowering dogwoods or silverbells. *Waldsteinia* is an underused creeping ground cover with bright yellow flowers in spring. It complements spring bulbs and woodland perennials and creeps under the edges of evergreen and deciduous shrubs. Use it to flow among *Cimicifuga, Kirengeshoma,* or *Astrantia.* Foliage is a lively green, well suited to modern architecture and to bridging formal and more relaxed garden areas. Foliage works equally well with cottages and historic houses.

W. fragariodes

fray-gair-ee-OY-deez. Barren Strawberry. This wide-ranging native of eastern North America forms a foliage carpet to 6 inches high. It is not fussy as to soil and is fairly drought tolerant once established. For best growth, plant it where it will receive some sun during the day. Useful in Zones 4 to 7.

W. ternata

P. 149

ter-NAY-tuh. Barren Strawberry. The common name is the same as for the previous species, but this native of northern Asia and Europe makes a handsome, glossy, evergreen ground cover in humus-rich, moist soil and partial shade. Foliage is not as tall as that of *W. fragariodes*, but it spreads vigorously once established. This is one of the very best ground covers for sites with partial shade in Zones 4 to 8.

❦ Zauschneria

zawsh-NER-ee-uh. Evening primrose family, Onagraceae.

California fuchsia is the common name for the few species in this gloriously showy genus. All are native to the western United States, primarily California and Baja California (Mexico). *Zauschneria* is related to *Fuchsia* (true fuchsias) and *Oenothera* (evening primroses). Leaves are very narrow, usually ½ to just over 1 inch long. They are green to silvery gray and deciduous or semievergreen, depending on the species and where the plants are grown. The riotously bright red flowers are tubular, up to 2 inches long, and held prominently in front of the lax branches. They are absolute magnets for hummingbirds. Northern California was once the edge of the Russian empire, and the plant's scientific name commemorates a botanist from the period of czarist exploration.

HOW TO GROW

Zauschnerias require full sun and warm, well-drained soil. Plants will rot if moisture is allowed to stand in the soil at any time of the year. Where plants are marginally hardy they may benefit from a light cover of branches in winter, provided this does not trap water and moisture. The species listed here is useful in Zones 8 to 10 where summers are dry. Plants can be grown as curiosities, but not ground covers, with careful siting to Zone 6.

HOW TO USE

Plants can be somewhat lax and leggy, so they are ideal for cascading over rocks and down dry banks. On rocky slopes and gravel banks, California fuchsia makes a spreading ground cover of gray-green foliage with brilliant scarlet flowers. It shows well when planted with other California natives, such as *Ceanothus* or *Diplacus*. Or plant it with *Cistus, Helianthemum, Thymus, Rosemarinus,* or *Artemisia* to make an aromatic mix reminiscent of the Mediterranean. Note that some of the other *Zauschneria* species and some selections of *Z. californica* do not spread to form masses.

Z. californica (Epilobium canum)   P. 149

kal-if-OR-ni-cuh. California Fuchsia. This species spreads by rhizomes that send up wiry stems topped by tubular, scarlet flowers. Foliage is green, gray-green, or even very felted white, depending on the degree of hairiness. A number of named selections are available. 'Catalina' is unusually tall and broad, with nearly white leaves and brilliant flowers. 'Cloverdale' is a prostrate form with bright gray leaves and typical flowers. 'Dublin' (also known as 'Glasnevin', for the famous National Botanic Garden in Ireland) grows to 8 inches tall. It has scarlet flowers held above small, bright green leaves. 'Etteri' makes low mats of silvery leaves and scarlet flowers. 'Mattole Select' makes low mounds of silvery foliage and scarlet flowers, but it does not spread readily.

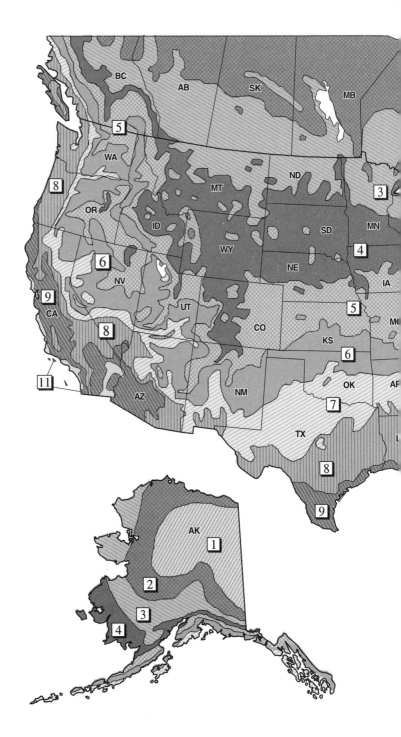

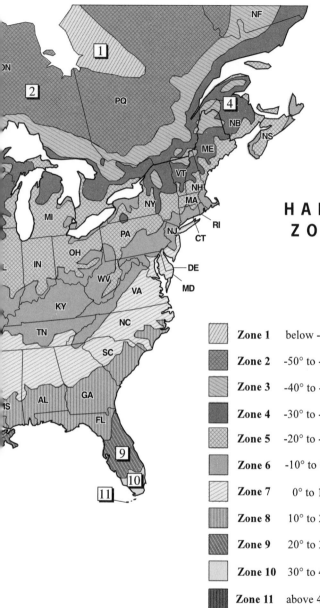

HARDINESS ZONE MAP

	Zone	Temperature
	Zone 1	below -50°
	Zone 2	-50° to -40°
	Zone 3	-40° to -30°
	Zone 4	-30° to -20°
	Zone 5	-20° to -10°
	Zone 6	-10° to 0°
	Zone 7	0° to 10°
	Zone 8	10° to 20°
	Zone 9	20° to 30°
	Zone 10	30° to 40°
	Zone 11	above 40°

❦ Photo Credits

THOMAS E. ELTZROTH: 19 top, 53 top, 55 top, 57 top, 60 top, 66 top, 74 bottom, 83 bottom, 110 bottom, 112 bottom, 115 top, 119 top, 128 top, 129 top, 131 top, 141 bottom

DEREK FELL: 31 top, 32 bottom, 33 bottom, 40 bottom, 44 top, 49 top, 50 top, 52 bottom, 53 bottom, 58 top, 59 bottom, 67 bottom, 69 top, 70 top, 79 top, 84 bottom, 85 top, 86 top, 86 bottom, 87 bottom, 89 top, 91 top, 103 top, 112 top, 117 bottom, 124 bottom, 126 bottom, 127 bottom, 129 bottom, 142 bottom, 144 top, 148 top

CHARLES MANN: 28 top

STEVEN NIKKILA C/O PERENNIAL FAVORITES: 29 bottom, 32 top, 40 top, 41 bottom, 49 bottom, 54 bottom, 64 bottom, 72 top, 72 bottom, 74 top, 75 top, 82 top inset, 87 top inset, 88 top, 94 bottom, 97 top, 100 bottom, 101 bottom, 102 top, 102 bottom, 105 bottom, 106 bottom, 107 top, 108 bottom, 111 top, 111 bottom, 115 bottom, 134 top, 134 bottom, 137 bottom, 142 top inset

JERRY PAVIA: 36 bottom, 50 bottom, 51 top, 55 bottom, 63 top, 68 top, 68 bottom, 73 top, 75 bottom, 84 top, 92 top, 95 top, 107 bottom, 125 bottom, 130 top, 130 bottom, 133 top, 136 bottom, 144 bottom, 145 top, 146 bottom, 148 bottom, 151

NAN SINTON: 23

NAN SINTON AND DAVID MICHENER: vi–1, 10, 21, 136 top

STEVEN STILL: ii–iii, 13, 26–27, 28 bottom, 30 top, 30 bottom, 31 bottom, 33 top, 34 top, 34 bottom, 38 bottom, 39 top, 39 bottom, 42 top, 42 bottom, 43 top, 43 bottom, 45 bottom, 47 top, 47 bottom, 48 top, 48 bottom, 51 bottom, 52 top, 57 top inset, 57 bottom, 58 bottom, 59 top, 60 bottom, 61 bottom, 62 bottom, 63 bottom, 64 top, 66 bottom, 67 top, 71 top, 71 bottom, 73 bottom, 77 bottom, 78 top, 80 bottom, 81 bottom, 83 top, 85 bottom, 87 top, 90 top, 91 bottom, 92 bottom, 93 top, 94 top, 96 bottom, 97 bottom, 98 top, 98 bottom, 99 bottom, 101 top, 102 bottom inset, 104 bottom, 106 top, 109 top, 109 bottom, 110 top, 113 top, 114 top, 114 bottom, 118 bottom, 121 bottom, 122 bottom, 123 top, 125 top, 129 top inset, 135 bottom, 138 top, 138 bottom, 139 top, 139 bottom, 140 top, 141 top, 141 bottom inset, 147 top, 149 top, 149 bottom, 150 top

MICHAEL S. THOMPSON: 2, 14, 19 bottom, 29 top, 35 top, 35 bottom, 36 top, 37 top, 37 bottom, 38 top, 41 top, 44 bottom, 45 top, 45 bottom inset, 46 top, 46 bottom, 54 top, 56 top, 56 bottom, 61 top, 61 bottom inset, 62 top, 65 top, 65 bottom, 69 bottom, 70 bottom, 72 top inset, 76 top, 76 bottom, 77 top, 78 bottom, 79 bottom, 80 top, 81 top, 82 top, 82 bottom, 88 bottom, 89 bottom, 90 bottom, 93 bottom, 95 bottom, 96 top, 99 top, 100 top, 103 bottom, 104 top, 105 top, 108 top, 113 bottom, 116 top, 116 bottom, 117 top, 118 top, 119 bottom, 120 top, 120 bottom, 121 top, 122 top, 123 bottom, 124 top, 126 top, 127 top, 128 bottom, 128 bottom inset, 131 bottom, 132 top, 132 bottom, 133 bottom, 135 top, 137 top, 140 top inset, 140 bottom, 142 top, 143 top, 143 bottom, 145 bottom, 146 top, 147 bottom

☙ Index

Page numbers in italics refer to illustrations.